MW00883944

ANCESTORS

OF

SOCRATES BACON

·

A GENEALOGICAL HISTORY

·

LaDonna Gulley Warrick

FORT WAYNE, INDIANA
1982

Revised a bit 2008

"Out of moments. . .

names. . .

words. . .

proverbs. . .

traditions. . .

private records

and evidences. . .

fragments of stories. . .

passages of books. . .

and the like—

we do save and recover somewhat

from the deluge of time."

FRANCIS BACON

CONTENTS

Socrates Bacon

It was 1838 when Socrates Bacon came to Indiana. He'd been born in Massachusetts, taken as an infant to live in the beautiful wilderness of Maine and, when grown and married, lived for awhile in Pennsylvania, the young, bustling, river city of Detroit, and in Ohio before settling for the rest of his life here in the dense forests of northern Indiana. He was an intelligent man with wide interests and many talents.

Socrates was told the stories of his forefathers and admired the Bacon men and women left behind in time and distance in New England. Probably he named his son Samuel after his father's brother, the Rev. Samuel Bacon, trained in the law, the Marines and the Church. After a hundred and sixty years, fragments of Uncle Samuel Bacon's story were still being told to the children.

When Socrates arrived in Indiana he settled on farmland deeded to him by President Van Buren. That farm is located on the Fackler Road near the town of Maples and is still owned by one of his descendants. Socrates' sister Cendarilla came from Charlton, Massachusetts, with money her maternal grandmother willed her, married, and settled on the farm next to Socrates.

In 1849, Socrates Bacon and George Buchanan repaired Fort Wayne's Fire Engine No. 1. It belonged to the German Fire Company and needed extensive work after a run-away fire destroyed all of the buildings on the west side of Calhoun Street between Main and Columbia and then burned farther westward.

In 1850, Socrates Bacon had at Maples the first post office in the township but "it was so much more to the inclination of the settlers to go to New Haven that the office was soon abandoned". By 1858 he deeded his farm to his son Sam and moved to New Haven to open its first tin shop, dealing in hardware, stoves and tinware. He also platted some open land in New Haven and sold lots.*

Socrates died in 1867 shortly after his sons returned from

*Green Street

1

the Civil War. Two, John and Charles, moved west to Oregon. He is buried, along with his wife, his sister Cendarilla, his daughter and son Sam and their families, in a circular plot in the I.O.O.F. Cemetary on the Hartzell Road, New Haven.

He was the eighth generation of the Bacon family in America.

Children of Socrates and Anne Bacon

Anne Earp,   b. September 15, 1827 in Pennsylvania
            d. October 9, 1884   Marr. Earl Adams

Charles W.,   b. 1831 in Bardstown, Pennsylvania
            d. in Ventura, Calif. Marr. Clara _____

Samuel B.,   b. October 10, 1834 in Detroit, Michigan
            d. May, 1917 in Allen County, Indiana
            Marr. Nov, 25, 1854 Virginia (Jane) Gerardot
              b. 1832, Stark County, Ohio
              d. August 16, 1872, Allen County, Indiana
            Marr. July 14, 1873 Josephine M. Didier
              b. 1855 in Ohio

Amanda,   b. 1837 in Lucas County, Ohio
            d. in Illinois
            Marr. William Earp of Livingston Co., Illinois

John Earp,   b. June 27, 1841 in Allen County, Indiana
            d. June 6, 1914 in Baker City, Oregon
            Marr. Elizor Elmer Holland, Nov. 5, 1865

Adeline E.,   b. Dec, 28, 1843 in Allen County, Indiana
            d. April 15, 1908 in Allen County, Indiana

Laura.   b. 1846 in Allen County, Indiana
            d. 1862 in Allen County, Indiana

Lucy M.,   b. Sept. 18, 1850 in New Haven, Indiana
            d. Oct. 3, 1904 in Fort Wayne, Indiana
            Marr. Milton M. Thompson, June 7, 1874

Further information available in *The Descendants of Samuel Bacon*
by Michael T. Biesiada   1984   Allen Co., In. Public Library

The Bacons in England

The name Bacon originated in Normandy, a land populated by descendants of Vikings. Scholars believe that the family living in England descends from Grimbald "the Norman", a member of William the Conqueror's invading force that attacked Hastings on English shores in 1066.

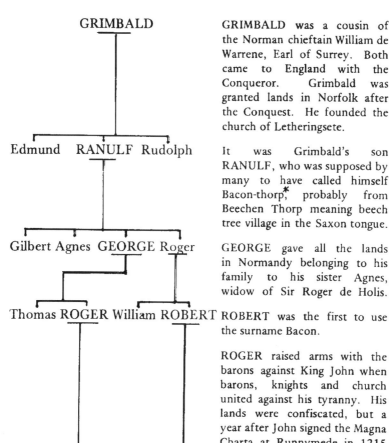

GRIMBALD was a cousin of the Norman chieftain William de Warrene, Earl of Surrey. Both came to England with the Conqueror. Grimbald was granted lands in Norfolk after the Conquest. He founded the church of Letheringsete.

It was Grimbald's son RANULF, who was supposed by many to have called himself Bacon-thorp,* probably from Beechen Thorp meaning beech tree village in the Saxon tongue.

GEORGE gave all the lands in Normandy belonging to his family to his sister Agnes, widow of Sir Roger de Holis.

ROBERT was the first to use the surname Bacon.

ROGER raised arms with the barons against King John when barons, knights and church united against his tyranny. His lands were confiscated, but a year after John signed the Magna Charta at Runnymede in 1215 his lands were returned by favor of King Henry III.

3

see *Corrections*, page 337

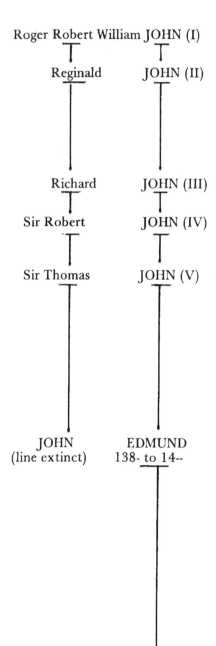

Roger Robert William JOHN (I)   JOHN (I) of Hesset and Brad-
field married Alice

Reginald   JOHN (II)   JOHN (II) lived in the time of Edward I. He married Cicly Hoo (Howe) in Hesset in the County of Suffolk. John and his brother-in-law were probably the builders of the beautiful church there.

Richard   JOHN (III)   JOHN (III) married Helena Geddings.

Sir Robert   JOHN (IV)   JOHN (IV) married Helena Tillots, daughter of Sir George Tillots of Rougham, Norfolk.

Sir Thomas   JOHN (V)   JOHN (V) married Margery Thorpe, who through her great grandmother, Beatrix Bacon, was directly descended from Grimbald and also Charlemagne through William the Conqueror, from a great grandson of King Henry I of England, and two granddaughters of King Henry I of France. This line is detailed in the last chapter.

JOHN (line extinct)   EDMUND 138- to 14--   EDMUND óf Drinkston, County Suffolk, married Elizabeth Crafts (Crofts).

JOHN was "the studious and eloquent Carmelite styled the *Resolute Doctor*. He studied at Oxford and Paris and was remarkable for his "high sprit and low body". It was claimed "his penknife, ink horn, one sheet of paper and any of his books would amount to his full height. As for all the books of his own making put togehter, their burden was more than his body could bear". He died in 1346.

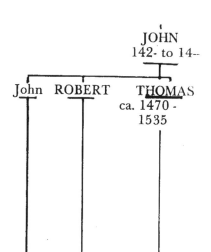

JOHN
142- to 14--

John ROBERT THOMAS
ca. 1470 -
1535

JOHN married Agnes Cokefield, daughter of Sir Thomas Cockfield (Cakefield, Cokefield).

THOMAS of Helmingham, Norfolk,* married Joan . "Will of Thomas Bakon of Helmingham. Proved at Ipswich 28 February, 1535, [excerpted] In the name of god Amen I Thomas Bakon of Helmynghm in the dioc of Norwich hole of minde & goode of rememgraunce being the last daye off Julye in the yere of our lord god MCCCCCXXXIIIIth do ordeyne & make this my present testament & Last will in the manr & fourme folowing. . . Itm I will that myn esecutors or John my son shall dystrybute & geve to all people att my buriall ther beying prsent praying for my soule& for all Chystian souls pennye doles. . . Itm I will that Johan my wyff shall have all thos my lands & tentts aswell Arabyll as pasture & medows wt all th apprtenances both free & copye sytting & lyeng in Helmnghm, Otley, Wynston & Pethawe. . . And after the decease of the said Johan by wyff I will that all my pecys of lands inclosed called Goldsmith. . .To have & to hold to the said John my son his heyres & assyneis for and on this condycon followyng that is to saye that he shall kepe or do to be kepte my Obyte Mays in the yere the daye of my deptying out of this present worlde or any other day as he shall thynke most convenyent for ytt to be kepte

see *Corrections,* page 337

5

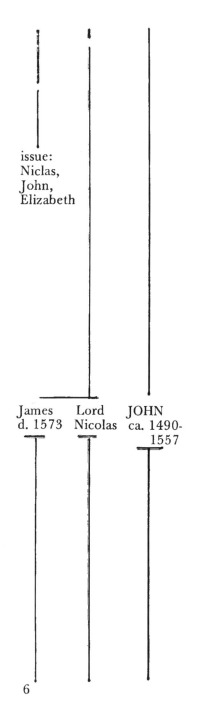

issue:
Niclas,
John,
Elizabeth

James Lord JOHN
d. 1573 Nicolas ca. 1490-
1557

6

wtin the said cherch of Helmynghn the space of XII yeres after my decease ther dysposying for my soule. . ."

ROBERT was the father of Sir Nicolas Bacon, Lord Keeper of the Great Seal for Queen Elizabeth I of England, and Grandfather of Lord Francis Bacon, whom Voltaire called the father of experimental philosophy and "his works are, for expression as well as thought, the glory of our nation and of all later ages". Through another son, James, the alderman of London, Robert was ancestor to Nathaniel Bacon, the leader of the Virginia Colony's **Bacon's Rebellion** and of the Governor of the colony, also called Nathaniel. And also of the Bacon s who emigrated to Barnstable, Massachusetts Bay Colony.

JOHN married Margaret His will was proved March 19, 1557 by Michael Bacon, executor, and Margaret, *relict*, Ipswich. Excerpts: "Itm I bequeath to Margaret my wyef my tenement called Rystheblemys with the lands thereto belonging therme of her lyef...and after her decease I give it to Willm my eldest sone and to his heyres forever. . ." John bequethed lands in Ottleye to Margaret and son Thomas, twenty pounds to be paid at age twenty one to son Richard, a "medowplot" in Barkinge Ashe to Margaret and youngest son William. The eldest son

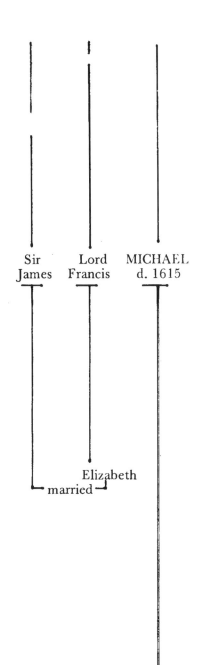

Sir   Lord   MICHAEL
James Francis   d. 1615

Elizabeth
married

William died in 1574, "a single gentleman". The youngest William died in 1610 leaving a granddaughter, Rose Ballet. "...Itm I give to Mihell Bacon my sone my tenements lands medow and pasture lyinge in Wynston and Pettaw called Rosland with their purtenacces fre and coppye to him and to his heyres". Ten pounds at age twenty one to daughter Barbara and "X pounds at xxi yeres of age" to daughter Rose.

MICHAEL BACON married Elizabeth Wylie August 16, 1565, at Helmingham, Suffolk County, England. He was buried March 25, 1615. Eldest son, John, had been baptised with his mother and father on May 31, 1566. "Will of Michael Bacon of Winston in the countie of Suff. Yeoman, beinge of good healthe & perfect Memorye...I bequeath to John Bacon my sonne all that my messuage or Tenemant wherein I noe dwell...I geve...unto Thomas Bacon my sonne...All that my tenemt sometyme buylded called & Knowne by the name of Thomazines & eight Acres of lands and pasture...lyinge in Winston...Item I give and bequeath to Michael Bacon my sonne all the ffrehold Lands and Tenemts within Winston and all lease lands whatsoever and wheresoever they doe lye... to Katherin Bacon the daughter of Elizabeth Bacon my daughter ...I will that my sonne Michael ...shall at his p'ticular costs and charges kepe mayteine &

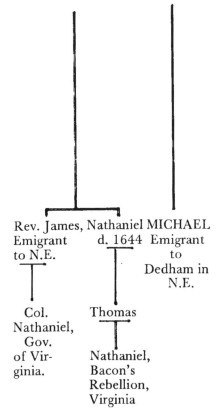

bring upp Katherin Bakon. . . with sufficient meate, drincke apparell & all other things. . ." Michael also gave to his "sonne Michael Bacon my best feather-bed bowester & my best Coverings. A pott Tipped with silver Six silver spoons marked with M and B." Michael, the emmigrant to America, bequeathed in turn the spoons to his eldest son, Michael, when he made his will in New England.

Rev. James, Nathaniel MICHAEL
Emigrant   d. 1644 Emigrant
to N.E.   to
                       Dedham in
                       N.E.

Col.   Thomas
Nathaniel,
Gov.
of Vir-   Nathaniel,
ginia.   Bacon's
              Rebellion,
              Virginia

Sources:
Bacon, E.B., *English Ancestry of Michael Bacon*
Bacon, J.D. and L.L., *Bacon and Allied Families*
N. E. Historical and Genealogical Register
Baldwin, T.W., *Bacon Genealogy*
Battle Abby Roll
Galaise Roll
Linzee, J.W., *Peter Palmer and Sarah Ruggles*
Sever, J., *Stone Genealogy*

The Bacons in America

For five hundred years Bacons were true Englishmen, yeomen, scientists, peers of the realm. In the sixteenth and seventeenth centuries political upheavings battered a growing group of Puritans, Michael Bacon among them, who acted in accordance with their belief that the Church and the State, which were the same as one, were not obeying God's laws. The Puritan preachers called widely and often for reforms and King James I, and then King Charles I, tried to "harry them out of the land".

As Puritans resisted new laws made by the king without approval of his parliment they were jailed. Some, largely country people, separated themselves from England and the Church and went to Jamestown, some others to Holland and some on to Plymouth Plantation in the New World. But most Puritans felt that to leave was to fail their fellow man and did not want such a complete separation. They decided to stay and work to save England and their church. England did not respond the way they had hoped and very soon they felt a "general callamitie" was looming so made the decision to look for a home elsewhere--with the approval of their King and without seeming to repudiate their own churches and the Christians in them.

In 1628 several Puritans obtained a grant of land between the Merrimack and Charles Rivers in New England and the next year they formed a group called the Massachusetts Bay Company. Sir Richard Saltonstall, John Winthrop, Thomas Dudley and Isaac Johnson, with a large following, decided to sail to New England with the intention of colonizing that land.

In March, 1630, about seven hundred people were ready to cross the Atlantic. They sailed on eleven small ships, ordinary freighters of the period, with the *Arbella* as the flagship. The *Ambrose*, the *Mayflower*, the *Whale*, the *Jewel*, the *Success* and the *Talbot* carried passengers. The *William and Francis*, the *Hopewell*, the *Trail* and the *Charles* carried freight and livestock.

John Winthrop organized the trip and was sole authority on the voyage. Happily, he kept a detailed diary commencing the day the grand fleet sailed:

"Anno Domini 1630, March 29 Monday Easter Monday. Ryding at the Cowes, near the Isle of Wight." At Gravesend the Reverand John Cotton "provibited from preaching any more in England", spoke to the company going to New England. Friends and relatives came to say goodbye to the departing emigrants. They "had their speach strangled from the depth of their inward dolor with heart breaking sobs. . .adding many drops of salt liquor to the ebbing ocean".

The worst of a stormy crossing was over June 6 when three of the ships sighted land "about five or six leagues off" and the next day, in calmer water of thirty fathoms, they were excited to find a sea of codfish. Sixty-seven codfish were caught.

The three sped down the coastline of Maine. Then, on June 12, the *Arbella* reached Cape Ann and those voyagers who were able went ashore to gather "a Store of fine strawberries". The *Mayflower* and the *Whale* dropped anchor two weeks later and the *Talbot* the day after. The *William and Francis* and the *Hopewell* arrived the next day, the the *Trial* and the *Charles* the next, and one day later, on the sixth of July, the *Success*, the last of the fleet, safely arrived at Salem Harbor.

At Salem, they found sickness wide-spread and the colonists began to look for a better site for their plantations. Some formed shore-side Charlestown, some Boston, with grants for inland towns soon following, Dedham, Sudbury, Wenham, Rowley, Watertown and Woburn among them.

Ninety, or more, of Socrates Bacon's ancestors arrived in the first few years of settlement and all but a very few have been identified. A complete list of passengers of the first fleet was never made. About two hundred people who died and nearly one hundred who returned to England immediately are lost from the records forever. Of the Bacon family, Thomas Dudley, his wife and children, Ephraim Child and Rev. George Phillips sailed on the flagship *Arbella* and, of course, many on the other ships of that small fleet.

Michael Bacon of Dedham

Michael Bacon, son of Michael Bacon and Elizabeth Wylie, had his fate tied up with the new plantation Deham.*

The town was founded by the revered churchman John Rogers of Dedham in England. He had been forbidden to preach in England and many of his own people emigrated with him to this new town.

Each town was allowed to make its own laws, for the busy Massachusetts Bay government could not all at once make enough general laws. Dedham's covenant (constitution) began:

"We whose names are here unto subscribed, do in the fear and reverence of our Almighty God mutually and severally promise amongst ourselves, and to each other, to profess and practice one faith according to that most perfect rule, the foundation whereof is everlasting love. .

"Secondly, we engage by all means, to keep off from our company such as shall be contrary minded, and receive any such into our society as will in a meek and quiet spirit, promote its temporal and spiritual good.

"Thirdly, that if any differences arise, the parties shall presently refer all such difference unto one, two or three of the society, to be fully accorded by them.

"Fourthly, that everyman who shall have lots in the town shall pay all such sums for the public charges, as shall be imposed upon him rateably, and shall obey all such by-laws and constitutions as the inhabitants shall judge necessary for the management of their temporal affairs, for religion, and for loving society.

"Fifthly, for the better manifestation of their intentions herein, they suscribe their names, and bind themselves, and their successors forever to the true observance of this covenant."

Some of the signers were, Michaell Bacon, Jonathan Fayerbanke, Michaell Metcalfe, George Fayerbanke and James Draper.*

This covenant is typical of the rules of the colony as a whole. Eventually there were many laws made, many very stringent, but by the close observance of such laws dedicated to the good of the many and the survival of a whole colony, John Winthrop, as Governor of the Colony, is credited with making the great experiment work and acually prosper while settlements elsewhere in the new world either nearly failed or did fail entirely.

11

see *Corrections*, page 337

The large tract of land called Dedham was given to only a few persons. These "grantees" were the sole owners until they admitted new associates. This they did at first without asking compensation. A man was admitted as an inhabitant if he would sign the covenant and was then entitled to a share of the division of lands and house lots, house lots which were, by law and necessity, near each other and near to the meeting house. But ownership of this land was subject to Indian title. They were bound by the law of the colony to "extinguish that title by equitable contract". And seldom abused that law.

In 1640, Michael Bacon arrived in Dedham from Ireland where he had fled seven years before to escape the troubles in England. But trouble was growing, too, in Ireland and he left just before the Irish suddenly rebelled in a protest against the unprecedented execution of England's King Charles I. They massacred 30,000 Protestants. Michael's brother William barely escaped to New England with his family. William's brother-in-law was killed in the riots.

Michael Bacon was baptised in Winston, County Suffolk, England. Tradition says he held the office of Captain in a company of Yeomanry there.

His wife Alice and his four children were offered land in Dedham in May of 1640 when it was agreed by seven men chosen to govern the town for one year that, "being called together for advise therein upon deliberation. . .assented unto that the Towne of Dedham shall entertain Mr. Sam'l Cooke, together with his estate and also Mr. Smith and Mr. Bacon all from Ireland and afford to them such accomodation of upland and meadow as their estates shall require". There is a solid theory held by historian Cutter that Michael Bacon was in Watertown as early as 1630. Also, there is evidence that he was in Dedham in 1633 to sign the Dedham agreement before he went to Ireland. What is indisputable is that in June, 1640, Mr. Smith, Mr. Cooke and Mr. Bacon had applied for land but had not yet arrived in Dedham for the record continues,

"Whereas Mrs. Smith & Mrs. Bacon being lately arived heer from Ireland, have ben in our towne & not only well appved of, but also gcnally desiered yt they might inhabitte wth us: And howesoev'r their housbands are not yet come, yet liberty is graunted unto them to purchase in our towne for al habitacon. And such other accomidacons both of upland & medowes to be given unto them as their stocks and estates shall Requier as appeth by a former order conc'rneing ye same."

(The title of Mr. was used to identify a gentleman.)

Later,* whereas Michael Bacon hath parted with some of his plantinge Lot. . [Part of a ten acre lot down to the Charles River. . .] reserving for the Towne for ever a high way three Rods broad. . . where the Towne shalle think most convenient: Always p'vided yt the sd Michael shall have all the wood & timber growinge or yt shall grow upon the sd high way. . .to enjoy the sd land with out paying any Rates for it for ever."

Except for the home lot, all the lands to be cultivated were enclosed in common fields. The common plough field of 200 acres on the village plain was surrounded by a fence made at common charge. The wood reeves [1] decided the number of rods of fence to be made by each owner.

"And it is agreed betwene them yt if the towne shall se cause to desire a fence to be set up to fence ye high way from ye land of Michael Bacon: in his planting field abovesd the sd Michael is to provide ye fencing stuffe ready & ye towne is to be at the charg of the Carrage of it & ye sd Michael is to set it up at his owne prop charge and to maintaine it at his owne Charge for ever And in the meane while he is to provide a gate or gates to secure his corne & to maintaine them."

To enrich his field, Michael would have "fed the ground" with the fish, shad and alewives, as the Indians were teaching the planters. He would have needed about a thousand to an acre of cornfield. In 1644,

". . .it is ordered that all doggs, for the space of 3 weeks after the publishing here of, shall have one legg tyed up. If such a dogg should break loose and be found in any corne field, doing any harme, the owner of the dogg shall pay the damages. If a man refuse to tye up his dogg's legg, and hee bee found scraping up fish in the cornefield, the owner shall pay 12s., besides whatever damage the dogg doth."

1. Wood reeves held authority over the use of the Colony's forests.

see *Corrections,* page 337

Michael's dog could have been a hound or a beagle, or possibly, a mastiff.

> ". . .for the better destroying or fraying away wolves from the town, it is ordered. . .every householder, whose estate is rated f500 and upward shall keep a sufficient mastive dog; or f100 to f500, shall provide a sufficient hound or beagle, to the intent that they be in readiness to hunt. . ."

Alice Bacon was admitted to the church September 17, 1641, thereby joining the elite of the colonies, the "visible saints." It showed the community that she had been baptised and had made a public profession of faith. Dedham was a town made up of the more moderate puritans and the new settlers it attracted were of the same love of peace and distain for bigotry. These settlers were the first to state the doctrine of religious liberty as we understand it now. When the General Court seated in Boston sent a proclamation against the Quakers over all the Colony it was ignored in Dedham.

"1648 Michaell Bacon deceased the 18th of the 2 mo.", [1] the Dedham Vital Records state. Alice died on April 2, sixteen days earlier. His will was dated four days before his death and mentions all his children but daughter Alice who died only a month before.

> "14: 2: 1648 unto Michall Bacon, my eldest sonne, one tipped pot, [torn off] silver spoones, after my decease, [and] my stuff coate and my stockings. Unto Daniell Bacon, my second sonne, the best kowe & the best steere that shall be mine at the time of my decease, p'vided, said kowe or steere be let out upon hyer at [torn off] of my decease. At the end of the tearme of hyer they shall be delivered unto said Daniell. In case of losse of said cattell, my executor shall make it good. Unto sonne Daniel, my best Iron kettle, and three pewter dishes, of middle sort in value; my own best [torn off] coate, & my wives best Gowne. Unto John Bacon, my third sonne, my p'cell of upland, Comonly called the twelve Acre Lott, with all buildings, &c therupon; also that p'cell of Meadow adjoyning, allso, four Acres of Meadow Lying in ffowle Meadow in

---

1. Until September, 1752, the Julian, or "old style", calendar was the legal standard. The year began March 25. March was the first month so sometimes the year given, by later writers, with the months January, February and March is written, for example, 1648/9. M.B. died April 18, 1648.

Dorchester; all woodlands & swamps granted me by the Town of Dedham, excepting that Swampe that Lye one the North of Charles River. To sonn John, my best ffeather bedd, except one, [torn] twoo pillowes & pillow bieres, one blancket, best coverlet except one, one payer of [torn] fine ope seamed sheetes, my bigg [torn] pott, & one trammel. [1.] Unto Sarah Bacon, my dau. my Tenement, wherin I now dwell, with all the houses, lands, &c. ther unto belonging, also seaven acres in Broade Meadowe, & twoo Acres of my p'cell of six acres in ffoule meadow, to be differently devided from the other four Acres. . .given to my sonn John; also four Acres of Land upon the great playne, lately purchased of Richard Ellice; allso, that p'cell of woodland I formerly purchased off Edward Cullver. . .To Sarah, all my cattell not formerly deposed of: all my swine living or dead, my household stuffe not herein bequeathed, wth all instruments of husbandry my Cart wheeles with what doe belong to them, reserveing the Corne & debts due me, to the use of my executor; To Sarah, my [orchard?] being on the Island playne. Unto Thomas Bancroft, my sonne in Law, 20s to be payd within one yeare after my decease . John Bacon my sonne Executor, unto whom I give all by goods not disposed of.

> Michaell (0   Bacon
> in p'resence of
> John (K   Kingsberry,
> Eleazer Lusher,
> Daniell ffisher.

Memorandum Anthony Hubbert[2.] is to paye to for that bullock he bought, the same price he agreed for upon purchase he is to paye the executor; as for that bullock of 3 yeare old, Anthony Hubbert receaved upon condicion to bring up another steere to the same age, he is discharged of that engagement, if the Testator recover not. Anthony Hubbert is to pay for the testator 10s. to Mr. Allen, pastor, & 7s. 6d. to John Morse.''

---

1. trammel, in this case a two-piece hook, adjustable for length, used to suspend cooking pots from a fireplace crane.

2. Hubbard.

The silver spoons mentioned for the second time in a Bacon will were possibly the five divided between the two daughters of Benjamin Bacon III in his will of Nov. 24, 1810. ". . .to my daughter Esther Emes one bed & bedding, also three silver tea spoons. . .to my daughter Katherine Emes eighteen dollars . . ., also two silver tea spoons. . ." If these are the same silver spoons they must have been inherited by Michael III of Billerica, 1688, who was an only son. His son Benjamin inherited Michael Bacon's house and contents as did his son Benjamin II and his grandson Benjamin III. Perhaps the silver spoons, "marked with M and B" still exist.

The children of Michael and Alice were:

Michael,   born about 1608 in England, died in 1688, lived in Charlestown and Woburn. His son Michael's house still stands in Bedford (Billerica) on East street.

DANIEL,   born about 1615.

John,   of Dedham; freeman 1647; died 1683. Married Rebecca Hall.

Alice,   married Thomas Bancroft of Dedham. Died 1648.

Sarah,   married Anthony Hubbard of Dedham who died four days before Sarah's father died, the day her father wrote the will. Sarah died in 1652.

Some descendants of Michael Bacon:

David Bacon (1771-1817). The son of Joseph Bacon, Woodstock, Connecticut, Congregational Clergyman and missionary. Explored among the tribes beyond Lake Erie for the Connecticut Missionary Society, making the journey "alone, on foot, luggage strapped to his back." He "concieved the idea of a community built. . .upon the foundation of New England Puritanism" and started a town in the Western Reserve, now Tallmadge, Ohio.

Delia Salter Bacon (1811-1859). Daughter of David Bacon, above, born in a log cabin which was the first house in Tallmadge. She published a collection of short stories and a drama and lectured on literature and history. She devoted all her energy from 1852 to her death to her conviction that Shakespeare's plays were written by a "liberary coterie" headed by Lord Francis Bacon.

Leonard Bacon (1802-1881), Congregational clergyman, son of David Bacon, above. Was "regarded as the most formidable polemical writer and speaker in the American Congregationalism of his day," pastor for Noah Webster and Eli Whitney for 23 years at New Haven, Conn. and a leader in the anti-slavery cause. In 1846 he published a volume on the subject that made an impression on an unknown lawyer in Illinois. The lawyer, Abraham Linclon, later paraphrased one statement in the book when he made his famous declaration, "If slavery is not wrong, nothing is wrong."

Frederick Asa Bacon (1812-1839). Commanded one of the ships sent by the U.S. Navy to look for Antartica under Lieut. Charles Wilkes. Sailing through "the windiest seas in the world", Wilkes proved that the southern continent existed. Frederick Bacon was lost in a gale off Cape Horn on the expedition.

John (1801), Ezekiel (1807), and William (1877), father, son, and grandson, were all members of the U.S. Congress.

Johathan Bacon of Needham, Mass. (1760-1844), was a member of the Constitutional Convention in 1820.

Josiah Bacon of Boston (1785-1852) was in the Battle of Tippecanoe on the staff of General Harrison. And taken prisoner at Detroit in 1812. His wife Lydia published an account of the campaign.

David Francis Bacon (1813-1865). Son of David Bacon, above, was sent by the American Colonization Society as principal colonial physician to Liberia around 1843. He published a book, *Wandering on the Seas and Shores of Africa.*

Henry Bacon (1866-1924), architect. "The history of American architecture records no more impressive occasion that in May 1923, when Bacon stood, under the evening sky, on the steps of the Lincoln Memorial, his crowning work, at Washington, and received from President Harding the Gold Medal of the American Institute of Architects, the highest distinction it was in the power of his fellow craftsmen to confer . . .He executed a great deal of work jointly with Augustus Saint-Gaudens and Daniel Chester French." He worked on the buildings for the World's Fair in Chicago and innumerable other buildings.

Edward Woolsey Bacon (1843-1887). Son of Dr. Leonard Bacon, above, was chaplin on Farragut's flagship "Hartford" during combat in the Civil War.

Sources:

Cutter, *Genealogical and Personal Memories*
Hudson, A.S. *History of Sudbury*
Worthington, G., *History of Dedham*
Dedham Town Records
Bacon, J. D. and L. L., *Bacon and Allied Families*
Leiby, C. C., Jr., *Michael Bacon and His House at Shawshin*
Baldwin, T. W., *Michael Bacon of Dedham*

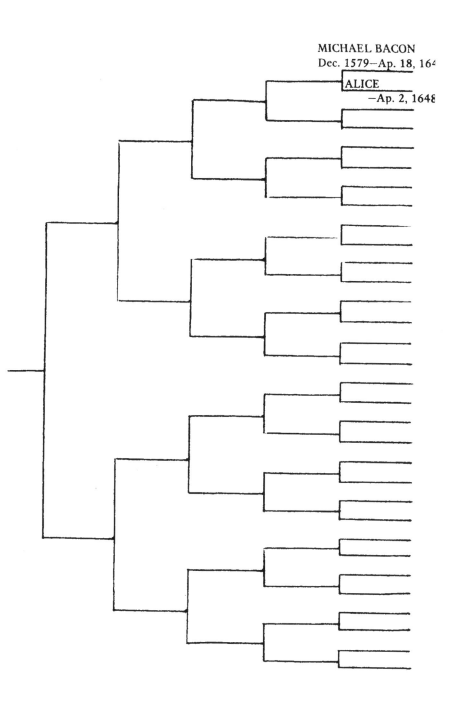

MICHAEL BACON
Dec. 1579—Ap. 18, 164

ALICE
—Ap. 2, 1648

DANIEL BACON

Daniel, second son of Michael Bacon of Dedham, was born in England about 1615 and came to New England with his parents, brothers and sisters from Ireland. Although his father stayed in Dedham, Daniel and his brother Michael went to Charlestown where they joined the group that founded Woburn, Massachusetts in 1640 out of Charlestown's land.

This group, petitioning to form Woburn because Charlestown's agricultural population was increasing, asked for two additional square miles on its western border. This request was immediately granted provided the land would be built upon within two years. The area was soon enlarged to four square miles, so many young men wanted to move to the new site.

Commissioners were appointed to explore this place of unbroken forest, heavy underbrush and swampish wetland. When they walked the new tract they were concerned about the "wandering savage natives" but the worst part of their treke was the November weather. As they were exploring the land around the Shawshin River they were lost in a snow storm and forced, as night approached, "to lye under the Rockes, whilst the Raine and Snow did bedew their Rockye beds".

They decided on a location for the town center and all who intended to inhabit the town met, forty strong, on February 16, to mark trees and lay out bridges. The records say, though, that the place "was so playen backward, that divers never went forward againe". So they located at a better spot near by and in March and May laid out house lots so that buildings were erected that year. Another commission was appointed ". . . to give and grant lands unto any persons who are willing to take up their dwellings within the said precinct and to be admitted to all common privileges of the said town; giving them such an ample portion both of medow and Upland, as their present and future stock of cattel and lands were like to improve. . ." Daniel was given a house lot near the center of town and the meeting house and agreed not to cut down any young oak tree "like to be good timber, under 8 inches square".

20

1·Thirty families made up the town and by 1642, the records state, "Charlestown Village is called Wooburne" from now on.

Daniel Bacon married Mary Reed of Bridgewater, daughter of Thomas Reed of Colchester, County Essex, England. They had six sons and three daughters:

Daniel,	born within Woburn boundries about 1641; shipwright in Salem in 1664, married Susanna Spencer. When he died he left a large part of his property to "the children of his brother John deceased."
Thomas,	born 1645, died young.
John,	died young before 1647.
JOHN,	born September 8, 1647, married SUSANNA DRAPER.
Isaac,	born 1650, probably died childless. He was a taylor in Cambridge.
Rachel,	born 1652, married Thomas Pierce.
Jacob,	born 1654, died at Newton, married Elizabeth Knight. He was a weaver.
Lydia,	born 1656, married Samuel Pierce, brother of the Pierce her sister Rachel married. President Franklin Pierce came from this Pierce family.
Hannah,	married James Trowbridge, Jr.

1.* "As the Indians resided on a spot, till they had consumed the trees around them, and then sought another place. . .they thought that one reason, why our ancestors emigrated to this country, was, that they had burnt out their fuel in England". . .Felt, *History of Ipswich.*

21

see *Corrections,* page 337

Daniel Bacon, taylor, he stated in documents while he lived in Woburn. He, Thomas Chamberlain, John Pierce and Robert Pierce were among signers of a petition regarding religious ordinances in Woburn about 1653, just after their first church was founded and had accepted a minister. He was a member of the jury chosen to lay out the highways in 1664. In 1672, he was chosen constable.

On May 26, 1647, Daniel was made a freeman. Before any man could vote or hold office, he must have been made a freeman by the General Court. He was required to produce evidence that he was a respectable member of the church. Of course Daniel had helped build the church in Woburn. "None have voice in the elections of Governor, Deputy and Assistants, none are to be Magistrates, Officers or Jurymen, grand or petit, but Freemen." The Massachusetts Bay Colony Charter gave "powere forever to the freemen of the company to elect each year these officers on the last Wednesday of Easter term and to make laws consistant with those of England". About one adult male in eight was admitted as a freeman.

The Freeman's Oath proceeded,

"I [Daniel Bacon], being by God's Providence an inhabitant, and Freeman, within the Jurisdiction of this Commonwealth; do freely acknowledge my self to be subject to the Government thereof: and therefore do here swear by the great and dreadful Name of the Ever-lasting God, that I will be true and faithful to the same, and will accordingly yield assistance & support thereunto with my person and estate, as in equity I am bound; and will also truly endeavor to maintain and preserve all the liberties and priviledges thereof, submitting my self to the wholesome Lawes & Orders made and established by the same. And further, that I will not plot or practice any evill against it, or consent to any that shall so do; but will timely discover and reveal the same to lawfull Authority now here established, for the speedy preventing thereof.

"Moreover, I doe solemnly bind myself in the light of God, that when I shal be called to give my voyce touching any such matter of this State, in which Freemen are to deal, I will give my vote and suffrage as I shall judge in mine own conscience may best conduce and tend to the publike weal of the body, so help me God in the Lord Jesus Christ."

After being qualified by the vote of the court and taking the oath, the freeman was allowed to vote in the elections in the following manner:

"It is ordered by this Court. . .that for the yearly choosing of assistants, the freemen shall use Indian Corn and beans–the Indian corn to manifest election, the beans the conntrary;. . ."

The freemen were at first required to appear at the General Court held in Boston to vote but it was inconvenient, and even dangerous, for all of them to assemble in one place and leave their homes unprotected, and so it was ordered that they should send their sealed votes in by deputy.

Some of Daniel Bacon's land in Woburn consisted of a sheep pasture, 60 acres of upland meadow near the cedar swamp called Ladder Pole Swamp bounded by Settle Meadow Brook and Maple Meadow River, a 1648 grant of "that piece of meadow in Loose Meadow sometimes called Lost Meadow", some land received from his nephew Michael Bacon, Jr. consisting of "Sixty acres of uplands part whereof is broken uplands, part pasture land, and part woodland" which included the homestead, (West End, Woburn, later Burlington, at Angier's Corner), "also eight acres in Rock Meadow and one acre in Pine Meadow" and parts of wood lots.

In 1668, Daniel purchased some land in Cambridge and signed the deed,

"This witnesseth that I Daniel Bacon the above named grantee do acknowledge yt the one moyty[1] or halfe parte of the above granted pr'mises is by mee purchased with the legacy that was given by Thomas Read my father in law for the benefit & beooffe of my children by my loving wife Mary his daughter and I do hereby assigne the said moyty or halfe part thereof to be & remayne after the decease of myselfe and my wife to them their heyres and assignes forever to be divided among them in such way as the last Will of their grandfather have nominated & appointed."

1. Moiety; a half, a small portion.

Daniel moved to Cambridge Village, later called Newton, in 1660 where William Clements, Jr. conveyed to Daniel 25 acres for £60 which was partly in Newton and partly in Watertown. His sons Isaac and John settled on this tract, John within the boundry of Watertown. There Daniel died September 7, 1691. His wife mary died October 4.

Inventory of the Estate of Daniel Bacon	£	s	d
His wearing Apparell	3	10	00
In ye Kitchen or Lower room one bed & bedsted with ye furniture belonging to it	4	00	00
One trundle bed with ye furniture belonging to it	3	00	00
Three sheets one Table Cloth and six Napkins	1	00	00
one flock bed 1 Brass Kettle 1 Brass Pott 1 old Copper	1	10	00
In Pewter	0	16	00
One Iron Pott, 1 Iron Trammell; fire shovell & Tongs 1 Gridiron 1 Smoothing Iron & Heaters	1	00	00
One Gunn one old Cubbord	0	14	00
In books 2 old Tables 1 Table leafe 1 joint Stool 5 chaires [It was unusual to own chairs]	0	16	00
In ye Chamber			
Three old Chests Two old Ruggs	0	14	00

24

Tubbs and Lumber	0	04	00
Three old sacks	0	04	00
In Leather	0	01	00
8 pound of hemp	0	02	00
one old Sadle & Pillion & old bridles	0	05	000
In old Iron	0	12	00
One Cheespress; one Crosscutt saw, one Tennent saw, one hand saw	0	10	00
Tubbs and Lumber in ye Cellar	0	10	00
In Hay In Ry In Indian Corn	3	14	00
One horse on*Cow Three Swine	3	07	00
In Cotton Yarn	0	01	06
Due to him in money by bond	17	00	00
one Dwelling & Barn & Seven acres and a halfe of Land on wch is a small orchard	40	00	00
More sixteen acres of Land	40	00	00
More Ten acres of Land	20	00	00
	143	17	06

see *Corrections*, page 337

Sources:

Jackson, F.,   *History of the Early Settlement of Newton*
Fogleberg, J. E. ,   *Burlington*
Sewell, *History of Woburn*
Historic Homes and Families of Middlesex
Winthrop's Journal
Felt, J.B., *History of Ipswich, Essex and Hamilton, Mass.*
Wyman, T. B., *Charlestown's Genealogies and Estates 1629-1818*
Baldwin, T. W.,   *Michael Bacon of Dedham 1640*

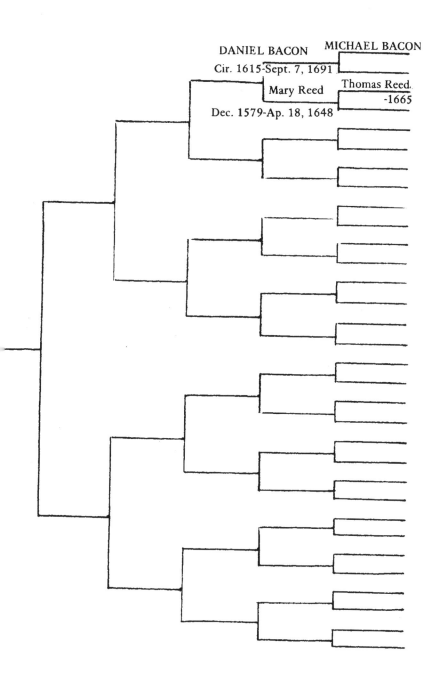

DANIEL BACON
Cir. 1615-Sept. 7, 1691

MICHAEL BACON

Mary Reed
Dec. 1579-Ap. 18, 1648

Thomas Reed.
-1665

JOHN BACON

John was Daniel Bacon's second son; born September 8, 1647, probably in Woburn. When he married Susanna Draper, daughter of James Draper, a weaver later called *The Puritan*, he lived in nearby Charlestown. (The history of the Draper family is in another chapter.) In February, 1667/8 Daniel gave John a deed of the land he had in Watertown "in observance of the last will and testament" of John's grandfather Reed.

John was 'impressed' in 1675 to serve in Captain Davenport's company to fight the Indians in King Philip's War.

The war originated with a Wampanoag chieftain. His father had been a friend of the Pilgrims at Plymouth, but Philip, called by the Indians Metacomet, felt that the English were encroaching upon the forest and greatly feared a time when his people would be crowded out. He sought an alliance with the tribes of New England in order to conduct war and before long the entire frontier was aflame. Crops were burned, captives murdered. Sixteen towns in Massachusetts and four in Rhode Island were completely destroyed. Everywhere, settlers were apprehensive of all unusual sights and sounds. Houses in each town were fortified and officially designated as garrisons where the inhabitants of the town collected in time of trouble.

The colonies of Massachusetts, Plymouth, and Connecticut, involved in the terrible war instigated by the Chief, ordered a thousand men raised for an expedition to the Indian Narragansett Fort built on a piece of high ground in the midst of a large swamp in the Narragansett country.[1] It was defended by four-foot palisades, provided with loopholes that were in turn backed up by a stockade of logs. It was completely hidden from sight in a thick stand of cypress trees.

Massachusetts furnished 527 men making up six companies of foot soldiers led by Major Samuel Appleton and Captains Mosely, Gardener, Davenport, Oliver and Johnson and a troop of horse. Captain Johnson also led a group of praying Indians.

1. Now within the boundries of South Kingston, Rhode Island.

28

After spending the cold and stormy night of December 18, 1675, camped in the open they struggled all morning to the site of the fort guided by an Indian prisoner. The snowstorm still raged as they attacked. "Massachusetts men. . .in advance of the rest. . .made a bold effort to throw themselves into the fort", rushing across the only entrance, a long log spanning an icy stream where just one man could cross at a time. "The brave and intrepid Capt. Johnson", alone on the tree, and Captain Davenport were "instantly shot down, mortally wounded". Wave after wave of colonials stormed the fort, many died, and late in the day a few found their way in over frozen swamp water at the back. Indians were forced to die in the fort or to run into the swamp, some to die there of cold. The fort was set on fire and the army collected its wounded and some of its dead. "The snow fell so deep that night that it was difficult the next day for the army to move."

"The Great Swamp Fight" didn't end the war. It didn't end until the next year when King Philip died. John Bacon went back to his land in Watertown.

On March 20, three years later in 1678, Susanna, John's wife, died of small-pox. On April 7, John also died of the rampaging disease. He made a will the day before his death.

"The sixt of aprill one thousand six hundred and sevety and eight I John beecon in this massachusst colony in the county of midlsex in Charles town being weak in body but right in my understanding sound in memory do comitt my sowll to god in christ and my body to be desently buried and being of a disposing mind do [   ] after all my debts are paid do will and bequeath my Eldest Sonn John a dubl portion of my estatt and the other children a equall proportion my desir is that my daughter may bee put to missris Eliott of Roxsbury to bee brought up in the feare of god and that my two Sonns bee left at my fathers dispoas to bee brought up in the fear of god and in what calling Shall bee thought fitt and I do impour and apoynt my honored father James draper of dedham to be my Sole exequtor to whom I comitt all power and trust of this my last will and testament and I do desire my loveing frinds goodman pentecost and Joseph Linds to bee the over seers of this my last will and I do desier that twenty Shilling bee given to my boy Robert miller to this my last will and testament I have hear to Sett my hand and Seall

John Beecon   his mark

29

in the presens of us

Thomas Brigdon
Samuell Hunting

John and Susanna's four children were:

John,   born 1670. He lived in Roxbury when he
                         married Mary Baker. He had twins Benjamin
                         and Robert in 1709 and several more child-
                         ren by his second wife. He was admitted
                         a freeman in 1690.

Susanna,   born in 1673.

EPHRAIM,   born November 17, 1675. He lived in
                         Roxbury and married ELIZABETH
                         GRIGGS.

————— ,   infant, died of small-pox March 18, 1678.

"July 10, 1677. The vessal arrived at Nantasket which brought
that contagious Distemper the Small Pox, which was soon taken by
some of Charlestown going aboard, since which time many
thousands have taken the infection, and more than 700 already
cut off by it."

Note:
   Baldwin's *Bacon Genealogy* states that Daniel's son was a John
Bacon who died in 1723 but John's own brother, dying as early as
1720, left property to "children of my brother John, deceased".

Sources:

Bacon, L. B., *Michael Bacon and His Descendants*
Felt, J.B., *History of Ipswich, Essex, and Hamilton, Mass.*
Magazine of American Genealogy 1930 No's 7-13
————— , *The Draper Line*
Necrology of Historic Genealogical Society

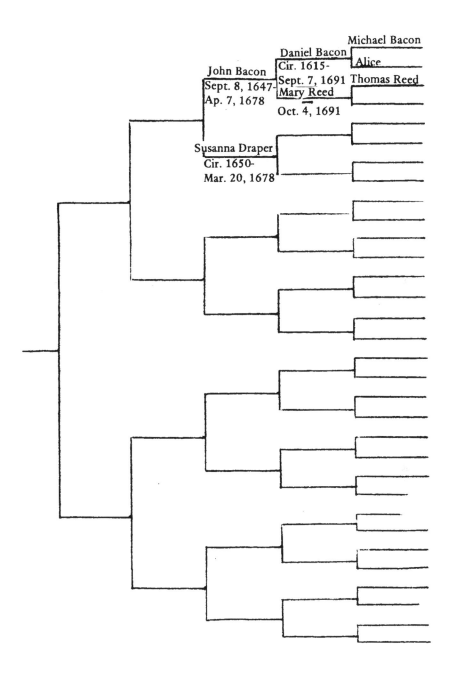

Michael Bacon

Daniel Bacon
Cir. 1615-
Sept. 7, 1691

Alice

Thomas Reed

John Bacon
Sept. 8, 1647-
Ap. 7, 1678

Mary Reed
Oct. 4, 1691

Susanna Draper
Cir. 1650-
Mar. 20, 1678

EPHRIAM BACON
and
ELIZABETH GRIGGS

The young family of John and Susanna Bacon was divided and there seems to be no record of the life of little Susanna who was sent to live with Mrs. Eliot in Roxbury. No doubt it was one of the best homes possible, for the Reverend John Eliot, the famed Apostle to the Indians, had earned the highest admiration from his fellow puritans.

As for the two small boys, most historians state that Ephraim and John were sent to live with grandfather James Draper although their father's will says "that my two sonns bee left at my father's dispoas". That sounds like he means Daniel Bacon——but not necessarily. In the time of the Puritans, in-laws were treated as blood relatives even after the death of a spouse and a remarriage. Parents, brothers and sisters, and even brothers and sister-in-law of the deceased spouse, no matter how many other marriages had taken place on their part, were considered one's own family and close contact was forever maintained. Calling James Draper "father" in a legal document would be the normal thing.

It is sure that Ephraim and John lived in Roxbury when they were grown, the same place James Draper and his family had lived since they moved from Dedham where James Draper was one of the original settlers. Grandfather Daniel Bacon lived in Cambridge Village at Woburn.

Ephraim married Elizabeth Griggs on August 28, 1700 in Roxbury. She was the great granddaughter of Thomas Griggs who helped settle the town in 1639. (the history of the Griggs family is in another chapter.)

In 1706, Ephraim Bacon and forty-four other residents from the west end of Roxbury toward Dedham called Jamaica End "prayed the General Court "because of their great distance from John Eliot's meeting-house and the "great travail and time in going and returning", to be made a separate parish, to be freed from paying taxes for the old parish and for aid in building a meeting house. ". . .In the extreme difficult seasons of heat and cold we were ready to say of the Sabbath, Behold

32

what a weariness". Their request was not an unusual one because, as the towns spread, travel to church and meeting became a real hardship. Settlers did not build their own house of worship without permission, it took ministers and members and money away from established church districts. And, of course, there were only so many ministers. Among the earliest records is a list of badly needed articles from England that included, "beans, peas, vine planters, potatoes, hop roots, brass ladles and ministers".

Ephraim's group was different. They built a church and started services without leave. In April, 1711, they sent a "humble address" praying for pardon to their "fathers and elder brothers" assembled in town meeting "with a sincere design to give Christian satisfaction for any wrong, disorderly steps in our late proceedings. . .for we humbly acknowledge it to be offensive for us to presume. . ." They asked again to be dismissed from their old church.

"As for the season & opportunity we took for our aboves'd mismanaged enterprise whether this was the time agreeable to the approving will of god, we dare not assert, but the event proves it to be his permissive and determinate will, else it had not been so far effected. . .

"We subscribe at the western end of Roxbury Feb. 7, 1710/1

Nat. Holmes	Jonathan Curtice	Timothy Whitney
Isaac Bowen	Daniel Whitney	James Griggs*
Thomas Mory	Samuel Holdridge	Eliphalet Lyon
Ebenezer Lyon	Thomas Bugbee	Ichabod Davis
Joseph Weld	John Case* [Cass]	John Weld
John Fuller	Thomas Mayo	Ephraim Beacon*
John Whitney	Thomas Lyon	John Curtiss
John Griggs*	Samuel Lyon	John Parry
Ephraim Lyon	Peter Hanchet	Samuel Lyon, Jr.
Joseph Lyon	Nath. Draper	Joseph Parry
Thomas Parry	William Lyon	

*Members of the Bacon family tree.

Then, only a few years later;

"Bacon, of Roxbury, perished of cold while returning home from Boston in his sled with three horses. Jan 19, 1713/14."

A narrow mile long strip of land originally connected the peninsula of Boston with the mainland and was the only passage for more than one hundred and fifty years. From the old gateway to the town and the fortifications at Dover Street where it was its narrowest, it gradually widened until at Roxbury's line it was about a half mile wide. In the seasons of full tides parts of the Neck were covered with water making it almost impassable. It is hard to imagine how dangerous this narrow pass with close-lying marshes once was. Now it is broad and paved, lined with parks and filled with traffic.

From the *Boston Transcript* genealogy column of January 29, 1913,

"Ephraim Bacon of Roxbury died before May 20, 1714, on which date his widow Elizabeth took out administration papers. . . He left four children: Elizabeth, born about 1701, Ebenezer, born about 1706, Susan, born about 1708. . .and Ephraim who was baptised February 21 or 25, 1713/14 in the West Roxbury Church."

". . .born about 18 days after its father was lost upon the Neck in a storm." says another notice.

New born Ephraim would have been baptised on the Sunday following his birth, wrapped in "a staniell or baise[1] bearing cloth".

There were three more children, claimed a researcher from the early part of this century, and he mentions Ebenezer again, and Susan, and another, Mary, whom he says was born about 1710. Abigail, born in 1703, is mentioned in the town records.

Ephraim Bacon left a homestead of twenty-two acres and real and personal estate valued at £388 5s.

With in a few years, the widow Elizabeth Griggs Bacon married Captain Ebenezer Edmunds and they moved their family far out onto the frontier to new, raw Woodstock.

1. Stammel: a linsey-woolsey of a dull scarlet color. Baize: a plain, loosely woven cotton or woolen fabric, usually dyed green.

Sources:

Boston News-Letter
Roxbury Vital Records
Thwing, *First Church of Roxbury*
Dedham Vital Records
Drake, *Town of Roxbury*
Index of Obituaries 1704 - 1800
Boston Transcript

WOODSTOCK

In October 1683, the selectmen[1] of Roxbury, Joseph Griggs, (Elizabeth Bacon's brother), and John Ruggles among them, felt that new land was needed for the young men of town who were not first-born sons. "This Bay township was filled with very laborious people whose labors the Lord had blessed with Godly [goodly] fruit trees, fruitful fields and gardens and great store of cattles." They petitioned the General Court of the Bay Colony for a tract of land in the Nipmuck country. In October, 1684, Roxbury enpowered "Lieut. Sam'l Ruggles, John Ruggles, senior, John Curtice, and Isaac Morris" (all to someday make up part of the Bacon family) to "spy out this wilderness the Indians call Wabbaquasset".

The new colony absorbed the attention of everyone in Roxbury and at town meeting people were spoken of as "Goers" or "Stayers". When it was proposed, March 9, 1686, that a group of capable men should go in advance and break up the land for the main body of colonists, the town offered them even more land that had been offered before, with only one condition: "That whosoever desired to enter as a Goer shall be twenty-one years old by June 10, 1686."

By April, more than the requisite thirty families were ready to migrate. All were Roxbury people and members of the parish and church of the Reverend John Eliot and very devoted to him and his projects to benefit the Indians.

Arriving at their new home, called at first, New Roxbury, they drew lots for their homesteads. Lot number one was drawn by cousins of Ephraim Bacon, Thomas and Joseph Bacon. Lot number nine went to an uncle of Ephraim's wife Elizabeth, Ebenezer Cass. Lots were reserved for a common burying ground, a meeting house, and a quarry for hearth and building stones.

When winter set in, after the cabins were built, the ground broken, the highway made passable, the only news the settlers

1. Selectmen, a board of town officers, usually of the weathier or upper middle class, chosen to conduct the affairs of the town.

were able to receive was from the few travelers on the old Bay Path, a trail with a long history. Indians from the Nipmuck country had taken corn to Boston that first winter in 1630 along the old Bay Path and had been using its network from time out of memory. In 1633, John Oldham and his three Dorchester companions had come this way intending to learn something about the Connecticut River country. "They lodged at Indian towns all the way." The Bay Path was also the route of that band of colonists lead by Rev. Thomas Hooker and Rev. Stone who with one hundred of their church members and families left Cambridge and settled Hartford, Connecticut in June, 1636, passing through the heart of what was to later be New Roxbury, Woodstock.

With only the Bay Path to connect them the mother town of Roxbury prayed each Sunday for the welfare of the new colony. It is said that at one service John Eliot "arose in his pulpit and exclaimed, 'Alas! Alas! I forgot to pray for our sons and daughters in New Roxbury, and therefor, let us pray again!' This he did much to the comfort and relief of the congregation who feared his neglect would cause their children there to be devoured by the wild beasts or destroyed by the Indians."

The town thrived. It acquired a mill (built by William Bartholomew), a meeting house, roads to the clay pits, the quarry and the woods and planting fields, a minister's house, and a teacher. It dealt with Indians, had some marriages, planted on the minister's land the town's first orchard, recorded the ear marks of all the cattle that grazed on the common and added to their grants. Fifty pounds due Woodstock by Roxbury was paid and so the new minister, Reverend Mr. Dwight, finally received his salary "for preaching from the beginning of the world unto the sixth of May in the year 1696." Officers were elected. A salary of ten shillings was voted the tax collector, with the stipulation that he should pay out of his own pocket whatever taxes he could not collect. Aged people and prompt taxpayers were assigned the best seats in the meeting house.

40

In 1693, James and Jabez Corbin built a trading post to receive furs, turpentine and surplus farm produce which they traded in Boston for rum (a principal trade item), ammunition and supplies. In fact, "James Corbin's cart" was the only vehicle of communication with the outside world. Wagons were unknown even as late as 1747 and the Bay Path was still "very rocky, bushy, in many places miry". Corbin testified that "they had much ado to get their loading to Boston, breaking two axel-trees between Woodstock and Mendon." In June, 1702, the bill sent with this load that broke the axel-trees tells of the abundance of game they carried; nine hundred deer skins, three hundred beaver skins, thirty bear skins, twenty fox and the skins of four wallenegs[1], eighty-one racoon skins, nineteen cat, nine minx, twelve musquash, four marten and four wolfskins.

Woodstock had serious Indian trouble as it tried to settle itself. Even though many Wabbaquassets lived in the town, Indian alarms continued to 1710 before abating.

After a lull of ten years, another Indian disturbance in 1720 caused Colonel John Chandler to receive orders from Boston to impress twenty Woodstock men for service on the frontier which was then in central Massachusetts very close to home. All the women and children were moved to garrison houses for safety.

Kept inside, they soon tired of dried foods so Bathshua Holmes slipped out to raid their gardens of "cucumber, leeks, melons, onion and garlic" and returned with a basket full. Years later, an old Indian told her he had watched her slip to the gardens and back and although he raised his bow to shoot at her, was unable to do the deed, as if "the Great Spirit held his arm". He'd always considered her since under the special protection of the Indian's God.

It was to this Woodstock, a long way inland from the familiar Bay, that Ephraim Bacon, ten years old, his eldest brother Ebenezer, and three of his sisters came to live.

1. Woolleneg, could have been wolverine. Wollaneg was often mentioned in New England papers.

Some of the Woodstock families that had an interesting future, Edward Morris, an original settler, was the father of Commodore Charles Morris, famous in the War of 1812, and grandfather of Commodore George N. Morris, Commander in the Civil War of the U.S. Sloop-of-War *Cumberland.*

David and Bathshua Holmes were the grandparents of Oliver Wendell Holmes.

Deacon Jedidiah Morse was the father of Jedidiah Morse, America's foremost geographer of the late 18th and early 19th centuries, and grandfather to Samuel F. B. Morse, inventor of the telegraph.

Sources:

Converse, E., *Genealogy of Converse*
Connecticut Towns Origins
Bowen, C., *History of Woodstock*
Bowen, C. Winthrop, *An Historical Sketch*

EPHRAIM BACON II
and
SARAH FAIRBANKS

In the summer of 1723 Ebenezer Edmunds and his wife Elizabeth, mother of the Bacon children, purchased 300 acres of Woodstock land. He paid 330 pounds, cash, and the next summer they lived with friends or family in Woodstock while a house was built.

Ephraim was ten years old, Ebenezer was eighteen, and their sister Elizabeth, twenty-two, had already been married for four years to a Woodstock man, Lt. Ebenezer Child, son of Benjamin and Grace Child. The Childs were early proprietors of Woodstock. In fact, Ebenezer Child was one of seven brothers who migrated there with parents and aunts and uncles. The young couple raised eleven children, some in Woodstock and some in Union, Vermont, where they died in the late 1700's.

The two other Bacon sisters also married in Woodstock. Susan married James Corbin of the trading post family and Mary married Eliphalet Carpenter.

Many tangled family relationships were represented in Woodstock. George, Joseph and Benjamin Griggs and Ebenezer Cass were all uncles of young Ephraim's mother, and besides, Uncle Ebenezer Cass was married to Patience Draper, sister of Ephraim's paternal grandmother, Susanna Bacon. Her nephew, James Draper, III, had lived in Woodstock since before 1695 and his daughter was married to a Griggs. Thomas and Joseph Bacon were original lot owners and were cousins of Ephraim. There were many more.

The Edmunds bought land a little outside Woodstock near the Childs', the Holmes', the Lyon's and the Morse's, all newcomers from Roxbury.

In 1728, Ephraim Bacon chose his older brother Ebenezer "of or near Woodstock" to be his guardian, having been previously under the guardianship of his stepfather Ebenezer Edmunds. It is probable his mother had died shortly before this.

43

On March 10, 1741, Ephraim stood up in church after regular service and "published his intentions" to marry Sarah Fairbanks, the daughter of Samuel Fairbanks and Susanna Watson of Woodstock. The Fairbanks were from a good Puritan family that built in 1636 the house of Dedham, Massachusetts, that is today the oldest wooden house in the United States. (See the Fairbanks family on page ✳

Ephraim built his house in the same area as had his brother and step-father Edmunds, the strip of land fought over by Massachusetts and Connecticut since 1713 called the Middlesex Gore and, much later, the Bacon District. The founding fathers had mistakenly built Woodstock on Connecticut land.   A compromise in 1714 put it back on the Massachusetts side but in 1747 Woodstock applied for a reversal of that decision and it was granted to all but 3000 acres on the northern border. That 3000 acre gore came under the jurisdiction of neighboring Sturbridge, Massachusetts.   Later, in 1794, the Gore, breaking away from Sturbridge, became a part of Southbridge on the petition of Ezekial Brown, Cyrus and Joseph Ammidown, Benjamin Stoddard, Jeremiah Morse and Ephraim Bacon, III.

The Quinaboug Historical Society Leaflets describe the Woodstock area the summer before Ephraim married Sarah when bear, wolves and deer still prowled around the farms:

> "We can see here and there a good farm house, but generally the pioneers are lodged in small frame houses built of hewn oak timber with thick planks nailed upright on the frames with no other covering. . .The later settlers are still living in houses built of logs hewn on two sides, laid closely together, forming warm, comfortable dwellings. The windows are few with small 6x8 panes of glass. We realize that not more than one tenth of the land has been cleared of its original big forest trees, giving the farms a secluded, isolated appearance."

The average pre-revolution New England farmer cleared three acres of land a year, half of which he planted in corn. He had corn pone on his table nearly every day. He ate wild game just as often and wild apples were a staple. Often "apples" meant crab apples.

44

see *Corrections*, page 337

The author of the leaflet was a boy that summer and was invited

"...to partake of pot Luck...one July evening...it appeared to us in the guise of salt pork and corned beef boiled together with four kinds of vegetables left over from yesterday's hot dinner. This with rye and Indian bread made a royal feast for us. We could see that the bulk of the cooking was done in the enormous oven beside the kitchen fireplace, which only did duty to warm up the viands cooked in the oven. The cradle and the spinning wheel appeared to be the most used articles in the house."

In 1745, that part of Woodstock was still so unsettled that danger from Indians was always possible and men from Woodstock were dying at garrisons even closer to the frontier.

Ephraim Bacon and Sarah Fairbanks had twelve children recorded in the Woodstock town records:

EPHRAIM,	born Jan. 10, 1742, married Hannah Chamberlain.
Moses,	born 1743.
Asa,	born 1744.
Benjamin,	born 1746.
Abel,	born 1747.
Daniel,	born 1749.
Sarah,	born 1751, married Moses Corbin.
,	year of birth unknown.
Levi	born 1757.
,	a daughter born 1759. Possibly named Jemima.
Ebenezer,	born 1761, died 1838. Fought in the

Revolution and lead a colony from Connecticut to settle in Otsego Co., N.Y.

Simeon,   born 1765.

A war between France and Great Britain was declared in 1744. When the news reached Boston fifty men in Colonel Thomas Chandler's Woodstock regiment went to guard the frontier. History declares that this regiment "rendered efficient service" in the important victory at the French Louisburg on Cape Breton Island in 1745. In March, 1755, Connecticut recruited a thousand men to build and defend a fort at Crown Point. Ephraim would have been the right age to fight in these campaigns but the only documentation of his part in the conflict is for the year 1759 as the war reached its zenith.

That year Ephraim, Sr., joined the expedition to Crown Point under Captain Daniel McFarland, head of a Massachusetts troop. He served from March 25 through the summer to November 29.

Ephraim Bacon, Jr., seventeen years old now, was on the muster roll of Captain David Holmes of the Seventh Company in the Fourth Regiment of Connecticut Troops commanded by Eleazer Fitch, Esquire, also bound for Crown Point. This troop included Jonathan Child, 2ond Lieutenant, Lemuel Lyon, Corporal, John Chamberlain, Jr., drummer, Carpenters, Corbins, Eastman, Johnson, May, all of the neighbors. This, too, was the regiment of Israel Putnam, Lieutenant Colonel and Captain of the Second Company. Putnam lived just over the line from Woodstock at Pomfret, Connecticut, and was married to Sarah Bacon, great, great, granddaughter of the first Michael Bacon. It was Israel Putnam who almost twenty years later, while in the fortification at Bunker Hill, commanded, "Don't fire 'till you see the whites of their eyes!"

English on both sides of the Atlantic were concerned about the French encroachment on lands the English considered their northern frontier. In the 1750's relations between the two countries approached a crisis. The English had the greater numbers with which to fight but the colonies were not

46

see 'Corrections, page 337

accustomed to act together. Indians who thought that because the English had been defeated a few times the French must be unbeatable joined the French side and boldly attacked English settlers along the western frontier. By 1756, the French controlled the whole Great Lakes country and the Indians were their close allies.

Major General Amherst was sent to New England by William Pitt, new Prime Minister of England, determined to unify the colonies and drive the French out. He organized the largest army America had ever seen, fifty thousand troops, of whom twenty thousand were provincials. Consequently, as 1759 began, the French no longer controlled the Mississippi and Ohio valleys. Young George Washington and Governor Shirley decided the English should arm to take Forts Niagra, Crown Point and Ticonderoga. They knew that for generations New England men had been required to train in the militia and felt well-prepared to fight. And too, Massachusetts was so exposed to "massacre" from Canada it was not hard to raise men.

Both Ephraims learned it was ordered that,

> "each man shall furnish himself with Sutible Cloaths a Powder horn and Shot bag to the acceptence of the Muster Master Shall be intitled to Recive fore Pounds the one half on his inlistment and the other half to gather with one Months wages a blanket and Knapsack before he Marches oute of this Colony and that the waiges for Each Priviet Soldier for his Service in the Campaign Should be one Pound Sixteen Shillings Lawfull money acouinting 28 days to a month."

All men were required to be able-bodied and between seventeen and forty-five, and must measure to a certain height.

> "Particular stress was laid upon marksmanship. The gun of that day, seldom trustworthy in aim or velocity, was the long-barreled weapon, the ammunition was not the fixed ammunition of today; the paper cartridge and ball were carried in cartouche boxes,
>
> the powder generally in a horn which was often carved in an ornate manner in token of the campaigns the owner participated in."

The two Ephraims, father and son, met the New England troops of Massachusetts, Connecticut and Rhode Island gathered at Springfield, May 15.

"Let every man take out his provisions one days allowance. The rest with all his baggage to be sent to the river immediately in order to be conveyed by carts & that five men with one Sergt. one Corporal out of every Company be peraded att the Black Horse forthwith in order to march as guards for the carts, By order of Generall Ruggles."

They marched up to the well-fortified Dutch village of Albany where Amherst was preparing for the expedition to Ticonderoga and Crown Point.

On May 26, a detail of 200 men of the Massachusetts troops, loaded the supplies on "battoes" and planned to work their way up the Hudson River to Lake George in stages while, still at camp,

". . .all the guards of the Royal Highland Regt. are relieved by the Conn. Troops."

The remainder of the Connecticut troops were ordered,

". . .to provide themselves immediately with everything they will have occassion for that they may be ready to march att the least notice."

By the 7th of June they were camped at Fort Edward. The troops were "regaled" with spruce beer and discipline was tightened. Indiscriminate firing was prohibited, arms were ordered to be kept clean and in good order.

On June 18 they were at Half Way Brook where they stopped for two days. Special orders were given the guards and the pickets; officers were to be extra vigilant on their outposts, to permit only two men to lie down at one time and to make their rounds very regularly; no man on any account to stray beyond the line of sentries. At the same time the morals of the men were not overlooked. Card playing in camp was fobidden, an hour a day for exercise prescribed, profanity barred, and whoever found guilty of disobeying the injunction against making noise in camp after tattoo, "will be took as a dispicer of the Marshal law."

June 20th Amherst issued orders for the main force to march to Lake George, where they "encamped on its woody banks on an intolably hot day". The rest of the troops, the two Bacons, and Roger's Rangers, waited there in a very disorderly camp, owing to half of the troops being "not regular soldiers". ". . .all officers. . .especially take the greatest precaution after the tattoe is beat, that there be no hollowing or singing in the camp." J.H. 1

They waited there for another four weeks doing "piquit" duty, building and repairing roads, clearing brush, parading, "falling trees" on the road and testing their aim.

"our men are pretty healthy, they dont want for work. By ye appearance of things it seems as if we should soon go over ye lake, face ye danger of ye field, be surrounded with ye thunder of war and I exhort our men not to be faint. . .There are different reports of the strength of ye enemy. . .some say yr number is superior to our . . .we have no certain intelligence. . .Capt. Jacobs went out last week with about 30 men, was surrounded at ye narrows with birch cannoos, fired upon by ye emeny. Capt. Jacobs and 10 of them are not yet come in. . .I expect yt we shall engage ye enemy in 3 or 4 days. . .how it will turn out God only knows. . ." H. T. 1

On July 21st, twelve thousand strong, they started out onto the lake in the bateaus.

"The men must row in turns. . .The whole will move on gently. The men that are not imployed in rowing must go to sleep that the men may be ellert & fit for service when landed. . ."J. H.

There on dark Lake George they "lay all night on their oars, wind something high, Weather lowering". H.T. Finally, a calmer morning came. They landed,

". . .in their wastcoats and. . .as light as possible. . .no hurry or huzzaing on any account whatsoever, no man to fire with out orders from his officer. . .The enemie must be mett with fixed bayonets . . .Silence amongst the men must be kept. . .They must expect to ly one night or 2 on their arms."J.H.

Though they expected to meet French soldiers, they were not opposed in the takeover.

"After landing imediately some of our men marched to ye saw mill, there they surrounded about 20 French and Indians. . .we killed some of them. . .the rest fleeing. . .Our men immediately took possission of ye breast works. . .confining ye enemy all in ye fort." H. T.

1. J. H., Orderly Book and Journal of Major John Hawks
1. H. T., Letter of Rev. Henry True to His Wife.

The pressure on Quebec had forced the French commander to weaken the support at Ticonderoga. Bourlemaque had seen the hopelessness of his stand and had quickly withdrawn his main force leaving Hebecourt with four hundred troops to give only the appearance of a fully-manned fort and with instructions to blow up the works as soon as the British batteries were established. Bourlemaque struck out for Crown point and Canada.

The provincial troops with their British leaders entrenched themselves after a "sally or two". Fitch's batallion, with Ephraim, Jr., furnished a guard to take post,

". . .halfway betwixt the camp and saw mill. . .taking care no straggling Indians may pick of their people. . .The General would on no account have the men fire in the night unless they are very sure of their shotts, but recieve the enemy with their bayonets."J.H.

The enemy continually fired,

". . .ball and bombs. . .The General was present and was ready to say that ye French bombs could not hurt us. . .Our men were exceedingly active, ready to laugh under their toyls and burthens. Regulars and provincials all united, New Hampshire men helped, had ye cannon and mortars onto ye intrenchments.

"July 26th, at night when we had got our artilery ready to play, the enemy blew up ye magazine and so fled all of them. . .which we took. . .they left some cannons, some mortars and balls." H.T.

They had loaded and pointed every gun, charged several mines and lighted a fuse that connected with the over-stocked powder magazine. The explosion made the ground move. The next day the flames were extinguished and the Brittish flag run up.

By August first the men were preparing to go on to Crown Point. Some had "stop'd up the great rhode to make it impassable from Lake Champlain to the saw mill" by cutting down trees. Fitch's Regiment was one that was assigned to repair the fort "with the utmost expedition." Others readied for the move by putting their whale boats and bateaus into the river. Then the regiments cut boughs to cover the bottoms, cushioning the provisions being loaded. At two o'clock in the morning of August 3rd the men sent their tents and baggage to the sawmill river to be ready to move off by day-break to join Major Rogers.

". . .Collo Fitch is to leave Serjt Eddy with the masons of his Regt who are att present att work with him for the repair of the Fort. . .the proventials are to recieve 4 days provisions tomorrow att the revalley. . .each to receive 2 pints of pease, which compleats them to the 6th inclusive. . ." J. H.

Possibly, Ephraim, Jr. stayed to work on the fort but it is more likely that he joined the rest of the 4th regiment, ". . . they are to man the Artillary boats. . ." No one relished the idea of the trip in the bateaus "but we shall have good Oswego bass I hope."

The next day when they arrived at Crown Point they found Bourlemaque had also blown up those works, leaving everything to the British. Today that is a picturesque ruin.

August 6. Major Rogers sent back "2 batoes immidiately to Ticonderoga" for spruce beer and brewing utensils. They also received "flower to bake their bread" and a schedule for the use of the fort's ovens.

September 1. The camp received supplies of New England rum, "Madara Wine", molasses (to mix with the rum, no doubt, for what the Red coats later called the "Yankee drink"), Indian meal, soap and chocolate, and "one Sack Containing Forty Seven Pair Shoes it Being on the Acco't of the Colony Connecticut and for the Service of the Troops in Colo Eleazer Fitch Regiment".

On the 13th of October the army sailed up Lake Champlain, "but the weather proving boisterous" it returned on the 2oth after capturing several French.

In November, as the war in America was almost over, the troops started gratefully home to families that, in almost every case, had not heard from their husband, son or brother since spring and to farms that had been worked all summer without the help of any of the men of the family. It was young Ephraim Jr's first taste of war.

Ephraim Bacon, Sr., died sometime before April 13, 1773 It was on that date that his widow, Sarah, "Administratrx of all and singular the Goods, Chattells, Credits and Estate of Ephraim Bacon Late of Woodstock Deceased, do make or cause to be made a true and perfect Inventory. . .".

The inventory was taken by Elisha Child and Daniel Lyon.

"Armory

Large Gunn 24/ two Small at 18/

Wearing apparrel

Brown Coat 12/ Striped Jacoat 4/ Great Coat 12/
Leather Breeches 20/ two Woolen Shirts 16/
Beaver Hat 4/ Handkerchief 3/ Shoes 4/
Two pair Stocking 4/ Leather (stockings (?) 2/ Boots 10/

Stock

L--e Back Cow 4 lbs White fac'd Heifer 55/
Bull 54/ two Steers 60/ Bull 26/
Three Heifers 4lbs Two ditto @ 52/
four Oxen 21 lbs two Steers at 7 lbs twenty four sheep
four Swine at 5lbs Seven Cows 32lbs
two Steers at 50/ two Heifer at 40/ Yearling Coult 4lbs
Roan Mare 4lbs Young ditto 11 lbs Three Calves at 10/ Each
two tun of Hay 40/ four Hives of Bees 4 lbs

Farming tools

Two Iron Bars 26/ ten Axes 27/6 three Hoes 7/2
Bedle and Wedges 10/ Shovel 2/ Rope 2/
Grind Stone 14/ Iron fetters 1/6 Old Iron 8/4
Cou-ter 3/ Cart Irons 1/0 Tobacco Knife 1/6
Iron Dogs 1/6 four Sickles 2/ Hand soew(?) 7/
Tinners tools 7/ three Cythes 8/ Broad axes 10/
Cythe 2/ Port Axe 2/6 Square 4/ Shave 2/

Six Chains 76/ three Yokes 15/ Augur and other tools 7/8
Sled 4/ Dragg 4/ Plow 12/ Cart and Wheels 6lbs
Timber 6/ Stub Cythe 2/ Old Cythes 5/8 Horse Trases 10/
Coopers addstt ax 8/ Cythe T--king 2/ Sheep Sheres 1/
old Iron 2/8 two Steel traps 17/ Curry Comb 1/6 fork 0/8
Stub Cythe and old Iron 9/ Tininers Screws (?) 3/4
Boards and Clapboard 40/ Steel Yards 4/ Shingles and bark

Library

Great Bible etc 15/8

Household Goods

Mans Saddle 40/ Woman ditto 35/ old Saddle 14/ Hobbel 6/
Crain and Hooks 10/ Trammels 6/ fire Shovel and tongs 7/
Loombs 28/ Tea Kaster 6/ Brass Kettle 20/ Small ditto 6/
Iron Pott 4/ Small ditto 4/ Iron Kettle 1/6 Spider 2/
Scummer 1/6 fork 1/ Churn 4/ Chopping Knife 1/
Bullet molds 6/ thirty Barrels and Cyder 11 lbs
ten Barrels 20/ Hogshead 3/ New and old Casks 23/6
Pork 50/ Pewter 16/ tin 1/0
Knives & forks 4/ Trays 4/ Piggin[1] 0/6
Earthen 4/ Wheels 10/ Tub 1/0 Salt 18/
firkin[2] 1/6 Beehives 4/ Pigeon Net 10/ baskets 6/
Chest 2/6 barley 4/ Trushoops 10/ Bedsted 3/1
Ox Shoes 8/ flax 6/8 Tallow 5/6
4 Beds and fruniture 15 lbs 5
Glass Bottles 3/6 Candlesticks 0/10 Chain 20/
tables 12/ Beer Barrel 2/ Slays and harness 12/

1. Piggin, a small wooden vessel having one stave projecting above the rim for a handle; also, a pitcher.

2. firkin, a wooden vessel for lard, or, an English measure equal to one fourth of a barrel.

Meal Chest 3/4 Cheese Press 8/ Small Chest 2/
Malt 15/ Cedar tub 6/ ditto 2/ Reel 1/0 Grease 4/
Butter tub 2/6 roling Pin o/8 basket 1/0
Baggs 2/ Chest 3/ Linen 16/ Case Drawr 45/
table 2/ Box and heators 3/6 Chest 9/
Brass Seales 2/0 Stone Jugg 1/0

In the Corn Barn

Indian Corn Rie & Oats tog. 9 lbs 6
Sundry Articles of Lumber 1 lbs 15 4

Notes

Ebenezer Edmunds [half-brother?] 1 lbs
Josiah Somnor 5 lb
David Smith and Caleb Rogers 5 lb 17
Asa Bacon 7 lb 3 11
Zachariah Newton 16 lb
Joseph Ainsworth 10 lb
Moses Bacon 2 lb 4 7

Lands and Buildings 685 lbs 18

Taken May 1 1773

Ephraim died without a will and so his widow was given her
"thirds" by the Court. Part of her thirds included,

"The West Room of the Dwelling House with the Chamber
over it & a Celoar under the Bed Room & a right of passing thro'
the other parts of the House to & from said Cellar & Chamber.
Also the part of the barn that is West of the Floor with a Privi-
ledge in the floor. And also about Forty-two Acres of land. . .in
Woodstock. . .Also about 20 Acres of woodland. . .
Also set out to Ephraim Eldest Surviving. Son of said Deceased
in the following manner – certain tract of Land lying in sd Woodstock one of which lieth in the third Range of the Second division

54

of Lotts in the North Half of Woodstock in No. 34 laid out in Right of Edward Moriss & contains by estimation 44 acres more or less also one other tract or lot of land in the second range of Third Division land in said North half in right of Jn. Griggs & contains 47 acres ½ more or less the third tract contains five acres ½ & bounds as follows North on Dudly line 48½ rods, East on Jonathan Bacons land 18 rods, South on Land set off to Levi 48½ rods and West on a highway 18 rods, the corners are heaps of Stones – Also of the moveable Estate amounting in the whole to the sum of 104 lbs 19."

Those old farms with their corner boundries marked by heaps of stones inspired the keeping of a special spring Sunday when all the families "walked the boundries" of their land. Often the boys in the family were bumped against a boundry stone or tree in fun or playfully dunked in a boundry stream, a good way to remember the mark he would someday be responsible for.

April 19, 1810, the division of widow Sarah's thirds, or Dower, was made as she was "now deceased". Ephraim, as the eldest son, again received his two shares, nine acres of land.

Sources:

Hawks, J., *Orderly Book and Journal of Major John Hawks*
Rolls of Connecticut Men in the French and Indian Wars
Andrews, *Connecticut Soldiers in French and Indian Wars*
Child, *Genealogy of Child Family*
Quinabaug Historical Society Leaflets
Woodstock Vital Records
Dudley Vital Records
Virkus, F. A., *Compendium of American Genealogy*
Converse, *Family Record of Deacons J. W. and E. S. Converse*
Boston Transcripts
Bowen, C. W., *Woodstock Genealogy*
Bowan, C. W., *Woodstock, An Historical Sketch*
Letters From Rev. Henry True to His Wife, Mrs. Ruth True
Plimpton, *History of Southbridge*

EPHRAIM BACON III
and
HANNAH CHAMBERLAIN

Ephraim Bacon, son of Ephraim and grandson of Ephraim, grew up in the Gore and built his own home nearby in 1756.[*] If you had the opportunity to walk down Bacon's Lane today, you'd see the foundation for the chimney and the cellar walls, made with large flat pieces of New England granite, hiding under the fallen leaves and soft moss. A hundred old trees and an army of new-sprouted ones surround and cover the old walls. The lane and the road to the Bacon farms are walled three feet high with rough granite slabs placed there by Bacon men over two hundred years ago.

Mr. H. Porter Morse now owns the abandoned Bacon farms in the Southeast corner of Southbridge. (Nee Woodstock, then Sturbridge, now Southbridge.) He will tell you that the town took the "beautiful wall" of Ephraim's barn for the under-pinnings of the road close by at Notre Dame Church, Route 169, the Woodstock Road.

Ephraim had 30 acres of apple orchard where he raised, mostly, Northern Spys. When H. Porter Morse was a boy, many decades ago, he watched the deer gather early in the morning to feed on the seeds in the soft apples that had fallen to the ground in that remote and abandoned orchard.

Ephraim married Hannah Chamberlain, May 28, 1767, and they started their family and tended their farm[1].

To chop ten cords of wood a day out in the forest was not an unusual day's work for the ordinary colonial farmer like Ephraim. And the forest offered the chance to become a good hunter and to make a day's entertainment out of it. Squirrel hunts were often organized in the fall with two teams

chosen by a pair of captains lasting from dawn to dusk. As did Turkey shoots. There were fox and partridge hunts and

---

1. Eighty-one acres purchased January 4, 1765, for £20. Book 51, page 283, Court Records.

see *Corrections*, page 337

pigeons were chased and caught with a large net. More entertainment was furnished by husking-bees and barn-raisings; both of which ended with serious wrestling matches watched with intense interest. A good supper ended the day. Beans were a favorite and housewives were skilled at baking beans or brewing a bean porridge. Hasty pudding was another favorite and a bowl of baked apples and milk was a choice dish many days out of the year. The farm yielded almost all the ingredients for the needs of the Bacon family. There was little or no sugar, chocolate, coffee, tea or potatoes before the Revolution. And for drink there was plenty of home-brewed beer and cider and stronger spirits. Turnips were their potatoes.

The first Baptist Church was built in the area in 1766 as a result of almost twenty years of strife there between the established Congregational Church of New England and a small group calling themselves Separatists. The dissention arose because this group, who became Separatists as a result of a wave of evangelism in the countryside, did not want to pay for the support of any other minister but their own. The town insisted upon the payment which was a part of the townspeople's taxes. The law said everyone must support the minister chosen by the people. Assessors took what they could from the Separatists to get their payment. One irate observer wrote,

> "Kitchens were robbed of their shovels and tongs, trammels and andirons; larders of their pewter ware; housewives of their spinning wheels, warming pans, tankards, and quart pots, the mechanic of his broadaxe, saw and other tools; and farmers of their cows, oxen and smaller stock in great abundance. And, to complete this scene, from Deacon Newell, they took a flock of geese, besides his cow and pewter ware."

When Ephraim's (III) son, Samuel, was grown he reflected on this and wrote,

> "The 'standing order' will probably grow more and more arrogant and powerful, if the law in their favour be not relaxed. . .It is predicted that the unnatural union of church and state will take place in [New England] if not guarded aaginst."

Each side took a long look at itself. The town held a meeting and offered to return "all the creatures and all the goods" if there could be peace.

Just how early the Bacons were involved with the Separarists or with the Baptist Church is hard to tell but Ephraim and Hannah were already members, according to Samuel, when he was born in 1781. By then, most of the town was Baptist. In 1800, Ephraim and his eldest son, Enoch, signed the petition asking to be "set off with our lands "to form a new parish and build our own church". In May 1816, Ephraim Bacon sighed the Constitution of the First Baptist Society and was on the ministerial committee. Ephraim, at the end, attempted to will all he had to the Baptist Church.

Another storm hovered on the horizon even before that was settled. Since the beginning of the eighteenth centry, the colonists had been restless under an uncaring King and parliment. Between 1764 and 1774, Great Britain imposed upon the American colonies a series of measures that caused a hundred small rumblings of protest. Town meetings were called. Actions were proposed and some dramatic ones, like the Boston Tea Party, were taken.

In Sturbridge, the Selectmen called a meeting. They spent the hours discussing their grievances and lead the town to vote unanimously to not purchase any goods imported from England after a certain date.

Those rumblings of revolution built suddenly into a great thunderhead when the powder stored in Cambridge by the patriots was found by the British and removed in September, 1774, to Boston. The news flew as fast through New England towns as horses hooves could take it. The men of the scattered towns, unorganized as yet, hurried to Cambridge and were barely restrained from marching into Boston to demand, with their loaded muskets, the return of the powder.

In Sturbridge town meeting it was voted "to provide four half barrels of powder, 5 cwt. of lead, and 500 flints' to the emergency store. Timothy Newell and Erasmus Babbit stepped forward and generously offered to furnish one half barrel of powder at at their own expense, which was received with applause. A committee of seven were then chosen "to make provision for the men who should be called away." At the same meeting they appointed Capt. Timothy Parker a delegate to the Provincial Congress "to be convened soon after at Concord".

Other meetings followed. At one they decided to see how committed the townspeople were to military action and too, how well prepared. They would adjourn the meeting until the first Monday in December at 10 o'clock A.M. and,

> "all the men in town, from 16 years old and upward, then meet at the Meetinghouse in Sturbridge with arms and ammunition in order for reviewing."

That Monday the training field (today called the Common) was a military camp. The elders of the town formed into a company of "Alarm Men." Capt. Parker was marshalling the men into a band of "Minute Men." And there was Ephraim, probably with his gun he used for squirrels. Capt. Newell with his company of Grenadiers was assembled in another part of the field, while a body of Cavalry under Capt. Craft occupied another. Almost every male citizen over 16 had become a soldier. After review, they marched into the church in military order for prayer and a sermon by the Rev. Joshua Paine.

> ". . .It was then proposed by the town to call over the list of the Alarm men, the number of which was 103, some 60 -- some 70 years old. Most of them were deficient as to arms or ammunition, and some as to both. The Clerks of the other companies, [the Minutemen, the Grenadiers, the Cavalry] returned that the men were generally present, and generally equipped, or would be soon. . . Captain Ebenezer Craft for the troop in this town returned an account of every one in particular, that they were well equipped and all prepared."

After that report the town voted,

> "that it is the sense of this town, that every man in town able to furnish himself with arms and ammunition do forthwith fit himself complete. . ."

That winter was an unusually mild one and it was easy for the Minutemen to drill. "Extraordinary weather for warlike preparations", wrote Concord's minister, William Emerson.

Came spring, 1775, and only a few knew that the British regulars were preparing to march out to Concord to look for the new military stores, collected and hidden by Minutemen. Paul Revere was ready to ride to notify all the towns between Cambridge and Concord that "the regulars are out", if the British staged one of their search missions into the countryside.

Early on the morning of April 19, Colonel Joseph Palmer, member of the Committee of Safety, was sent hasty word of the shots fired on Lexington Green and with borrowed quill, ink and paper he hurriedly began to write,

Wednesday Morng near to 10 of the Clock

Watertown

To all friends of American Liberty let it be known that this Morning before break of day a Brigade. . .marched to Lexington . . .where. . . they fired without any Provecation and killed 6 Men and wounded 4 others. . .we find that another Brigade are now upon their March from Boston. . .The bearer Israel Bissel is charged to alarm the Country quite to Connecticut, and all persons are desired to furnish him with fresh Horses, as they may be needed. I have spoken with Several who have seen the dead and the wounded. . .

J. Palmer - - one of the Comy of Sy.

Israel Bissel was a veteran postrider of the Boston to New York run, and he did ride "quite to Connecticut". He rode faster than anyone could hope he would and covered the hilly road to Worchester in two hours. Tradition says that his spent horse died under him near Worchester City Hall. Very quickly, he was spurring a new horse into the rolling hills of Sturbridge where distant bells and echoing drum rolls, now sounding across all New England, were calling out the men. He shouted his news that the British troops had fired on the people of Lexington. He showed his, by now, tattered papers signed by Palmer and endorsed by the scrawled signatures of key men in the towns he had been through. He rode over the close-by line for

Pomfret in Connecticut. "Old Put", Israel Putnam, left his plough in the furrow and rounded up his command. He was on the way to his moment in history when he was to command his men not to shoot "til you see the whites of their eyes!"

In Woodstock, the McClellans were planting elm trees along their drive when Col. McClellan (later General McClellan), answered the call. Mrs. McClellan, after he was gone to meet his troops, finished the planting and solemnly dedicated the trees to the men at Lexington. The trees stood more than a hundred years. [1]

Ephraim Bacon, in the Gore, heard the long drum roll that was the order for assembly, and hurried with his gun, powder horn and bullet pouch, to the Common to join his neighbors in the Minutemen ranks before the pacing Captain Timothy Parker. Forever after, they were part of that group of men remembered because they "marched on the alarm of April 19". H. Porter Morse will confirm, while walking down between the old stone walls of Bacon's Lane, that "Ephraim Bacon answered the call of the 19th". He says that as if he were there. There is no need, in New England, to explain what the call was for or what month or year "the 19th" belongs to.

The weather was fair, windy and cold. The drummers beat a marching rhythm, the ranks grew as now and then another new American in brown hunting shirt and farm clothes, musket on his shoulder, came down their lanes to join the men maching towards Concord. These were men from outfits the British had never heard of before, men who fought like Indians. Or, "like bears, and I would as soon storm hell as fight them again".

The British found their way through the gantlet to the safety of Boston by night time but they were prisoners, for the

---

1. McClellan was the great grandfather of Gen. George McClellan of the Civil War.

Minutemen stayed, forming a ring around the town. Not all the Minutemen remained throughout the long vigil leading to Bunker Hill, some had to go home after a few days but others came to take their place and kept up enough of a military force that the King's army was penned up. General Ward arrived and from these Minutemen slowly and surely built an army.

This is where Ephraim and the men from Sturbridge stayed for the fourteen days service they saw this time. On Captain Parker's muster roll, you can see that Ephraim stayed as long as any one in his company. Joseph Morse, Jr. stayed six days, Benjamin Bacon, fourteen days. Everyone stayed either three, six, seven or fourteen days. Perhaps there was gunfire each of those days, perhaps they were wounded. And, too, there was little in the way of supplies. Someone had to start the essential items flowing towards Boston. Some had to go home and check on the mill or finish a field. If there was no crop how would the colonies survive? So they walked back seventy miles to check, to finish, to instruct.

Of the Bedford Minutemen who led the attack at Concord Bridge, nine out of the twenty-six were named Bacon. At Lexington Green and Concord these men were killed and wounded; Jacob Bacon from Woburn, wounded, from Natick, Captain David Bacon, killed. From Bedford, Reuben Bacon was said to have died from the day's exertions.

Records kept during the Revolution were hit and miss and many have been lost, but there is record of Ephraim returning to service at least twice more. Undoubtably, he joined his townsmen many times to form a regiment as emergencies arose. He likely helped move the desperately needed cannon to Boston from captured Ticonderoga, captured just to get those cannon. The Americans pulled them over the snowy Berkshires for fifty bitterly cold days.

December 10, 1776, Ephraim served with Captain Able Mason's company in Colonel Jonathan Holman's regiment on an alarm at Rhode Island. He was stationed at Providence for forty-three days with the 1st Sturbridge and the 5th Worchester Companies.

It was this winter that Thomas Paine's first pamphlet was published,

> "These are the times that try men's souls.. The summer soldier and sunshine patriot will, in this crisis, shrink from the service of their country; but he that stands it *now* deserves the love and thanks of man and woman."

This was, too, the December of George Washington's attack across the Delaware River.

The next September, in 1777, Ephraim marched on secret expedition to Rhode Island as a corporal with Daniel Eame's company and Benjamin Hawe's regiment. The expedition was formed to force the British out of Newport where they had "forty sail" of transport ships. The Americans in Boston constantly expected an attack from that direction. But now the French, too, had a fleet here and if they could land a force Washington would send men to join the militia of Rhode Island, Connecticut, and Massachusetts. Major Hitchbourn would lead his independent Cadets. Colonel Revere would command the Boston artillery train, which was very much thinned. John Hancock was the major general of the Massachusetts militia, three thousand of them in all, and Lafayette himself was present.

The French fleet sailed. The men marched. The heavy artillery bumped over the bad roads, all converging upon Rhode Island. The attack began well but soon lost power and the Americans had to leave, their ranks very much smaller.

Ephraim was gone from home one month and three days that time. There were probably more expeditions for him and in some one of them the Americans began to gain. The war was over with the signing of a treaty on September 13, 1783. And Benjamin Franklin wrote, "There never was a good war or a bad peace".

Now Ephraim stayed home. Listed in the records of Sturbridge are his and Hannah's first four children:

Kezia,   a daughter born in 1768.[*]

Enoch,   born 1769.[*]

66

see *Corrections*, page 337

Ichabod,   born 1771, died 1772.

Lois,   born, 1773.

From other sources we learn of:
Hannah,   no date.*

Ephraim,   born in 1776.

Samuel,   1781.

Samuel stated in a journal written when he was grown that he was the youngest of nine children. A memoir was written about him after his death in 1820 by a man who worked with him and admired him. It contains a description of the family from Samuel's point of view,

"The paternal ancestor from whom his branch of the family descended, came to America about one hundred and twenty years ago, [sic] and settled in the province of Massachusetts bay, near Boston. Passing alone in the night, during a violent storm of snow, across the isthmus which connects Boston with Roxbury, he lost his way on the narrowest part, plunged with his horses into the wintry surf, and miserably perished. On the same night was born the grand-father of Samuel. The father had been induced by the expectation of this event, to visit the town on the preceding day, in order to procure necessaries for the occasion. This is the family tradition.[1]

"Mr. Bacon's American ancestors were farmers – the proprietors of the soil which they cultivated with their own hands; procuring by incessant industry and strict frugality, a moderate competency for themselves, and their numerous families.

"The family constitution is remarkably vigorous. Of the eight children of Ephraim Bacon, seven are sons, and all are believed to be living at the present time.[2] The age of the youngest is sixty, and of the oldest, about eighty-four. Sickness, except from casualties, is almost unknown to the family: all of whom "bore the appearance of the freshness of youth, even to middle age.

1. But like most traditions, lost some accuracy over the many years of retelling.
2. Actually, there had been twelve aunts and uncles for Samuel to try to recall and nine, or perhaps ten, were sons of that Ephraim.

see *Corrections*, page 337

"Ephraim Bacon, the eldest of these brothers, removed at the age of twenty-four, to Sturbridge in Worchester county, about thirty miles [1] from the paternal residence of Woodstock; where he obtained one hundred and fifty acres of land, then in an uncultivated state; built a house with his own hands, and married Hannah Chamberlain. His removal took place about the year 1762 . . .Samuel's mother who died in 1790, is thus characterised in the affectionate language of her late son: 'her spirit was that of gentleness; kind, pious, charitable, and humble. She knew but little enjoyment in this world. I never but once recollect seeing her out of her room. She was five years sick of a cunsumption, and nearly all that time confined to her room, – commonly to her bed. Her parentage was respectable. So much was she beloved and esteemed by all, that a general joy seemed to pervade her christian friends, when they heard of her release from sufferings, by an exchange of worlds. Her last words were a charge to her husband respecting her young children. . .'

"The surviving parent continues, at the age of eighty-four years, to occupy the same farm, surrounded with the scenery of his youthful days, from which he seems never to have been many weeks absent. 'it is there. . .he has laboured nearly sixty years at the plough, the scythe, the axe and the flail. It is there, his nine children were born. The spot is rendered sacred by the death of three children and a wife. There, often, very often, has the morning sun found him upon the hills before him, and the evening star has a thousand times lighted him at his labours. It is that spot which had been moistened by his sweat and his tears: there, have the wild and rugged rocks echoed the expressions of his grief, and his mirth. It is that soil, which, for many years sustained the firmness of his youthful tread, and now feels the tottering footsteps of his age.'

"Of his mother, the subject of this memoir remarked, that, 'for the time at which she lived, she exhibited uncommon evidence of a truly pious character,' and took much pains to impress his mind with the truths of religion. . .During Samuel's minority his father occasionally observed the forms of religion in his family; but appears at that period, very imperfectly to have understood its nature. . .He did sometimes pray in the domestic circle. [2]

1. Not so. He built very near the land his father and grandfather had lived on in the Gore. Only the name of the territory changed.
2. From 1805 to 1814 the Southbridge (Sturbridge) churches were unable to find ministers to hold meeting for even half of the Sundays in a year. ". . .remote from any other convenient place of attending church, to be destitute of any preaching one half of the time would naturally lead to an habitual disregard of the Sabbath. . ," Plimpton. This may✶

68

see *Corrections*, page 337

apply to the Bacon experience.

"His parents, being Baptists, are to be ranked among the nonconformists of the time. and experienced in consequence, inconveniences which gave to their son's mind an early bias against the principle of religious taxation, which he never afterwards entirely dismissed.

"A general trait of the laborious yeomanry of New England. . . is roughness, and severity of temper. . .It may easily consist, as commonly it does, with perfect inflexibility of principle, and correctness of moral deportment. And such, until advanced much beyond the limit of mature life, was the father of Samuel Bacon. 'He possessed, 'according to his son. . .'a good education, a strong and masculine understanding, equal to all the affairs of life; sound reasoning powers; fertility of invention; a good judgment, and an enterprising, intrepid character: but no gentleness. But. . .the scene is now changed. The religion of Jesus Christ had imparted its meekness to that ridged bosom, and the sun-set of his life is almost without its clouds. It is serene, and mild, and peaceful, as the closing eve.' "

In 1824, a year before Ephraim died, General lafayette received a hero's welcome as he toured America, a country he seemed to love as well as his own. He visited each of the twenty-four states and in Massachusetts he stopped at Southbridge.

"The artillery and a splendid band of martial music were stationed on the meeting-house hill. The gathering, from all the neighboring region, exceeded in number, three thousand. The approach of the cavalcade was announced by the artillery. When it arrived, a large man, plainly dressed, of dignified and venerable appearance, alighted from a carriage. . .The most touching spectacle was the meeting with his old fellow-soldiers, who, in early manhood, had shared with him the perils and conflicts of our revolutionary struggle. They had taken their position, in military style, by themselves, where the interview took place. Most of them had seen him. and some had been under his command. They related incidents

. . .which he remembered. The triumphant result of the mighty struggle was spoken of with the highest satisfaction. They had all become old men. Forty years had passed away since they had terminated together their labors."

Surely, Ephraim Bacon was there, "in military style".

Hannah Chamberlain Bacon died in 1790. Ephraim married

see *Corrections*, page 337

69

Mary (Molly) McKinstry, widow of John O'Layha, in 1793. He died in August, 1825, and both he and Hannah and some of his children and grandchildren are buried in a small cemetery at the corner of the road to Bacon's Lane and Woodstock Road. In that time, the Eddy family owned the corner and had their own cemetery there. They told Ephraim that "all the offspring of Bacon forever" could use that ground for burying.

IN THE NAME OF GOD AMEN. . .

Know all men by these presents that I, Ephraim Bacon of South-bridge in the County of Worcester, and State of Massachusetts, Farmer, being blessed with a sound disposing mind and memory nevertheless knowing, "It is appointed unto men once to die", for certain good reasons, think it my duty to make my last Will and Testament which is in manner and form as follows, (viz.)

1st I give and bequeath to my wife Molly Bacon the use and improvement of one third of all my real Estate during her natural life, and one third of my personal Estate.

21y I give and bequeath to the first Baptist Society in South-bridge and their successors, all the remainder of my real estate, including the reversion of that part the improvement of which is heretofore given to my said wife (meaning to except only that part of my real estate heretofore conveyed by deed to my son Samuel Bacon, deceased, and daughter Hannah, which Deed is to take effect after my decease,) the use and annual income or avails of which, to be appropriated for the support of the gospel ministry in this place, agreeably to the articles of faith adopted by the Baptist Church now in this town, to the end of time, reserving such a part of the improvement or avails of said real estate given to said Society, as may be necessary to pay certain legacies hereafter mentioned.

31y I give and bequeath to my daughter Keziah Farnum Forty Dollars annually, during her natural life, together with the use of my small House situated between my two Barns, to be paid out of the improvement of avails of the real estate given to said Society, and paid out to her by sd Society.

41y I give and bequeath to my daughter Lois Farnum Twenty Dollars annually, during five years, if she shall live so long, to be paid out of the improvement or avails of said estate given to said Society in manner aforesaid.

51y I give and bequeath to my two sons Enoch and Ephraim Bacon, and my grandson, the son of Samuel Bacon deceased all my wearing apparel to be equally divided between them.

61y I give and bequeath all the remainder of my estate, after the payment of my just debts, and expense of settling my estate together with funeral charges, and erecting suitable grave stones, at my grave, to all my children to be equally divided among them.

And lastly I do constitute and appoint Joshua Vinton and Decon Samuel Fiske, both of said Southbridge, Executors of this my last will and Testament – In testimony whereof I do hereunto set my hand and Seal this Sixth day of July in the year of our Lord One Thousand Eight Hundred and Twenty Two, In the presence of witnesses as my last will and Testament.

Ephraim Bacon

A very upsetting will. In 1822 an eldest son had a right to expect at least two full shares of his father's estate, particularly, a goodly amount of farm land.

In September, 1825, Samuel Fiske declined the trust of Executor of Ephraim Bacon's will. In November, Joshua Vinton did the same. In October, Enoch Bacon "judges himself to be aggrieved by will and claims an appeal". A note was sent to the judge claiming "father not of sound mind", and later a note was received by Judge Nathaniel Paine to the effect that,

> "We consider Ephraim Bacon died Intestate and by law each is entitled to 1/6 part of said Estate and Pray your honor to order division."

In May, 1826, "Enoch Bacon, yeoman" was appointed administrator and Ebenezer D. Ammidown, Esquire, Jason Morse, gentleman, of Southbridge, and David Wright, Esquire, of Sturbridge, were appointed to appraise the real estate and "distribute among children. . .preferring Males to Females and Elder to younger sons. . .". June 5, 1827, all who were interested appeared at the Court of Probate for the appraisal and division of the remainder of the Real Estate. They included, "widow Molly Bacon, Enoch Bacon, Hannah Higbee, of Union, N.Y., wife of Erastus and daughter of said Ephraim Bacon deceased, Kezia Bacon Farnum, widow of Luther Farnum, Lois Bacon Farnum, wife of Chamberlain Farnum, and Oliver Mason, agent for Ephraim Bacon, Jr., living in Philadelphia." John McKinstry was agent for Jacob Barnitz Bacon of York Co., Pennsylvania, the only child of Samuel. They claimed themselves to be satisfied with the division.

"An inventory of the estate of Ephraim Bacon late of South-bridge in the county of Worcester deceased appraised upon oath by us the subscribers duly appointed to that service by the Hon Nath'l Paine Esq'r Judge of Probate of wills in foesaid County viz Real Estate — The farm of said deceased situated in said South-bridge containing about 180 acres of land with the buildings thereon standing. $15.00 pr acre $2700.

Inventory of stock tools household furniture clothing books and money. Viz cash in the hands of Samuel Fisk — $15.00

1 yoke Beef cattle	$75.00
1 black beef cow	18.00
1 brindle cow	13.00
2 brown Milch cows @13.00	26.00
1 Red Milch cow	15.00
1 Brindlc Milch cow	15.00
1 Black Bull	9.00
1 Red heifer	11.00
1 Black Horse	10.00
1 bull calf	3.33
1 heifer calf	3.50
2 Steers calf	8.00
3 Hogs	57.09
10 tons of Hay straw & corn up in barn	70.00
3 Rakes	.30
1 cask & Hayseed	1.00
1 cart	3.00
77 bushle oats @30 cts	23.10
89 bushle corn @58	22.62
1½ bushle beans @4/6	1.13
1½ bushle flax seed @3/	.75
2 bushle salt @ 6/	2.00
Lot of old casks	1.00
1 old Sleigh harness	1.50
ox yoke 2 saddles	1.25
waggen & Harness	8.00
1 halter	.50

1 new bridle	.75
2 old bridle	.12
Sheepskin	.25
cords & old collars	.20
Lot of old Iron	5.00
1 bas of Iron & Steel	.67
Dry measures	.60
old axes & hammers	1.00
Saw sq'r Camp[?] & Shave	.25
Fro. butte & weges	.50
Axe helve plaines chisells	
& gauge	.50
4 sickles	.50
2 curry combs	.20
1 pr Steele yards	.25
12½ lbs old brass kettle	
@15c	1.87
winnowing seives	.38
12 lbs wool	3.00
chaines	2.50
traces	.34
2 iron bars	1.50
dung fork Shevel	.50
2 Pitch-forks	.84
Old Pot mettle	.25
27 plates -- 4 cups & saucers	1.70
3 bowlls 4 teaspoons	.35
1 clothes basket	.25
1 bed bolster & pillows	7.00
1 pr cotten & wool sheets	2.25
1 wool blanket (striped)	1.00
1 bed quilt	3.50
6 pr pillow cases 4 pr	
sheets	5.50
2 towels 1 table cloth	1.54
1 old coat	.25
3 pr pantaloons 3 old vests	1.13

3 pr cotton pantaloons	
1 silk vest	$ .50
1 pr. cotten & wool shirts	.25
2 pocket 1 pr shirts·	.95
7 yds all wool cloth	5.25
1 tin trunk	.40
1 pr Decanter	
1 doz buttons	.52
1 old steel	.25
Barrel & cider 1 honer	1.75
4 old Ploughs	1.00
5 tons of hay in two small barn	25.00
1 stack good hay	7.00
1 stack poor hay	3.00
7 cider barrells	2.34
lot of old casks	.50
1 grind stone 1 cheese press	1.25
hand cart & hay knife	.34
5 kegs & cider tunnel[1]	.84
2 wash tubs 1 iron pot	.94
2 Dish kettles 1 bake kettle	1.17
2 table cloths 1 ditto	1.84
1 old blanket 1 coverlid	1.25
1 bed bolster & pillowes	5.00
1 bedsted & cord	1.50
1 bedsted quilt 1 ditto	1.30
1 hat 1 great coat	5.00
2 old great coats	.75
1 surtout[2] 1 coat	4.00
1 coat & spencer[3]	.60

1. tun, (1) a large cask (2) A brewer's fermenting vat. Or, tunnel, a funnel.
2. surtout, a long, close-fitting over coat.
3. Spencer, A man's short jacket of early 19th century.

2 cotton coats 2 old vests	$ 1.67
1 cambrich coat	.25
1 callico gown 4 pr stockings	1.50
4 cotten handk'fs (for neck)	.40
1 pr shirts 2 pr mittens	.50
1 pr. boots 1 pr shoes	.75
Raisor & case	.12
1 bottle	1.31
1 hymn book	.37
1 case of pine Drawers	3.00
1 Maple Desk	3.34
1 small pine table	.67
lot of Leather	1.50
pr saddle bags old clock	1.34
1 table (cross legs)	.25
1 chest old cherry table	1.25
1 fauling Piece (gun)	1.50
Sheep shears bayonet spars & etc.	.12
1 pr sad irons toast iron	.75
gridiron & fry pan	.42
small brass kettle	.40
4 arm chairs 4 dining chairs	2.80
2 large arm chairs	.67
7 kitchen chairs	1.75
1 case of cherry Drawers	7.00
(see Ephraim II's will -- is this the same "fine chest"?)	
1 large setlement[1]	.25
12 milk pans	1.00
3 milk pails	.50
4 trays	.67
2 tubs	.50
1 teakettle	.50
3 Piggons	.30

1. settle, A long seat or bench, generally of wood, with a high back, originally to direct the draft up the chimney and to provide a warm nook.

1 hand wheel	$ .50
1 side saddle	2.50
worping bars Looms & ect.	3.00
1 foot wheel	2.00
Powder horn jug (?) &	
sugar box	.20
Bellows shovel & tongs	1.25
long kitchen table	.50
1 small kitchen table	.50
bread-trough cheese tub	
& chain	1.50
6 Pewter plates	.50
3 Pewter platters	1.50
3 basons	1.00
lot of tin ware	.50
1 Bras skimmer	.25
bottles & candlestick	.20
1 tin tea-pot skimer & diper	.30
choping knife	.25
6 barrels full of cider	6.00
40 bushl. Potatoes	7.00
4 kegs butter 14c lb	28.28
42 lbs flax @ 8c	3.36
3 meat barrells	.50
64 lbs skim cheese @ 2c	1.28
237 lbs 4 Meal(?) cheese @4c	9.48

When Molly died three years later, she did indeed possess only about a third of this list. In the accounting of the estate, she owed Enoch Bacon*

> "for the use of my Bull to your cow 34c
> to mending fence & damage done by cow. . . . . 50c"

The eldest son, Enoch, lived in Southbridge, a successful farmer, until his death in 1845, aged 75 years -- the only son to stay in Massachusetts. In 1806 Ephraim had made an arrangement with Enoch to give him some of his land early that he would pay for with work. Enoch said his father wanted to keep

76

see *Corrections*, page 337

from him the power to sell the land. Ephraim, Sr. had said it ". . .should not go out of the family whilst he lived".[1]

The youngest, Samuel, struggled against the wishes of his father and managed to get more than the usual schooling, eventually studing* at Harvard. He made a great impact on everyone he came in contact with, particularly his brother, Ephraim, Jr.

Ephraim, Jr., left Massachusetts to pioneer in Maine as a young man and in middle age made an effort to finish his brother Samuel's work in Africa. He was the father of Socrates Bonapart Bacon, emigrant to the West.

From the diary of Alexis de Tocqueville, written as he toured the United States in 1831:

> "Mr. Sparks said to me today; 'Landed estates in Massachusetts are no longer being divided up. The eldest almost always inherits the whole of the land.'
>
> 'And what happens to the other children?' I asked.
>
> 'They emigrate to the West.' "

1. The abandoned Bacon farms are located off Rt. 169, Woodstock Road. Route 131 passes through the Southbridge business district and joins Rt. 169 about one mile later. Turning right onto 169 and traveling two to three miles toward Woodstock brings you to the area of some scattered houses numbered in the 900's. A lane turns off to the left at the corner where the small Eddy cemetery lies, also on the left of the highway. H. Porter Morse lives at 984 Woodstock Rd.*

Sources:

Quinabaugh Historical Society Leaflets
Bowen, C. W., *Woodstock, an Historical Sketch*
American Patriots Who Fell at the Battle of Bunker Hill
Minute Men and Mariners
Forbes, E., *Paul Revere and the World He Lived In*
Lancaster, B., *From Lexington to Liberty*
————————, *The Minute Men and Their World*
Ashmun, J., *Memoir of Rev. Samuel Bacon*

77

see *Corrections*, page 337

Sturbridge Vital Records
Whipple, S. L.,   *Puritan Homes*

EPHRAIM BACON (IV)
and
LUCY CHAMBERLAIN

Ephraim grew up on his father's farm in the Bacon District, the Middlesex Gore. He was the next in age to Samuel, the youngest child. Enoch, his only other brother, was much older. Hannah, Ephraim's mother, died when he was fourteen years old and by the time his father remarried, three years later, Ephraim was well grown. His father was strict and certainly not rich but the farm must have been a pleasant place to grow up on with orchards, the horses, cows and sheep his father had. The woods were full of deer and game. The house was full of children.

Ephraim met Lucy Chamberlain in the Baptist Church and published his intentions to marry her on December 20, 1801. They were married January 24th, 1802. Lucy had been born in Charlton, a few miles away, and came from a large family headed by Eliakim Chamberlain, fifth generation from the Puritan forefather, Edmund Chamberlain; the same Edmund Chamberlain Ephraim's mother descended from in another line. (See Chamberlain family in another chapter.)

Ephraim and Lucy had three children born in Sturbridge:

Lucy,   born in 1802.

Cendarilla,   born in 1805.

SOCRATES BONAPART, born 1807.

There were just a few other Cendarilla's in N.E. but probably not another Socrates, and the *Bonapart*? Well, Napoleon conquered his fourth army in 1807.

That spring of 1807, Ephraim and his brother-in-law, Samuel Chamberlain, left for a new colony called Foxcroft in what is now Maine, a lovely country of pine forests and rivers. How long they had been listening to stories of cheap, rich land and planning to make such a move is hard to say, but many from long-established towns were pushed by circumstances to look toward the frontiers.

The Spalding brothers were first to live there in the wild center of the 7th Range and they hurried to have a mill built by January, 1807. Six more men arrived very early that spring; Timothy Hutchinson, Joseph Morse, John Bigelow, Eliphalet Washburn, and Ephraim and Samuel. These two "felled openings" and began the range's first frame house, cutting the timber from their own lots and making the shingles by hand. It was a double house made for two families to live together, with a brick chimney, a combination of two cabins with a wide, roofed-over opening between. Its site was where the soldiers monument now stands in present day Dover-Foxcroft.

In August, Samuel and Bigelow returned to Charlton to gather the families of the men in the new settlement. Samuel married Abigail Tucker while he was home and chartered a 'sailing vessel' for the little company and their belongings, "everyone considering that to be the most comfortable way for the ladies and the young children to make the trip". The household goods and provisions were to be sent by wagons from Charlton to Boston. On board were Isaac Wheeler, his wife Betsey and two children; Sarah Murray, Betsey's sister; Mrs. Nizaula Hutchinson and five children; Mrs. Prudence Morse and four children; Mr. and Mrs. John Bigelow and infant; Mr. and Mrs. Samuel Chamberlain; and Mrs. Lucy Chamberlain Bacon and her three children. Little Lucy, Jr., was five years old, Cendarilla two and a half and Socrates Bonaparte Bacon was seven months old. Mr. Bigelow become ill in Bangor and died and his family returned to Charlton.

Ephraim met the ship in Bangor where he and Samuel,

"procured a strong ox team to move with from Bangor to the settlement. They brought their household effects and a large stock of provisions to supply both familys until they should raise crops. They were four days in reaching Charleston, thence the road in many places had to be cut wider, sloughs and bogs bridged. One required a causeway no less then thirty feet in length to make it passable. They were two days in getting from Charleston to the settlement, 15 miles, and compelled to camp in the wilds one night with their women and children, their six oxen having only two bundles of corn-stalks for forage. . .Mr. Eli Towne went to meet them and found them building the long bridge and sending Mrs.

Chamberlain forward on his horse, took hold and helped finish. Mrs. Chamberlain arrived safely at Mr. Towne's but was so anxious for the others, she was sleepless through the night."

Sam Chamberlain cleared another opening for a new house and for a barn in August, 1809, where he raised a family of eleven. His first born, Sally, lived to ninety-three. All but two of his children taught at the school.

Sam Chamberlain was a delegate to the convention in 1819 that met to frame a state constitution and represented his district in the legislature, held many town offices, was trustee of the Academy that he gave to the town, and was thought to be,

". . .one of the greatest mathematical geniuses in the region. Though he never went beyond the common arithmetic, he could solve many questions impossible to all others not acquainted with higher mathematics. Captain Chamberlain was a model farmer, knowing how to make the farm pay. In the most unfavorable seasons, he always raised his own bread and some to spare. . .He was an excellent economist, giving shape to many judicious measures in town, as well as on his own premises. His moral character was beyond reproach, and in all his dealings with men he was the soul of honor. He was a friend to the poor. He reared up, and gave an academic education to a large family, A wild horse upset his chaise in 1838, at age 54, and he was fatally injured. He was taken to the dwelling of J. H. Loring [husband of one of his daughters], gave directions for the settlement of his estate which had grown to $8,000, lingered for 24 hours and expired June 6."

When Samuel built his new farm, Ephraim took down the house they had built together and moved it. His house still stands in Dover-Foxcroft where the two matching parts can be clearly identified.*

In August, 1811, Ephraim and Lucy's fourth child was born. Charlotte Anne Bacon was listed in the records back home as ". . .born at Piscataquis No. 5, in the 7th Range". Perhaps she was named after Lucy's sister, Charlotte, who had come up to live in Foxcroft and married Dr. Aaron Tucker. Lucy's brother, Nathaniel, also came to live in Foxcroft and was a skilled carpenter and cabinet maker.

Ephraim is listed as age 36 at the top of the poll of registered

83

see *Corrections,* page 337

voters in 1812 but after that there are no more notices of him in Foxcroft. Lucy died sometime before 1820 for her father's will of that year speaks of his "deceased daughter Lucy Bacon's children". The children were almost certainly living with Grandfather Chamberlain about that time and their world had changed.

So had Ephraim's. He had married Charlotte Ellis and in 1821 they both sailed for Africa to continue the work Samuel Bacon had devoted all of his energies to at the time of his death.

Sources:

Loring, *History of Piscataquis Co., Maine*
Lowell, M. C., *Old Foxcroft, Maine*
Charlton Vital Records

SAMUEL BACON

All through the time Ephraim was clearing land in the Maine wilderness his young brother, Samuel, was intent upon receiving a formal education.

When Samuel was a boy he'd had a contemplative turn of mind which made it,

> "impossible for me to work alone. Whenever I attempted it I soon fell into a profound reverie on the heavens, on the trees, the birds, the plants. . .my axe or hoe would fall from my hand, and I would think no more of it until roused by the approach of my father or some one of the family. I then would seize my implement . . .with the most poignant regret for the time I had lost."

When he was eighteen he was relieved to find work with a neighboring farmer and left the home he felt was too strict and quarellsome.

But a physician came to town the next year, greatly impressing the neighborhood and Ephraim, Sr., with his skill "and power of income". Samuel convinced his father it was advantagous to allow him more education. It was almost agreed that he could go to live eight weeks with the pastor of the Baptist Church of Sturbridge to learn English grammar until they found the charge for board and room was one dollar and twenty-five cents a week. Ephraim investigated Leicester Academy, sixteen miles away, where he found the tuition one dollar per quarter and board only one dollar a week so that in eight weeks time one dollar would be saved by going to that school. A dollar was worth something, just look at Ephraim's inventory. Samuel wrote,

> "I was able to read English correctly, and could spell well the common terms of the language, understood the simple rules of arithmetic, and could write as bad a hand, nearly, as at this time."

His father took him to Leicester on the first of April of 1801 on horseback, carrying provisions enough to last himself and the horses until their return. He found Samuel two or three elementary books and a place to board; paid the four shillings for his tuition and gave him twenty-five cents for incidental expenses, warning him to make his money last.

Samuel absorbed everything. It took him three days to learn the principles of English grammar and he felt he was at last at a place where he had the ability to succeed at something.

After spending the summer months on the farm, he coaxed his way back to Leicester where he was in charge of the parish school. He then obtained permission from his father to return for the next term and began Latin. Within five days he had memorized the Latin grammatical forms and by the end of the two month term was reading the easier Latin poets. He prepared for admission to Harvard and also taught a school near Leicester through the next two winters. Dutifully, a few weeks during each of those years he spent helping Ephraim bring in the harvest.

Samuel entered as a freshman at Harvard in the fall of 1804. He had traveled on foot "with his bundle" from home to Cambridge and now he needed to live with the most rigid economy. He applied for a partial scholarship, the "Holden Freshman", that required him to ring the bell twelve times daily for all exercises at college and to kindle and care for all the fires in the recitation rooms. He continued to teach grammer school through the winter and "showed an affectionate and interested regard for children".

The second and third year his servitorship duty was to wait on the common table of the college. These two winters he taught at Sudbury. Eventually, the extra work affected his health and, since he could not discontinue any of it, his health steadily worsened until he was forced to leave school to recover from a "pulmonary consumption".

He graduated from Harvard in September but because of his illness was not able to receive his diploma with his class.

Slowly, his health improved, and he started to read for the law in Rutland, close to home. Then in July, 1809, he moved to Worcester to manage the National Ægis, a respected weekly newspaper, and continued to read law under the guidance of Levi Lincoln, Jr., Esq., Lieutenant Governor of the state. But as the Massachusetts winter approached he decided to join a friend in Philadelphia where the weather was thought to be milder.

The job prospects in Pennsylvania were disappointing and money and health became a problem again. He wrote a letter to a physician friend, George C. Shattuck in Boston;

"Shippensburg, Jan. 6th, 1810

Dear Sir, Every thing, says somebody, has a beginning, a middle and an end. I wrote you from Lancaster, where I considered myself as beginning my enterprise. I now am I think about the centre and should deem myself inexcusable did I not write you something appertaining thereto. I do this the more readily as I am a little down at the heel and in writing to you, I shall entertain the comfortable idea of a *Doctor.* Besides I have the satisfaction of telling you that I have atoned for all those small sins and I could hope some of the big ones. Be patient, and I will answer you that old catechistical query, 'What is atonement?' It consists in doing as follows. The day after I wrote you I started from Lancaster on foot for York, the shire town of the county of that name. I did this because the stage would not go till the next week. . .It is 23 miles to York and half of that way I traveled in a wet snow of four inches deep with thin boots and of course with wet feet. York is in point of wealth and population the third town in the state, about 3400 inhabitants. They have a *'College'* there with small funds. It was said they were in *great want* of an instructor and much encouragement was given me by people acquainted with the place. I concluded it was the most favorable place for me in the State. I arrived in due time; and, after waiting three days, met the trustees in solemn conclave; portly Dutchmen by trade; and the amount of all the fuss was, I might open a school if I chose. I found they had one *professor,* who instructed in the A, B, C, and gave lectures on the A, B, ab, with a salary of *three hundred* per An. Were I to engage, I should have the income of seven latin schollars $24 each per An.; of perhaps fifteen english schollars at $8 each and the interest of their funds. . .But it is all a matter of *experiment.* Dutchmen do not like to be insulted with Latin and Greek. Their brain is so impregnably fortified with scull, that surprise is out of the question; and who, of common mortal composition, would not shrink at undertaking to carry them by a regular siege? I left York, to return if nothing better offered. I was told at that place, that by taking the stage for Hanover, (which, they said was only twenty-three miles from Carlisle whither I wished to go) I should find a stage there ready on my arrival to start for Carlisle. Thinking. . .such walk as

87

I had was quant. suff. I determined to go. . .by stage via Hanover. I. . .arrived in due order and time viz. very late and body bruised and partly frozen. On my arrival think of my disappointment, when I found I was two miles farther from Carlisle than I was at York; with the comfortable prospect of embracing one of three alternatives, wait seven days for a stage, hire a man and two horses to carry me, or walk thro' a mudy road where every step brought after it a sample of the soil of a pounds weight!! Good God! such a bore! a 'trick upon a traveller!' After mature deliberation I determined to mortify the flesh a little more. I started and tramped seven miles of it. There I would have hired a passage, had not the price there been the same as at Hanover. . .In short after wading the better part of three days in mud or clay nearly over shoes I arrived in Carlisle, worn quite out. I really fear serious bad consequences from the excessive fatique. In Carlisle I found no encouragement. . . I shall if nothing better is found here return to Lancaster for my trunk and settle at York. I must settle myself and recruit soon or I shall be settled with by the universal Accountant; be brought to a balance and may I not be found wanting! Sixty miles on foot in the very worst of travelling and four hundred and thirty with ninety more to get to York again. . .is enough to wear out all but the soul, which God be praised, rises in strength as difficulties increase. I could travel the last inch of skin from my bones (I have no *flesh*) and not repine could I but be assured by so doing I could pay my debts. To do that is the first wish of my heart and will draw my last sigh. . .But cheerly, Doctor, I am yet two thirds as stout as you last saw me and there is no telling what a little squad of a Dutch girl may do for me in case of necessity. I have been to one ball with them (a very genteel one when I saw *congressmen*) and squeezed the little cross cut rouges with a *righte smarte squeeze*. My Dear friend, tho' clouds and darkness rest on my prospects, I have faith well grounded of being bettered by my journey in point of property, if not health. Believe me your thankful friend

Bacon

Samuel reluctantly returned to Lancaster and after some struggle opened a school in the academy with five students. The school florished and soon had one hundred and fifty scholars. He poured all his profit back into his school, annually going into debt to try to perfect his own teaching system. He considerably raised the standard of education of York County, Pensylvania. He understood the relationship between student and teacher and once wrote to his teachers that every student must be asking, ". . .in the inimitable language of the Highland Bard,

"O come you in peace here, or come you in war?' " In his spare time he again edited a small weekly political newspaper, the *Hive*, to which he contributed some of his own writing:

THE GHOST OF A SACHEM

The war-song arose on the night's drowsy pinions,
It rose from the site, where his wigwam once stood:
On the banks of the Mohawk, his sire's wild dominions,
It roll'd in shrill echoes, -- the song of the wood.

The sky towering wilds of the untrodden mountains,
Reporting the full notes by distance made mild;
The Mohawk's rude billows, in haste from their fountains,
In consonance echoed, "the prince of the wild!"

By the flash of the far distant fire's dying embers,
I saw the red chieftain arise from the earth;
He review'd each old haunt; for the spirit remembers
Each scene, that to joy or to sorrow gave birth.

His shoulders o'er spread with his battle-worn blanket,
His ensigns of wildness all hung by his side;
His wounds weeping blood, while his native earth drank it:
For the "ghost of the sachem" appeared, as he died.

How oft," he exclaimed, "have my visits nocturnal
Been made to this spot, where my kindred all fell?
And let me still wander, "great spirit," supernal!
And still let the war-note on midnight's ear swell.

My old oaks, that stood like my tribe, long unshaken,
Brav'd the tempest, and storm, and the elements' roar;
My warriors, – my tribe -- the destroyer has taken;
The children of nature shall reign here no more.

The time-moulder'd stump of my forests now shew me,
They're pilfered, some towering wigwam to rear,
No more my own lands, as their sachem, shall know me;
Their vales are all furrowed – their groves are not here.

The buffalo, hence, with his bulky distention,
The elk and the deer from the river banks hie;
The mammoths, that bellow'd in dreadful convention,
No more shall here battle with powers of the sky!

The chase, that among yonder hill-tops resounded;
That fired the young red-man with enterprise high,
The yell, that exults, when the fleet deer is wounded,
No longer on wind or on breeze passes by.

The council-fire's blaze, where I oft quell'd commotion,
No longer illumines the gloom of the night;
No longer arises the fire of devotion;
No longer the war-dance leads on to the fight;

How oft have I buried the blood-thirsty hatchet!
For the white man besought, and the sachem was brave!
How oft did his treachery tempt me to snatch it;
And not e'en his wife or his little ones, save!

In an hour of repose the fell rifle was level'd;
It murder'd my boys, and my girls, and my wife!
The Mohawk received them; their straight hair dishevel'd:
It next sought their chief, and robb'd him too of life!

But the day-star approaches the darkness to banish;
I haste to the 'land of my fathers' in rest;
The breezy dawn comes, and each spirit must vanish;
The grave is my home, and the darkness my guest.

Samuel was a success at Lancaster and in March 1812 he was asked by the trustees of York College to take charge of that institution. There he wrote *Outline of the System of Government and Instruction Adopted in York County Academy* and was considered "an educator far in advance of his time." The "Outline" is now in the library of the Theological Seminary at Gettysburg.

The War of 1812 intruded and while Samuel waited for his commission as 2ond Lieutenant in the Marines he organized the Junior Volunteers of York County Academy. They marched to the defence of Baltimore where they fought in the battle of North Point. When his commission arrived, Samuel was ordered to New York to take charge of the Sloop of War, *Argus*. He became an ardent foe of dueling during that service after he fought a duel with a fellow officer, an old friend, and was wounded in the thigh.

On the last day of May, 1814, he married Anna Maria, daughter of Jacob Barnitz, Esq., one of those trustees of the York Academy he had written so disparagingly of in 1809. It was because of Anna Maria that he began to read the Bible. They were stationed in Washington that summer and Samuel was promoted to Captain, renewed his study of law and, by January 1815, was admitted to the bar. He opened a law office in York as soon as he was discharged.

In March a son was born they named Jacob Barnitz Bacon[1]. But Anna Maria never recovered from the birth and died in August, causing Samuel to turn more toward his wife's religion.

Samuel's practice grew and he "never departed from [an] unbending line of integrity". He was "habitually generous" to his poor clients.

> "Mr. Bacon not only spoke with great fluency, but often with eloquence, at the bar; and even in the dry details of a law-speech, he exhibited a richness and exuberence of mind that always excited interest."

One of the services Samuel's office supplied was to help Revolutionary soldiers apply for Government pension. He wrote on the application of Joseph Wren,

> "This old man's body and spirit seem to be equally light. He can

---

1. Jacob Barnitz Bacon, graduated from Gettysburg College, 1834, was "a scholar and expert employed for 17 years by the New York City Finance Dept. Among his outstanding public services" was his address to the city's Common Council "pleading that it prevent the opening of a new street through the graveyard of Old Trinity Church" where many York Co., Penn., Revolutionary soldiers were buried. The street was not opened. Jacob Bacon wrote several articles for magazines, one for "Frank Leslie's Chimney Corner", *Reminiscenses of New York in the Olden Days*. He had four sons (Frances Hause B., Charles Henry B., William H. Powell B., George Jones B.), and a daughter, Anna Mary (Bacon) Smith. He died May 18, 1896.

travel his thirty miles a day with ease. His appearance reminds you of the Egyptian Mummies so celebrated for their fresh and life-like appearance after the lapse of centuries. . .[has] had hair breadth 'scapes. . .and is spared to be made glad by something very unlike the ingratitude of republics."

And for another,

". . .Joel Gray -- He may indeed be addressed in the style of the old ballad,

O why do you shiver and shake Gaffer Gray?
And why does your nose look so blue?
I am grown old,
And the weather 'tis cold,
And my doublet is not very new."

Of course, he did not forget to state Gray's military service.

In 1815, Samuel was appointed District Attorney of the United States for York and Adams Counties. At the same time, he felt he needed the stablizing power of religion and joined the Episcopal Church. He began to use his spare time to form York's first Sunday schools for poor children and 'free blacks' and united people from all the different Christian societies in York to teach, two novel ideas for that time. He was soon teaching four nights a week. That, and directing the Sunday schools, he called his 'meat and drink'.

He then started to organize Sunday schools in other parts of Pennsylvania, traveling to them at first only on Sundays and then Saturdays and Mondays, too, to initiate rural people in the ways to form and support such schools. In the beginning he even managed them and continually revisited them on a circuit.

"Had you seen me at one time beating my way through the hills, with great difficulty, and some danger, --myself, horse, sleigh and all nearly buried in snowbanks: at other times, out late and early, in the wet and cold; drenched in rain; often so exhausted as to be hardly able to address an audience. . .you would exclaim that nothing but divine help could have sustained me."

Again, his health suffered. He drove himself to use every minute to teach and pray.

> "Last Sabbath, I visited two of our schools in the country. On my approach within two miles of one of them. I fell in with a little company of children, hastening to it, as cheerful as the birds of the forest where I met them. I followed them through the almost pathless woods. . .There the solitary place rejoiced in a song of Zion: amongst the wild shrubbery of the wilderness were seen these blooming plants of immortal growth."

On October 15, 1818, Samuel wrote of Ephraim Jr.,

> "My cup is full to overflowing. . .A brother of mine lately visited me. He was a confirmed deist. Being older than myself, I neglected . . .to invite him to our prayer meetings, fearing the ridicule of sacred things which might be expected from his satirical tongue. But a sense of duty compelled me to take him along. We went into meeting: in prayer, he was the only one present who stood. He kept his position as erect as a post: until, as I was kneeling near him, I pulled him by the coat, and he came upon his knees. –God. . . enabled me to wrestle. .for his salvation. I did so; and kept him with me about twelve days. In the mean time he was born both, 'of the water and of the Spirit '. . .He has left me, and all his sins behind."

Samuel's biographer wrote,

> the brother referred to in this extract, has since exhibited a life of consistent piety, and been usefully imployed in a public capacity, on the coast of Africa."

On the coast of Africa? Samuel had been for several years a member of the Abolition Society of Pennsylvania. He had also been writing essays for the papers to explain the aims of the Colonization Society. This society believed that freed slaves were, as a

> "class of people, freed indeed from personal bondage, but still separated by indelible characteristics, from the great body of citizens . . .every year witnessing an increase of their numbers. . ."

and that colonization would benefit both 'free blacks and the American community". Members included Daniel Webster, Levi Lincoln (with whom Samuel had studied law and who was later Governor of the state), Francis Scott Key and Bushrod Washington, President of the organization, Supreme Court Justice and, incidently, George Washington's nephew.*

The Colonization Society in Washington asked Samuel, now an ordained Episcopal Priest, to join their planned expedition to the west coast of Africa to form a settlement for free American blacks and in January, 1820, he received his commission and orders from President Monroe.

A likely site had already been scouted for the settlement and the merchant ship *Elizabeth* and a sloop of war, the *Cyane*, with twenty-four guns, were to be sent over. The sloop was to intercept any American slave ship and liberate the blacks aboard. These, and thirty families the Colonization Society had chosen from a great number of black applicants, would be landed at a place called Sherbro.

Before sailing, Samuel spent two weeks in Washington confering with "the executive officers of the general government and the managers of the Colonization Society". After their first meeting, one of these wrote,

". . .[he] inspired those he met [as] one of the brightest examples of piety and christian benevolence in the age. . ."

His biographer wrote,

"Mr. Bacon was tall. . .frame was masculine, and rather indicative of strength. . .features strongly marked. . .[his] expression . . .blended an interesting pensiveness. . .[he] was impatient of opposition, rapid in his movements. . .determined. . .[he had a] sincerity incapable of disguise. . ."

They were to sail on Monday, the 31st of January, and several thousand people came to see the ship off, causing a near riot. While Samuel spoke to the crowd he arranged to quietly send the passengers on board one by one.

Out on the seas, they suffered several frightening gales and near-mutiny by some of the crew. The instigators were summarily thrown overboard by the Captain's orders. The ship next developed a leak that allowed twenty-four inches of water in the hold an hour. It was repaired, but with enormous effort.

94

see *Corrections*, page 337

On March 30, the mission arrived near Sherbro at Campelar. Kissel, a native of the place, seemed to be helping them deal with the nearby African chieftans but he was very slow to help them to their own land where the ground and the water looked healthier than where they were camped. Samuel liked the people and thought the land could become a lush garden. He visited the chiefs and hiked far inland stopping at huts along the way to sip water offered in kindness.

But before the ships were even unloaded, the passengers began to suffer with fevers, and next the agents and the doctor and some of the ship's crew. Samuel was the only one strong enough to treat them. He fed the people, administered medicine, labored on the houses being built, rowed boats, handled casks while unloading the ship. And then the rainy season began. Several people died.

On April 16th, Samuel began to feel the fever himself and steadily worsened. On the 28th, a boat from African Sierre Leone anchored and two men, one a doctor, from that English-governed camp, came ashore. But they had come on their own special errand and were uninterested in the health of this colony. They returned that evening to their ship.

After long negotiations, they were persuaded to take Samuel with them the next day. But as his small boat approached the ship he was to board, it lifted its anchor and set sail. Because there was only a light wind, the natives in Samuel's boat were able to follow closely for six hours, only a silk umbrella protected the feverish man from the sun.

On the evening of the next day he was landed at Cape Shilling, almost unconcious. He was taken care of by Captain William Randle, superintendant of the station, all through the next day. Once Samuel seemed to be asking a question about what might be reserved for him in Heaven. Mr. Randle answered that he was sure Samuel would receive "a happiness that would abundantly compensate his present sufferings". Some of Samuel's last words were, "Ah, that is all I want!"

Before dawn the next morning he died and was buried next to the church in the settlement.

Every member of the crew of one of the ships died and only one agent, Rev. Coker, lived to administer the colony and the colonists, of which twenty had died. He worked there alone until March, 1821, when new agents arrived on the Nautilus with supplies and a reinforcement of colonists. She had sailed from Norfolk with agents for the government and the Society aboard. Ephraim Bacon was one of the agents.

Sources:

Carter, *History of York County*

Shattuck F. C. , *A Forgotten Hero, Atlantic Monthly Magazine, Vol. 142, November 1928*

Ashmun, J., Memoir of Rev. Samuel Bacon, A.M. From edition reprinted by *Books for Libraries Press*, 1969 Distributed by Arno Press, Inc.

Appleton, *Compendium of American Biography*

_____, *The York Co. Academy*

Fox, *The American Colonization Society 1817-1840*

ABSTRACT OF A JOURNAL

KEPT BY

B. BACON,

UNITED STATES ASSISTANT AGENT

FOR THE

RECEPTION OF RECAPTURED NEGROES

ON THE

WESTERN COAST OF AFRICA,

CONTAINING

An Account of the First Negotiations

FOR THE

PURCHASE OF LANDS

FOR THE

AMERICAN COLONY.

FOURTH EDITION

PHILADELPHIA:
CLARK & RASER, PRINTERS, 33 CARTER'S ALLEY.
1834.

PREFACE
***

The public have been already informed of the strenuous exertions of the United States government, in enacting numerous laws for the purpose of suppressing the slave trade; and of the successful vigilance of our naval officers, in detecting those desperadoes, the slave-traders, and bringing them to justice.

The public have also been informed of the benevolent operations of the American Colonization Society, in endeavouring to form a settlement on the western coast of Africa, composed of those free people of colour who choose to emigrate thither. It is moreover known that this settlement, if established, may prove an asylum for those Africans, who shall be recaptured by the United States' cruisers and sent to the coast.

Having been employed as an assistant agent of the United States, with J. B. Winn, Esq. principal agent in transporting to the coast of Africa a number of recaptured Africans and free people of colour; the author has had an opportunity of witnessing the degraded state of that section of the earth, and feels it a duty he owes to the souls of his fellow creatures, to lay before the Christian world a plain statement of facts in relation to the subject, which he doubts not will be interesting to all, and confidently trusts useful to many.

It may be proper to mention, that Mr. Winn, and the author, were accompanied in the expedition by the Rev. J. R. Andrus, principal, and Mr. C. Wiltberger, assistant agents of the Colonization Society, together with Mrs. Winn and Mrs. Bacon, in the brig Nautilus, Captain Blair, and further, that the author's return was cause by ill health.

E. B.

ABSTRACT, &c.

We left Norfolk on the 21st of January, 1821, and on the 23rd sailed from Hampton Roads. For about thirty days we encountered head winds and strong gales, and made slow progress. During this time I was very seasick, as were also Mrs. Bacon, and the Rev. Mr. Andrus. The other agents were less afflicted; some of the colonists suffered from the same malady. Our captain was remarkable kind and attentive to those who were sick, and particularly to Mrs. Bacon and myself, when we were unable to wait upon ourselves, for which kindness I shall always feel myself under very many obligations to him. Nothing uncommon occurred during our voyage, except that we experienced a very severe gale of wind, accompanied with a snow storm, which our captain told us was more violent than any he had known during the preceding twenty years. It was indeed a time to try our faith.

At the commencement of the voyage, we established morning and evening prayers in the cabin as well as in the steerage, where the coloured people were: in these we enjoyed the consolations of the religion we profess.

We had all recovered from sea-sickness, and having arrived within the tropics, where the weather was fine and the wind favourable, our passage was more agreeable, and during the remainder of our voyage, a continuation of the mercies of our heavenly Father were daily bestowed upon us. On the morning of the 8th of March, we had a distant view of the mountains of Sierra Leone, which was really animating after crossing the Atlantic. We felt ourselves approaching towards that much injured country, where we expected to labour, and to suffer many and great afflictions. We were cheered with the hope, that through the assistance of Divine grace, we should be, in a greater or less degree, useful among the degraded children of Africa. The wind was fair but rather light, as is not

Note: Ephraim Bacon's Journal has been edited to condense its great length.

uncommon in the dry season. We soon hove in sight of Cape Sierra Leone, when we discovered, for the first time, several native canoes approaching roward us. These excited our curiosity. They were manned by the native Kroomen, in a state of nudity, or nearly so. When I speak of naked people, it may be always understood that they wear a cloth about their loins, and that the men generally wear hats. These hats are manufactured out of a kind of grass. . .

We soon discovered a fine English barge approaching us, rowed by natives. In this were the harbour master. . .who very politely gave us much interesting information, relative to our American blacks at Sherbro. As we approached near the harbour, they gave the American agents a friendly invitation to go on shore in the barge, and take lodgings at their house. As the principal agent concluded to remain on board, Mrs. Bacon and myself thought proper not to slight their politeness, our accommodations in the brig being somewhat circumscribed, and the transition from Norfolk, where the cold was excessive, to Sierra Leone, where the degrees of heat were at noon day from 85 to 87½ in the shade, making a visit to land desirable . . .We accordingly went on shore, where we were politely and hospitably entertained for several days.

The agents. . .soon had an interview with the Rev. Daniel Coker, by whom we learnt the condition of the American settlers at Sherbro. . .Although very many of the settlers were extremely ill when they left Kizell's Place, and removed to Yonie, a more healthy part of Sherbro island. . .still no deaths by fever occurred at Yonie; but. . .a general recovery took place, notwithstanding there was no medical aid. The sickness at Kizzell's Place was evidently in a great degree owing to local causes: the water alone is said to be sufficiently bad to create malignant disorders, though Kizzell was base enough to assert that it contained peculiar qualities highly conducive to health. That, and other false assertions, induced the former agents to receive his offer of friendship; pretending, as he did, to unbounded influence among the native chiefs; an ardent desire to further the benevolent objects of our government and the Society; to benefit America; to meliorate the condition of the African race, and propagate the glorious gospel of God in a heathen land.

. . .A meeting of all the agents. . .took place, when it was unanimously agreed to relinquish the idea of making any further attempt to negotiate for lands in the Sherbro country . . .that Rev. Mr. Andrus and myself should be deputed to the service of exploring the coast, and (enter) into negotiations with the native chiefs. . .

The 22d of March. At 5 o'clock, P.M. all hands are on board, some of the sailors intoxicated; the captain appears to make unnecessary delays. At length we set sail. After doubling the cape, we stood out to sea, far enough to clear all the head lands and islands of the coast; and then proceeding coastwise, we made Cape Mount, about 250 miles distant from Sierra Leone, on the 27th. This part of the coast we had previously learned to be in the occupancy of King Peter, one of the most powerful and war-like chiefs of West Africa, and more deeply engaged in the slave trade than any of his neighbours. The known hostility of his views to the objects of the American government and Society, dissuaded us from incurring any loss of time or expense in procuring an interview with him. We accordingly proceeded onward to the mouth of the Mesurado river about 30 miles south of Cape Mount, where we came to anchor the next day, before two small islands, owned by John Milts, a yellow man, having an English education, and Cary, a black native African. Both of these men are slave dealers, and it is supposed that their islands are mere slave markets. Every appearance went to justify this suspicion. The neighbourhood of Cape Mesurado having been indicated as a part of the coast favourable to our purpose, we were induced to make the most particular inquiry and observations in our power, relative to the advantages and disadvantages that would attend a settlement here.

The appearance of this part of the left bank of the Mesurado river, which terminates in the cape of the same name, is sufficiently elevated, and inviting. The natural growth is luxuriant and abundant; many of the trees attain to a large size, and present every indication of a strong and fertile soil.*

While we were at anchor, a schooner under French colours appeared, laying off and apparently waiting for an opportunity to come in and receive a cargo of slaves. We saw a great number of young Africans, who appeared as if intended for that vessel.

. . .On the 1st of April, we brought the schooner to anchor off the mouth of the Grand Bassa river, at the distance of three-forths of a mile. We were soon surrounded with canoes, which brought on board a large number of natives. By one of them we despatched a small present to the king. This prince's name is Jack Ben, lately advanced to the supreme power, from the rank of principal head-man, in consequence of the death of King John, which occurred about four months before our visit.

. . .Monday morning, April 2d, Grand Bassa. Mr. Andrus and myself went on shore in our boat, below the mouth of Grand Bassa, to take a view of the point of land which projects out onto the sea. A fort, erected on this point, would completely command the whole harbour. After visiting the point, it was necessary to cross the Grand Bassa a short distance above its mouth, as the surf was turbulent below the bar. Our conductor was a Krooman, by the name of Bottle Beer. When we came to the left bank of the river, we saw no canoe or other means of crossing over as we thought; but Bottle Beer proposed to carry us over, and placed himself in a suitable position, and told one of us to sit upon his shoulders, when brother Andrus seated himself with one leg over each shoulder; then Bottle Beer walked deliberately through the river, carrying his burden safe to the other bank, and returned back and proposed to take me. I told him I was so fat and heavy that he would let me fall into the water; he put his hands upon his arms and legs, and

---

* This cape has since been negotiated for, together with a large tract of fertile country, and the American colony are settled on it.

This land was the nucleus of what is now the Republic of Liberia. L.W.

said, "Me strong, me carry you, Daddy." At length I seated myself likewise upon Bottle Beer, and though he was not as heavy a person as myself, he carried me safe over without wetting me; as the water was about half a fathom deep. After this we walked about 300 yards, to Bottle Beer's town, a little cluster of cottages inhabited by Kroomen, of which B. B. is head-man. . .The population is perhaps from 60 to 100; we were conducted to the palaver-house, where the people soon gathered together, and shook hands with us. After remaining a short time, we were conducted to another town (so called) where the people were boiling salt-water for salt, as they do at all the towns near the beach; this is called Salt-town; through this we passed to Jumbotown, which is about one mile from Bottle Beer's town, and much larger.

. . .About 1 o'clock, P.M. we returned back to our boat, which was at B.B.'s town. After the boat was in readiness, one of the Kroomen took me in his arms and carried me above the surf to the boat, and likewise Mr. Andrus, so that we were not wet; and all this kindness without being solicited. Indeed they are very kind and hospitable; they gave us water to drink, and palm wine, and made us welcome to such as they had. As is customary, they begged for tobacco, of which we gave a small quantity to the head-men, who always distribute among the people.

. . .Tuesday, April 3d. This morning brother Andrus was not in very good health, and did not go on shore, but took medicine. . .We. . .sent another message to the king. . .Davis saw some of the head-men to-day, who appear to be suspicious that we had some unfriendly object in view; but. . .he. . .is endeavouring to remove their doubts. . .I. . .Returned on board with not only my locks but my flannels drenched with perspiration. . .No prospect as yet of seeing the king. . .this evening brother Andrus's health is better. . .

Wednesday morning, April 4th. At six o'clock. . .we started in our boat, with four boatmen and our interpreters, making eight of us; and five natives, two of which were head-men, in two of their canoes. We ascended the river St. John to the first island. The banks of the river are rather low but suitable for cultivation. . .It was with great difficulty that we prevailed on the natives and our boat's crew to proceed any further, because they said, "White man never live above that place". It appeared that they doubted the efficacy of their gregres, which they never fail to wear when exposed to danger. . .We proceeded onwards. .15 to 20 miles. The land. . .becomes more elevated, with a fine growth of timber, admirably situated for settlements.

. . .At 7 o'clock, the boat arrived [back] at the mouth of the river, and before crossing the bar, brother A., myself, Tamba and Davis, went on shore, where we had a most fatiguing walk down the beach to Junbotown; our boat not being able to go over the bar before daylingt, as the tide did not favour. . . the native canoes were small and unsafe for us. Having been twelve hours exposed to the scorching rays of the sun, and having walked four miles in the damp of the evening, with our clothes drenched in perspiration, and being obliged to lay down supperless upon a floor composed of bamboo sticks, without any covering but our wet garments -- having no door to our cottage, and several hundred natives within twenty yards, drumming and dancing, until one or two o'clock in the morning, -- indeed these were times that the secret ejaculations of the heart ascended up to the throne of the Heavenly Grace, for grace to help in that hour of need. . .

Thursday Morning, April 5th. . .We this day learned from a head-man, that we could have land, but that we must go to the king's town tomorrow.

Friday Morning, April 6th. . . .We went on shore, and went to the king's town, but could not see him. . .Tamba and Davis. . . labour. . .to convince. . .that we have not come with any hostile intention. . .Brother A——, and Davis. . .saw the body of King John, who had been dead for moons, yet not buried; he was laid in state, in a palaver-house, dressed in a fine robe, with a pair of new English boots on the feet: a brick fire is kept buning in the room His grave is dug, which is eight feet square, for the purpose of admitting the body and the form upon which it lies, together with bullocks, goats, sheep, tobacco and pipes, as sacrifices!

Sunday, April 8th. . .King Ben. . .would meet us in Jumbo-town, in palaver, the next morning. . .

Monday, April 9th. . .we went on shore, with a present to the king, (as it is impossible to get a palaver with the authorities of the country, without a respectable present "to pay service") . . .we met his majesty. King Jack Ben of Grand Bassa, together with several of his head-men. . .with a large concourse of people. . .The king asked us what we wanted, although he could not have been ignorant of our wishes. We stated our object to be, "to get land for the black people in America, to come and sit down upon upon. .to occupy. We told him that the people were very many, and required much territory; that a few white men only would come along to assist and take care of them; that we should make a town where ships would come and trade with cloth, and guns, and beads, and knives, and tobacco, and pipes; and take in return, their ivory, and palm oil, and rice, and every other thing growing in the fields; that they would not then need to sell any more people, but might learn to cultivate the ground, and make other things to sell for whatever they wanted".

. . .We returned on board weary and faint. After partaking of some refreshment, and having implored the divine blessing of Him who has promised to give to his Son the heathen for his inheritance, and the uttermost parts of the earth for his possession, retired to rest.

Tuesday, April 10th. . .This day is expected to be a day of importance, as the palaver will be much larger. . .the king and his counsel withdrew to the shade of a large silk cotton tree, in conclave, for the space of twenty or thirty minutes. . . They demanded of us a positive stipulation, to make a contract, that the settlers and agents should act in consistency with this character, and in no way assist the armed ships sent to the coast to suppress the slave-trade, by communicating to them any information that might prove injurious to the Bassa people. We represented to them the advantages which would attend their relinquishing the trade altogether. . .

Thursday, April 13th. . .we directed our intrepretors (to) . . .describe it. . .The head-men readily agreed. . .They all took hold of the pen and made their marks; they then cried aloud, "Palaver set! Palaver set!" . . .At evening we took an affectionate leave of the king. . .

Grand Bassa, Saturday morning, April 14th. . .At twelve o'clock we set sail on our return to Sierra Leone. . .We are turning our attention to the state of our settlers at Sherbro . . . . .we are very anxious to hear from our friends. . .The pestilence which walketh in darkness hath not come near us; therefore, we are under renewed obligations to praise the Lord for his goodness, and for his wonderful works in the great deep.

Monday, April 16th. Last night there was a tremendous tornado, with much rain; at the appearance of a tornado it is necessary to take in all sail immediately, as the wind generally blows powerfully.

Our Kroomen are easily intimidated in bad weather; they have on their gregres, those which they think contain the most virtue and are best calculated to preserve them from the greatest danger. I endeavoured to persuade them that their gregres were useless, and advised them to throw them into the sea, but my entreaties were in vain; one had his gregre tied with a twine around his head above his ears; I took hold of the string and broke it. On examining it, I found it was composed of a ball of clay, tied up in a piece of white muslin, with a small feather in the end; he was angry and sorry for his loss. . .I threw the gregre into the sea, which grieved him very much.

Thursday morning, April 19th. We were within sight of the Shebar. . .[near Shebro]. Laying off and on with our vessel, hoping a pilot would come off to our assistance; several guns were fired as signals for pilots, but none came. . .As our sailors were unwilling to go in the boat, I prevailed upon them by proposing to accompany them. After approaching as near the Shebar as was thought prudent, the vessel was brought to anchor at four o'clock, P.M. The boat was manned with the mate of the vessel and three natives, one a sailor, the others

Kroomen. The mate although a tolerably good boatman, apprehended more danger than I did, for I had not much experience in crossing such bars. At length we started in the boat, and approached near the bar. It appeared dangerous indeed. The mate being at the rudder, gave directions to the oarsmen to obey him promptly; he told them he should watch the motion of the waves, and that, when he ordered them to pull at the oars, they must pull for their lives. We soon found our boat first soaring over the turbulent waves, then plunging into the deep, while the waves were tolling in quick succession after us, each appearing as if it would bury us in the ocean. One wave poured about sixty gallons of water into the boat, which cause me active employment in lading out the water; the boat having been brought quartering to the waves, it required quick exertion by the men at the oars, who were somewhat frightened, but were enabled to bring the boat to its proper position before the succeeding wave came, which wafted us over the greatest danger; by that time I had nearly laded out the water. Indeed, it was mercy to us that we were not swallowed up. . .We soon after arrived at Bohol, where we obtained a pilot. . .

I obtained a passage to Yonie, in. . .a canoe. . .where I arrived at nine o'clock, and found the American free people of colour who had survived of the first expedition. I went to the house where Nathaniel Brander resides;. .I was very much fatigued, from having been wet in the boat, and afterwards exposed to the damps of the evening. I soon learnt the condition of the people, and found they were in good health; they had previously received some small supplies from Mr. Winn, at Sierra Leone. After partaking of some refreshment which Brander caused to be prepared, I read a chapter in the Bible, and returned thanks to Almighty God for the great mercy and deliverance of the past day.

> "When waves on waves, to heav'n uprear'd,
>   Defy'd the pilot's art,
> When terror in each face appear'd,
>   And sorrow in each heart,

To thee I rais'd my humble pray'r,
To snatch me from the grave!
I found thine ear not slow to hear,
Nor short thine arm to save!"

I consider my preservation that day as one of the most extraordinary manifestations of Divine mercy to me during my life.

Wednesday morning, April 25th. We were between the Banana islands and Cape Shilling, and had a fair view of each; Cape Shilling is the place where the late Rev. Samuel Bacon died.

He left Campelar (Kizzell's Place) about the last of April, 1820, in an open boat, for the purpose of going to Sierra Leone, in order to procure medical aid. He expected to fall in with an English vessel, but he was not in time. Therefore, he directed his men to proceed on in the boat, he arrived at Cape Shilling on the first of May. Cape Shilling is an English settlement of recaptured Africans. A captain Randle was the English agent residing there. He received the Rev. Mr. Bacon into the mission-house, and hospitably administered to his wants, as did also Mrs. Randle. They affectionately acted the part of the good Samaritan, and redendered him every assistance in their power -- For which I gave them my most hearty thanks; as I visited them at Freetown, soon after our arrival.

Alas! the extreme anxiety of mind, of my dear brother, and his most arduous labours among the American people of colour, at Kizzell's Place; being as he was constantly employed with the sick and dying both day and might, while sick himself, with the use of that bad water, which it was said Kizzell did not use even in his own family of native Africans, proved too much for him. On the third day of May, 1820, he departed this life; and we have good reason to believe he is with Christ, which is far better. He was buried in a decent manner. Mr. and Mrs. Randle paid him the last acts of benevolence.

In him I lost an affectionate and dear brother, and a brother in Christ.

I did not go on shore at Cape Shilling; therefore, I could not visit the grave of dear Samuel. The wind was fair which wafted us along.

Sierra Leone, Friday April 27th. . .informed. . .that we had purchased land. . .I visited the Rev. Samuel Flood, chaplain of the English colony: he very politely furnished me with a horse, on which I rode to Regent's town, where my wife was sick of a fever; she had the attack on the evening previous, but it was not very violent.

Regent's town, Saturday morning, April 28th, My wife appears to be worse. . .

Regent's town, Sunday morning, 29th April. Mrs. Bacon is very ill: she is attended by Dr. Macauley Wilson, a native of the Bullum tribe; he was educated in England, is an assistant surgeon in this colony; a decent, well-behaved man; and is considered skilful in his profession. This morning the church was filled at six o'clock, as is usual, and a lesson was read, together with singing and prayers. . .O! these are the fruits of the labours of a faithful missionary, accompanied by the blessings of that God who has said, "in the morning sow thy seed, and in the evening withhold not thy hand; for thou knowest not which shall prosper, this or that". . .as I walk around the house in the piazza, I can see all parts of the settlement, and there is scarcely an individual to be seen--all are at church. . .

Monday morning, April 30th. Mrs. Bacon was worse last night than at any time previous. I remain with her while the family are at prayers, but it is deemed necessary that we should separate for a short time. . .As we know every thing which could tend to meliorate her sufferings would be undoubtedly done; and as there was business to transact at Foura Bay, discharging the schooner's crew, and consulting with the agents upon the propriety of removing the people from Sherbro, or sending them some necessaries of life. . .

Tuesday morning, May 1st. A messenger arrived with a note . . .that Mrs. Bacon had less fever than on the morning I left her. . .at 11 o'clock A.M. I felt somewhat indisposed; perspiration ceased; I was attacked with pain in the back part of the head, neck, and back. I immediately went on board the schooner. . .took some medicine and retired to my birth. . . after about two hours, the chill was succeeded by fever. . . The stomach being in a state for the reception of tonics, and brother Andrus having a small treatise of practice, by Dr. Winterbottom, which directed bark to be given in as large quantities as the stomach would receive, brother Andrus followed that plan. . .

Wednesday morning 2d May. No fever. . .continued bark . . .then two calomel pills. . .bark. . .

Thursday morning, 3rd May, Foura Bay. . .chill. . .succeeded by fever. . .bark. . .I had become very much debilitated for so short an illness. A message. . .Mrs. Bacon had not as much fever.

Monday morning, 7th May. Mrs. Bacon, who had heard of my illness, was brought as far as Gloucester, where she became too ill to proceed. . .during the following days, I received several notes. . .which informed me of the low state of Mrs. Bacon's health. . .however, her anxiety was so great, that it was thought by her physician, that a removal to Foura Bay would probably be beneficial. Mr. Johnson, therefore, again sent six or eight of his captured people with a palanquin. . .although she was unable to sit up. . .

Thursday morning 17th May. This day I walked to Freetown, a distance of about two miles, for the purpose of procuring a ship-carpenter, to examine the schooner and ascertain her condition. . .I visited Mr. Justice Craig, who very politely proposed that I should ride back, and lent me his horse for that purpose. This day's exertion nearly proved fatal. On my return, I also found Mrs. Bacon very ill, so that our hopes of speedy recovery were blasted, and the prospects of future usefulness clouded.

June 11th, Monday. . .We are so ill that brother Andrus has suggested to us the propriety of his remaining in my stead, and Mrs. Bacon and myself going to the United States. . .He had . . .learnt that a schooner. . .is about to be sent to Barbadoes

. . .Mr. Andrus went again to Freetown and obtained a passage for us. . .

Wednesday, 13 June. Our baggage was removed to the boat . . .at about 9 o'clock the heat become oppressive; Mrs Bacon was taken extremely ill, and had she not obtained immediate aid would probably have survived but a short time. . .At length we took leave of our friends on Saturday, the 16th of June, and sailed out of the harbour of Sierra Leone with the morning tide. . .In the evening I was much worse; indeed it was a time long to be remembered: I had no expectaions of surviving; accordingly I gave directions to my wife, and commended her, together with the cause in which we were engaged, to Him who has promised to be a father to the fatherless, and the widow's God. Death appeared fast approaching, and I must say that grim messenger had lost its terrors, and I could then exclaim, "O grave, where is victory!" The exercises of my mind, under these circumstances, I am unable to describe. . .For a considerable time I was unable to speak. Discovering our family Bible lying near, I made signs for it to be given to me. . .

After this, a gradual recovery took place. Still we found difficulties which were unpleasant. The captain and mate were Englishmen, and several of the crew; but several others were Spaniards, besides whom there were some negroes. To these the Spaniards took a dislike from the time of embarkation; several encounters took place; the Spaniards not unfrequently threatened the lives of the negroes; but Mr. Easton (the supercargo), and the captain, dissuaded them from excuting their horrid threats. We were, however, fearful that murder would be committed, as the Spaniards were of that class of perpetrators taken from the slave-ships, and were permitted to leave, or rather were banished from, the English colony--There was great danger of their raising a mutiny, so that the captain, supercargo and mate, were always on the watch, having their arms near at hand, even when they retired to rest. Those fears rendered our passage not as agreeable as it otherwise would have been: the officers were very obliging at all times. At length we arrived at the island of Barbadoes, the windward island of the West Indies, on the 10th of July, with our healths somewhat improved. . .Mrs. Bacon and myself were just able to walk from the wharf to the boarding house, about fifty yards distance. There we remained four days, after which we took passage in an English vessel for Martinique, where we arrived in about twenty-four hours. We remained in Martinique until the 29th of July. This island we found to be very sickly, and we were more debilitated when we left it, than we were when we arrived. We took passage from thence in an American schooner, commanded by J. Pennington, of Great Eggharbour, and for about eight days we had a delightful passage; after that we were almost becalmed, and at length a storm came on, the wind N. E. which carried us into the Gulf stream; we arrived within a short distance of Cape Lookout, then tacked ship and lay to under a short-reefed foresail about three days, the greater part of the time in the gulf, which caused me to be very sea-sick. At length the storm abated, and on Monday, the 13th August, we had a brisk wind, which wafted us into Hampton Roads, and Tuesday we arrived at Norfolk, in a convalescent state of health.

Notwithstanding our troubles have been neither few nor small, yet more abundantly has been the grace of God afforded us; therefore we give Him all the glory, both now and for ever.

E.B.

The Rev. Joseph R. Andrus departed this life on the 28th July, 1821, after a short illness, at Sierra Leone, on the coast of Africa. . ."When the glories of the mightiest and proudest conqueror that ever dazzled the world with the splendour of his exploits, shall have faded away, and have been rolled in that oblivious tide which sweeps away all that man calls good and great, the names of Andrus, and Bacon, and Mills, shall shine bright in the philanthropic page. The sons of Africa shall tell to their latest descendants, how these men of God left father and mother, and brother and sister, and all the sweet endearments of friendship and of home, to cross the wide ocean, and dwell beneath the burning sky, and the blasting heats of her inhospitable wilds, and counted not their own lives dear unto

112

them, that they might preach the unsearchable riches of Christ. Their infants shall be taught to lisp the names of these benefactors of their race, to lift their hearts in gratitude to Him who inclined these servants of the Most High to go forth in order to prepare in their desert a highway to the Lord."

Since the death of the above, we have to record the melancholy intelligence of the deaths of Mr. and Mrs. Winn, who died at the same place in the month of August, 1821.

E.B.

Ephraim's involvement with the American Colonization Society continued for many years. He is mentioned in a Society pamphlet of 1834 as then living in Philadelphia. In fact, he had lived there since his return from Africa. At first, reunited with his children, at 279 High Street, listed in the City Directory as "Bacon, Ephraim, gentleman". In 1826, the year his son Socrates married, he was listed as a *publisher* living at 39 Cherry. From that time he seems to have traveled for the Society.

Socrates was nineteen when he married Ann Earp in Philadelphia's 2ond Baptist Church at 112 "in Budd street between Poplar lane and Laurel street". Young Ann and her family were new to the United States arriving on the ship *Halcyon* from their home in Nottingham, England, only six years before[1]. Now, Ann and Socrates began to take giant steps toward Indiana.

And by 1834, when the Society pamphlet makes the last mention of Ephraim, his daughter Cendarilla was taking care of her Grandmother Chamberlain in Charlton. Socrates was living in Detroit and his son, Samuel is born. It will be four years before Socrates and Cendarilla meet again in Indiana, the only children of Ephraim to leave their history for us.

---

1. "10/10/1820", Ann , 16 years, and her twin, Betty, little sisters Mary and Ellen, brothers William, Joseph and John, disembarked with their mother, Sarah, at Philadelphia, From later histories, it appears that her

113

father William and eldest brother Charles came shortly before. Charles eventually settled in Amity, near Streator, Livingston County, Illinois, about 1840 leaving Earp family strung across Ohio and Indiana. He was a respected farmer, and the Bacon family of Indiana and the Earp family kept close touch. Socrates and Ann named their first son Charles William. Brother Charles Earp named his daughter Sarah Ann. Socrates and Ann's daughter Amanda married her first cousin, Charles' son William, and went to live with the Earps in Illinois where they named *their* first child after his mother and her mother, Esther Ann, and called her Annie.

Sources;

Ephraim Bacon's Journal
City Directory of Philadelphia
U.S. Census Records
Ship's Passenger Lists for Philadelphia
Genealogical Soc. of Penn. Publications, Vol. 12
Irving, Mrs. W., *Earp Family*

Joshua Meisler, a descendant of Ephraim and Charlotte Ellis Bacon, has added greatly to Ephraim's history by finding much of what was missing in the details of his life after Africa.

He finds that Ephraim continued to be deeply and enthusiastically committed to the work in Africa and traveled extensively on the eastern seaboard to raise money for the Domestic and Foreign Missionary Society of the Protestant Episcopal Church. He had ended his relationship with the American Colonization Society and by 1822 was appointed by the Missionary Society to establish and conduct a school for children on the western coast of Africa. Funds had to be raised and a history of the Society states that *"to make this appeal the directors sent out the man who had offered his life, that he might create interest and collect means for his own support and that of the school he was to found."* Ephraim was very successful and popular with the many people he met on the tours and soon Charlotte joined him. With local women, she visited merchants and asked for supplies and material to make clothing for the *'children received into the mission schools'.* They were grateful that *"all denominations were friendly'.*

Unhappily, problems between the two societies with transportation delayed those plans for many years and Ephraim became disengaged from the project.

And now, too, we know that Ephraim and Charlotte had at least one child. In 1830, in Pennsylvania, Josephine Andrus Bacon was born. We can only imagine that, out of gratitude and remorse, their daughter was named after Ephraim's partner in the work in Africa, Joseph Andrus.

During that time in Africa Joseph Andrus reserved a berth on a ship returning to the United States for himself but when Charlotte became ill with the deadly fever so rampant insisted that Ephraim and she take it. Tragically, after Ephraim and Charlotte reached home safely, Andrus himself became ill and died there in Africa.

Census records give us snapshots of the Bacon family. In 1836, they are in Tazewell County, Illinois near Pekin.

In 1850, Ephraim, 74 years old, and Charlotte are living with newly-wed daughter, Josephine, and her husband, David Kenyon, near Pekin.

In 1856, the family of five now; Ephraim, Charlotte, Josephine, David and two year old Isabel are living in Des Moines, Iowa.

In 1860, Ephraim, 80, is identified in the census as a teacher and it seems he and Charlotte have moved back to Illinois, leaving Josephine and David in Iowa.

January, 1861, Ephraim Bacon, 81, died. Charlotte, alone now, moved to live again with Josephine. Later in the same year, she also died.

By 1870, Josephine and David Kenyon and their five children are living in Winterset, Madison County, Iowa.

When she is twenty years old, Isabel marries Josiah B. Ferree.

Many newspaper articles for many newspapers were written by Ephraim Bacon relaying news from Africa. His many reports to the American Colonization Society were published. More than one edition of his journal was published. He wrote his autobiography and the publisher of that advertised *"a successful teacher, and founder of infant schools in the United States...Assistant Agent of the U.S. Government for persons liberated from Slave Ships on the coast of Africa..Explorer of the Western coast of Africa; Agent for the Protestant Episcopal Missionary Society; Publisher of Religious Books &c. &c."* He wrote, *A Manual of the System of Instruction Pursued at the Infant School.*

The farm boy, the Maine pioneer, the teacher who turns into the man who would plunge into an uncharted world of risky African endeavors.......what do we not yet know of the remarkable Ephraim Bacon?

FAIRBANKS FAMILY

Ephraim Bacon (II) married Sarah Fairbanks, daughter of an old Puritan family.

That family left us a legacy. The house that Jonathan Fairbanks built soon after he arrived in New England still stands in Dedham, Massachusetts. The great hewn oak timbers were brought on the ship with him and the house is furnished with the original pottery, pewter, the little diamond-shaped glass panes and solid furniture that made the same trip in 1633. Forty thousand bricks for the massive chimney he'd planned were used as the ship's ballast.

Jonathan Fairbanks was from a yeoman family of considerable wealth. It was understood of *yeoman* at the time that, "Many of these with us are gentleman -- descending from younger brothers -- or gentlemen's equals by estate". The earliest records that can be proved show that Jonathan was descended from William Fairbanke, born about 1455, of Manor Brigbothom, Sowerby Bridge, in the West Riding area of Yorkshire, home of the Draper and Griggs families.

His son John Fairbanke was born about 1480 and died in 1551. In 1506, "22nd [year of the reign of] Henry VII. . . William surrendered all his estate. . .of land and meadow called Brigbothame, and one croft called Pigilcroft in Soarbie to the use of John Faerbaink, son of said William. . . ."

Gilbert Fairebanke, son of John, was born about 1515. "1526, 19th Henry VIII, John Fairbanke surrendered 'Brigbotham" &c to the use of Gilbert Fairebanke, son of the aforesaid. . ." "1569, 11th Elizabeth, Gilbert Fairebank would not pay the stipent of the minister or curate of the Chapel . . .Fined 12d." He made his will on his death bed, March 4, 1578, and was buried on the same day. He gave to his wife, Jennett, one third of "my land and goods according to custom of the country."

George Fairbanke, son of Gilbert, was born about 1528. He sold a fulling mill in 1585 as he was, like most the Fairbanks family, involved in the woolen trade. He married Mary Farrer of Erringden, daughter of Richard and Margaret (Blackburn) Farrer. Their first child was Jonathan, the New England emmigrant.

Jonathan Fairbanks, a wool merchant, and Grace Smith of Warley were married in 1617. Six children were born by the time they sailed on *The Griffin* with Rev. John Cotton and Richard and Elizabeth Fairbanke[1] for Massachusetts where Jonathan supported his family in rough-hewn Watertown. He stored the timbers for his house for three years while he looked for a place to build.

He decided on Dedham and was made a freeman on the 23rd of March, 1637, and formally accepted by the town. He was the twenty-eighth person to sign the town charter and was from that time very active in the affairs of the town, "for he had a good education, strong common sense, sound judgement and good executive ability. . .It seems evident that he was a man of strong individuality. . ." He built his house in the center of the community with the pink brick from England for the chimney and furnished it with the heirlooms brought across the ocean. The mazer bowl was one of those. Well-to-do families considered their large, old, mazer bowls, usually made of maple and inlaid with silver, a treasure. The Fairbanks' bowl was probably used in the Crusades as a Wassail bowl, but Jonathan used it for Christenings. He and Grace brought one very old silver platter carrying the crest of King Richard III. An old oak chest is from the time of Elizabeth.

On hooks across the beams above the fireplace was hung Jonathan's flintlock. Generation after generation expected their Fairbanks successors to keep the old gun in the iron rests put up by Jonathan and so the six foot, four inch gun was cradled there until early this century. Then Rev. Henry Fairbanks of St. Johnsbury, Vermont, took it home with him for safekeeping thinking the house was to be sold. Many original things, like the mazer bowl, are still in the house which is now a public museum kept by the Fairbanks Family of America, but the gun is not there.

1. Richard Fairbanck, a relative of Jonathan, settled in Boston in his own tavern. "Richard's Tavern" was the first post office in America. The offices of the Boston Globe now stand there.

The house, made as draft free as possible with "wattle and daub" under the clapboards and sheltered by the way it fit into the lay of the land, was built on one of Dedham's usual twelve acre lot grants. The Fairbanks land straddled a well-traveled Indian trail which joined to the Pequot Path in Connecticut inspiring Jonathan to add a hiding place and escape tunnel from the house. Later, other grants added to his twelve acre lot included,

".. .so many Acres in Meadowe as he hath upland in his first grante for an house Lott. . .2 acres 2 roodes of upland ground fit for improvement with the plough. . .A grante of two acres of land upon the North end of the Wigwam playne. . ."

In 1646, the records of the church showed that,

"Jonathan Fairebanke notwithstanding he had long stood off fro' ye church upon some scruples about publike p'fession of faith & ye covenant yet after divers loving conferences wth him; he made such a declaration of his faith & conv'sion to god & p'fession of subjection to ye ordinances of Xt yt he was reddily & gladly received by ye whole church."

He and Grace had six children:

John,   appointed with John Rogers to survey the
                       Charles River in 1638. He was never made
                       a freeman because he could not "con-
                       scientiously make a public profession of
                       faith in the manner required of him by the
                       church".

George.

Mary,   married Michael Metcalf, first son of one of
                       Socrates' Puritan ancestors.

Susan.

Jonas,   "who, not being worth f200 was fined for
                       wearing great boots" and with his son was

killed by Indians in 1676 during a raid upon the settlement at Lancaster, Mass.

Jonathan, Jr.

Jonathan died at Dedham December 5, 1668, and an inventory of his estate was taken. In the *parlour* were mentioned (among many other things):

"In money 9s 8d the purse in which the money was 4d, the weareing woolen Aparill of the deceased, with one hatt, with boots & ect., . . .one blew Rugg. . .one trundle beadstead bed coarde and matts. . .a sea chest, one olde Warmeing panne, one Sunne Dyall. . . one Sworde 8s one Cutelas 4s, 2 gunnes 1f, one musket rest, One halfe pike, one grande staffe, one other small staffe. . ."

There were "2 old Tables and one Cheyer," "brasse" skillets, iron pots, kettles and pot hooks, a frying pan, pewter, china dishes and "sauchers", wooden platters and wooden bottles, a tobacco knife, a trencher, "aloamin spoones," "a painted Dish and one gully dish", and four spinning wheels. In the "parlour Chamber" were pieces of "new cotton cloath old and new linnen," one piece 15 yards long, and a "piece of english cotton, a powder horne with powder in it". In the new house, the part of the house that Jonathan built on for John when he got married, were many items of farming tools. In the "working cellar" were 2 vices and one "turning laeth". In another cellar were "cheese butter beefe, beere possets and a Churne". In the cellar "in the yarde" were "4 barreles with Cider, one pouldering [powdering salting] tubb wth some pork in it" and apples. In the "hafe chamber; many smalle tools for turning and other the like work. . .sheeps wool and cotton woole. . .linnen yarne and cotton yarne. . .scales and weights and. . .hopps in a bag". And in the yard was a cider press. In "cattell. . .3 swine. . . with the piggs belonging thereto, 4 Cowes and one yearling Calf, 2 Steeres about 4 yeares old. . .and "haye in the barn. . . the home Lott with the adition of Lande in the wigwam playne -- the orchayard and all the buildings thereupon, the 8 Cows Comons, 6 acres of meadowe in Broade meadowe, 2 acres at

118

forest meadow and Comon meadow shore, 22 acres uplands in purgatory playne. . .acres in the Lowe playne, 4 acres in North Devidens. . .in the Clapeboarde trees, Swampe in the great Ceader Swampe neer sawe mille, 3 Cow Comons at moolomun-upongo. . ." The inventory was made by Jonathan's "very loveing friends Eleazer Lusher & Petter Woodward Sen'e" and "Daniall ffisher".

In his book *The Fairbanks Family of America* (1896), L.C. Fairbanks wrote,

> ". . .and so John his eldest son, came into possession of the homestead. From that time down to July, 1892, the old house was continuously occupied by him and his descendants, Joseph, Joseph 2d, Ebenezer, Ebenezer 2d, Prudence, Sarah, Nancy, and Rebecca, the last of the family tenants. In July, 1892, the house was struck by lightning and considerably damaged. Miss Rebecca's pet dog, lying under the bed where she was sleeping, was killed, but she escaped with a severe shock. Shortly after this event, deeming the house no longer a desireable place of abode, she abandoned it, leaving a strange family in charge, and removed to Boston. Thus for the first time in over two hundred and fifty years the old house was occupied by persons not "to the manor born." But after spending several months in Boston whe returned to dwell in the time-honored mansion, of which she was then the sole owner, and is still living there."

In the house now hangs a photograph of Rebecca amidst her yard sale, held before she moved, showing precious old things up for bid in the grass. Most was retrieved.

In 1903, the house was acquired by the Fairbanks Family of America, Incorporated, all its low-ceiling rooms still filled with the Fairbanks antiquities. It is located at 511 East St., (once the Indian Pequot Path), Dedham, Mass., close to Boston. Visiting hours are set up through May to November and Fairbanks descendants are invited to join the association.

Among the descendants of Jonathan Fairbanks were the forty-four Fairbanks listed on the Alarm Rolls of April 19, 1775. Also:

Charles W. Fairbanks, U.S. Senator from Indiana, Vice-President

119

of the United States under Theodore Roosevelt and inspiration for the name of Fairbanks, Alaska. He was born in a log cabin in the wilds near Columbus, Ohio.

Thaddeus Fairbanks, (1796-1886), inventor of the platform scale in 1831; held many patents and was granted the last two in his ninetieth year. He also patented a cast-iron plow that was very slow to catch on. Farmers thought it would break into pieces.

Douglas Fairbanks, Jr., motion picture actor and television producer.

George was Jonathan's second son and came to New England with his father. He lived in Dedham until about 1657 and then moved to the new town of Sherborn (afterward called Medway and now Millis). He was the first settler there and was granted land to start a homestead along with Morse, Holbrook, Leland, Breck and Bass, men in the prime of life. He signed the first petition for the incorporation of Sherborn, was chosen as a selectman to stand for ten years and was on the committee to engage the town's first minister. The committee met on July 18, 1679 to ask Rev. Daniel Gookin to settle among them. George was also a member of the Ancient & Honorable Artillery Company of Boston and was considered a man "of sterling character".

George Fairbanks married Mary Adams on the "26 of the 8mo. 1646", in Dedham. She was very likely of the same Adams family whose forebearer was Henry; John and John Quincy Adams' family, rooted in the same place and time.* The Fairbanks had five children in Dedham; Mary, George, Samuel, Eliesur and Jonas. Jonathan and Margaret were born in Medway.

The house they lived in after they moved to Sherborn (the first settlers west of the river at Sherborn) was later famous in that area as the stone house. It was on the northern border of Bogistow Pond and originally one of the garrison houses built by the towns people as a place of refuge from the Indians.

120

see *Corrections,* page 337

The house was 65 or 75 feet long, two stories high, and made of flat stones laid in clay mortar. The openings were a double row of portholes on all sides and the inside walls were lined with heavy oak planks. It was inherited by four George Fairbanks in succession followed by two Silas Fairbanks before it went out of the family in 1820. Now the stones have all been carried away and there is no trace of the house.

In Sherborn, as in every other border settlement, people were watchful. There were numerous rules designed to protect settlers and stiff fines for breaking them. The fine was 12 shillings for going more than one mile away from one's house without carrying arms, unless one stayed near other houses, and 40 shillings for firing a gun after sundown. Certain arms were always brought to the meeting house, Sunday and every day, and must never be left unattended at home in the event Indians should find them.

In 1675, Philip, Chief of the Wampanoag Indians started his attacks on the border towns. Early on the morning of February, 1676, the Indians daringly attacked Medfield just across the river and burned about fifty houses. Fifteen or sixteen persons were killed or burned including members of the Adams family. Micahel Metcalf and George Fairbanks, Jr. lost their houses to the flames.

Years later, January 10, 1682, George Fairbanks drowned. His death was considered a severe loss by the settlement. His wife, Mary, died in August, 1711, in Mendon, Massachusetts, probably at the home of her son-in-law, William Holbrook.

Jonathan, George and Mary's sixth child, was born in 1662. He was Sherborn's first physician and lived in the old stone garrison house. He was a selectman for six years and town clerk for three. He married and had six children before his wife, Sarah died. In his second marriage he had one child. Benjamin was only three years old when Jonathan drowned in December, 1719, coming home from Medfield in the night. He fell through the ice while crossing the Charles River. The farm was left to Jonathan's sons, Samuel and Jonathan, Jr.

The six children were:

George,	born 1685, wounded in the French and Indian War.
Jonathan,	born 1689, became a physician.
Comfort,	1690.
Joseph,	1692.
SAMUEL,	1693, February, 27.
Jonas,	1697.

Samuel married Susanna Watson[1] June 30, 1718, in Sherborn. They had seven children:

Jonas,	born 1718.
Samuel,	1720.
Rebecca,	1723.
SARAH,	1724, October, 19.
Benjamin,	1726.
Jemima,	1729.
Levi,	1734. Killed in the French and Indian War.

Samuel's daughter, Sarah, married Ephraim Bacon (II) of Woodstock in 1741. Samuel and Susanna were living in Dudley, near Woodstock by that time and Samuel died there. An issue of the *News-Letter* of 1759 printed, "Fairbank, Samuel, at Dudley, a gross and heavy man dropped dead beside his horse at 66 years".

1. See Watson Family in another chapter.

Sources:

Barry, W., *History of Framingham*
____, *History of Worcester County, Mass.*
Fairbanks, L.S., *Fairbanks Family of America*
New England Genealogical and Historical Register
Fairbanks, C.H., *Fairbanks 1455-1897*
Macon, C.T., *The Fairbanks House*
Torrey, C.A., *English Ancestery of Jonathan Fairbanks*
Fairbank, J.W., *Ye Fayerbanke Historial*
Fairbanks, Thaddeus, *Fairbanks Family*
Dedham Town Records
Morse, *History of Sherborn and Holliston*

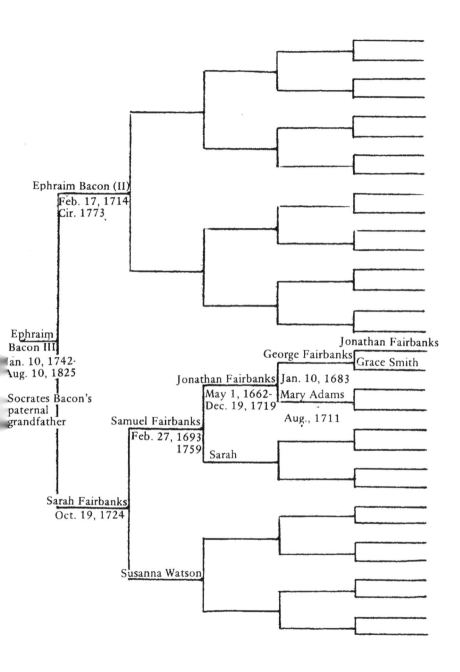

Ephraim Bacon (II)
Feb. 17, 1714
Cir. 1773

Ephraim
Bacon III
Jan. 10, 1742-
Aug. 10, 1825

Socrates Bacon's
paternal
grandfather

Jonathan Fairbanks

George Fairbanks   Grace Smith

Jonathan Fairbanks Jan. 10, 1683
May 1, 1662-   Mary Adams
Dec. 19, 1719   -
                    Aug., 1711

Samuel Fairbanks
Feb. 27, 1693
        1759   Sarah

Sarah Fairbanks
Oct. 19, 1724

Susanna Watson

WATSON FAMILY

It is almost certain that George Fairbank's wife, Susanna, was the daughter of Matthew Watson, an Englishman, a Presbyterian, believed to be descended from the Barons of Rockingham and who had lived many years in Londonderry, Ireland. He was a manufacturer and dealer in linens and cloth.

He'd married Mary Orr whose father was killed by Irish soldiers in the 1689 siege of Protestant Londonderry, his head "borne on a pike".

Matthew and Mary landed at Boston harbor in 1718 and made their home that first year in Framingham, a part of the town of Sherborn, George Fairbank's home. They later settled permanently in Leichester and Matthew Watson introduced potatoes to that part of the country. Before the year was over he was killed by a falling tree.

The recorded children of Matthew and Mary were:

Matthew,	born 1696, died very wealthy at 107 years old. Married Bethia Reed.
Samuel,	1698.
Patrick,	1706.
Robert	
William	
Elizabeth,	1709, died at 106 years.
Margaret,	married _____ McNeal.
John,	1716.
Oliver,	1718, born on board ship.

Sources;

Bemis, Watson Family
_____, History of Worchester Co., Mass.

DRAPER FAMILY

James Draper, called *The Puritan*, emigrated to America in 1647/48 for "Righteousness' Sake" with his wife Miriam Stansfield and others from his neighborhood in Yorkshire, England, He was very much caught up in the Puritan cause as was his father, Thomas Draper, and his brothers.

The home of the Drapers and Stansfields was a village near Heptonstall called Halifax Parish in the West Riding, Yorkshire, on the river Hebden. The Draper family had large landholdings in all the West Riding area from the 1400's, the time of William, John and Henry le Drapour.

The Stansfields descended from Wyon Maryon, member of a "noble line" in Brittany who was a companion of William the Conqueror from whom he received a grant of the Township of Stansfield. The family arms are "Sable with Three Goats Trippant Argent" They used two mottoes: *Nosce Teipsum*, Know Thyself, and *Virtus post funera vivit*, Virtue lives after the Tomb.

Records joining the two families go back as far as 1564.

A 1515 court roll gives early evidence of the Drapers involved in the making and fulling of cloth, an involvement that concerned Draper men even into this century in America. James Draper, The Puritan, was a weaver by trade.

Shortly after James Draper arrived in America he built a very substantial house in Roxbury which stood until the middle 1800's. There his daughter Susanna, who married John Bacon, was born about 1650 and later Sarah, James, John, Moses, Daniel, Patience and Jonathan. Susanna's two boys, Ephraim and John Bacon, were raised in that house after their parents died of small-pox in 1678.

James Draper gave large sums in goods and time to build the church in Roxbury and was made a freeman in 1690. He died in 1694. Joseph Warren, 'carpenter', was among the five men appointed administrators of his estate. Miriam died in 1697, and they share a common stone still standing in the West Roxbury cemetary.

They were forebearers of Connecticut Governor Eben S. Draper and Civil War General William T. Draper.

131

Sources:

Draper, T.W., *Draper Faimily in America*
_____, *The Draper Line*

GRIGGS FAMILY

The Griggs family is represented in Subsidy Return records as early as 1327 in County Suffolk, England, and owned lands in many places including Stansfield near where the Drapers and Stansfield families lived.

The family Arms were *Gules upon two feathers argent* (red upon two feathers silver) and the shield was topped with a helmet mantled with *gules and argent.* Their motto was *Secundo Curo.*

Thomas Griggs came from England to Roxbury in the Massachusetts Bay Colony in the spring of 1639 and was granted land on Muddy River next to Thomas Ruggles. With him were his two sons, John and Joseph, his daughter Mary and his wife Mary who only lived for a short time after they arrived. Thomas married again and died May 23, 1646, after a long illness.

An inventory of the goods "& Chattles of Thomas Griggs deceased, made this 25 May" mentions "one white backt cow" which his wife was to have during her life. A notice of his death was written by the Rev. John Eliot.

Thomas's son, John, was born in England about 1622. He married Mary Patten in 1652 in Roxbury, and they belonged to the Roxbury church. He was made a freeman May 18, 1653. His land abutted John Ruggles, John Johnson's and Joseph Grigg's, all, eventually, Bacon ancestors.

John was one of the many men impressed for the Narragansett campaign that ended in the Great Swamp Fight of December, 1675, designed to stop Indian Chief King Philip's ferocious attacks on English settlements.

John and Mary both died on January 23, 1692.

"The will of John Griggs of Roxbury in New England. . .my Eldest son John Grigs forty pounds; my dau. Mary ffelder ten pounds; my dau. Hannah Raynsford Twenty-two pounds; my dau. Abigail Cooke Twenty pounds; my dau. Sarah Kidder Twenty pounds; my grand dau. Sarah ffelder Ten pounds when she comes of age; these legacies to be paid in corne, cattle or pork or beefe within six yeares after the decease of the Testator. . .Remainder of estate both real and personal, to my two sons George and James. My son

John shall have his choice of my woolen coats, and so of one of my small chests, and a great sword, and his choice of any one of my bookes, the rest of my Bookes of divinity shall be divided amongst the rest of my children, but my Physick bookes I give wholely to my son George, my son James shall have my fowling peice and my Muskett & sword. . .And none of these lands should be put away by any sale, but to remaine with my two youngest sons and to their natural heires. Made 5 Jan. 1691 in the presence of Joseph Griggs, Robert Pierpont, John Searle."

His son, John Griggs, Jr. was born in 1659 and married Elizabeth Cass June 6, 1682. She was the daughter of John Cass and Martha Philbrick. (See the Cass Family, page 142.) Elizabeth "took hold on the Covenant" in Roxbury Church in 1685.

John, Jr., enlisted from Boston to fight against King Philip at the same time as his father was impressed, December, 1675. By the next year the colonists were able to end most Indian resistance. The loss of life among the English was as enormous as the enemy's. Not a settler was left in one community in Maine. Sixteen towns in Massachusetts and four in Rhode Island were completely destroyed. More than 6 percent of the men of military age were killed.

John and Elizabeth had four children recorded in the town records:

John, born 1685, died young.

John, 1688.

Joseph, 1703.

Elizabeth, married in 1700 to Ephraim Bacon raised in Roxbury by James Draper.

Griggses, Casses and Bacons removed to Woodstock in the early 1700's.

136

see *Corrections*, page 337

Sources:

Muskett. J.J., Suffolk Memorial Families
New England Historical and Genealogical Register
Griggs, Geanealogy of the Griggs Family
Linzee, Ancestors of Peter Parker and Sarah Ruggles
Bowen, Genealogy of Woodstock Families

PATTEN FAMILY

William Patten, probably the son of Thomas Patten of Hardington, Manfylde, County Somerset, England, came to Cambridge in New England sometime before 1635. He and his wife Mary were both members at the church in Cambridge, an important designation. Their children were Mary, Thomas, Sarah and Nathaniel, "the eldest being about 4 or 5 years old when her parents joyned, pabtised in Eng." William took the oath of freeman May 16, 1645.

"The 13 Mar. 1635. By a vote of the town. Agreed with William Patten to kepe 100 Cattell one the other side the River for the space of seaven Monthes."

The cattle belonged to the people of Cambridge and he was paid twenty pounds a year for several years for his ᵀvices. In 1646, "Brother Patten fined thrice one shilling, for a hog without keppr.", but in ᴗ 49 he and Andrew Steevenson were nominated to carry out the town orders concerning hogs and "to levy on all breaking the rule". He was a member of the Ancient & Honorable Artillery Co. of Boston but even before that he served in the Pequot War of 1637 where settlers fought the Indians back to their fort on the Mystic River. He was also a signer of the deed from the Cambridge proprietors to the Billerica proprietors granting Billerica (formerly *Shawshine*) the right to be its own town with its own government.

The site of William Patten's house was on the present Massachusetts Avenue opposite the Common and not far from Harvard Square. He died in 1668 and his estate was divided among his widow and children, young Mary, now the wife of John Griggs.

Sources:

Linzee. Ancestors of Peter Parker and Sarah Ruggles
Vircus, Compendium of American Genealogy

CASS FAMILY

John Cass was born in England about 1620 and came to Boston in 1644
He moved to Hampton, N.H. in 1647 and that same year, married Martha
daughter of Thomas and Elizabeth (Knapp) Philbrick from Watertown bu
new residents of Hampton, too.

John and Martha Cass had ten children. One son married Patience
Draper and moved to Woodstock. Daughter Elizabeth married John Griggs
and was the mother of the Elizabeth who married Ephraim Bacon. Thi
daughter, widowed, remarried and also moved to Woodstock taking witl
her Ephraim Bacon, Jr.

One source claims John Cass was a Quaker and, if that is so, would ex
plain his removal to New Hampshire. Boston was not tolerant of Quaker
although a few Massachusetts Bay settlements were. He was the ancestor o
General Lewis Cass, the Governor of the Michigan Territory, Secretary o
War under Jackson and nominated for President of the United States by th
Democratic Party in 1848. Cass Street in Fort Wayne was named for Lewi
Cass in honor of his oration at the celebration of the opening here of th
Wabash-Erie Canal, July 4, 1843.

Sources:

Bowen, Genealogies of Woodstock Families
Cass, E.M., Ada Ball Cass, Descendant of John Cass

142

PHILBRICK FAMILY

Thomas Philbrick came from Bures, County Sufflok, England. It is probable that this yeoman family was descended from the knightly house of Felbrigge, living in that vicinity since about 1285. Simon le Bigod, youngest son of Hugh Bigod, EArl of Norfolk, and his wife Maud, daughter of William Marshall, Earl of Pembroke. (See page 212.) Simon married Maud, the daughter and heiress of Richard de Felbrigge of Felbrigge and their decendants took the name of their manor. Excerpts from the Manor Court Rolls of Earls Colne state,

"Court with view holden 16 April 3 Henry V (1415)[1]. The jurors present that John Fylbryge has a ditch not scoured in the King's Highway, 1 perch in length. Amerced 3d..."

"The jurors present that Richard ffilbridge threw down soot in a common place to the common annoyance; he is amerced 3d and ordered not to do so again on paid of 12d..."

"Bures Rectory 26 October, 2 James I (1606)...Capital pledges include Thomas ffilbrigg... He is chosen to office of aletaster."

Thomas, likely a fuller of cloth, was born about 1545 and died after 1621. Register records of St. Mary's Bures show that he was the father of "Thomas Filbrigge, baptised 23 Sept. 1583", emigrant to New England. Thomas, Jr. married Elizabeth Knop (Knapp), daughter of William and Elizabeth (Read or Reed) Knop of Bures.

Thomas, Jr. and his family sailed on the flagship *Arbella* with Governor Winthrop in the first great migration of the Puritans in 1630. Thomas was one of that group that first settled in Watertown with Sir Richard Saltonstall. His homestead was on the N.W. corner of the present Belmont and Lexington Streets.

In 1646 Thomas Philbrick sold all his land in Watertown to Isaac Sternes and moved to Hampton, N.H., where his older sons already lived, for the "fishing, fowling, the best of clams, and the salt marshes almost ready for the scythe".

In 1655 he was a culler of staves. He also served his time on jury duty and was once paid 6 shillings, along with William Fuller, for "carring the votes to Boston". He had eight children and his youngest, Martha, born in 1631, married John Cass of Hampton. Thomas died in 1667.

145

see *Corrections*, page 337

Sources:

New England Historical and Genealogical Register
Moriarty, G.A., The English Connections of Thomas Felbrigge
Bond, Genealogy of the Families of the Early Settlers of Watertown.
Ipswich and Salisbury Quarterly Court Records

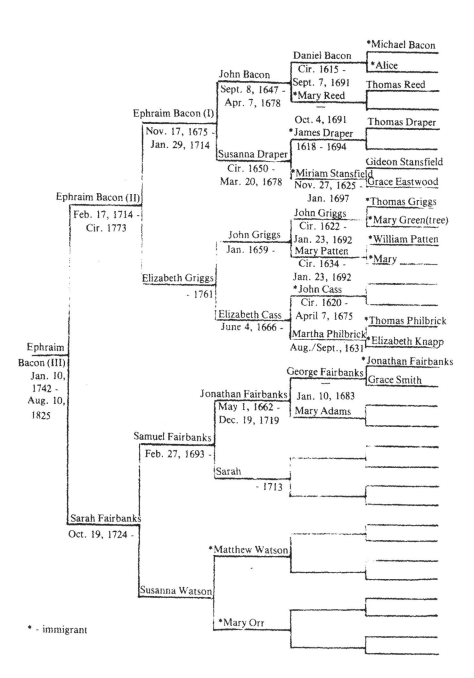

Ephraim
Bacon (III)
Jan. 10,
1742 -
Aug. 10,
1825

Ephraim Bacon (II)
Feb. 17, 1714 -
Cir. 1773

Ephraim Bacon (I)
Nov. 17, 1675 -
Jan. 29, 1714

John Bacon
Sept. 8, 1647 -
Apr. 7, 1678

Daniel Bacon
Cir. 1615 -
Sept. 7, 1691
*Mary Reed
—

*Michael Bacon
*Alice
Thomas Reed

Susanna Draper
Cir. 1650 -
Mar. 20, 1678

Oct. 4, 1691
*James Draper
1618 - 1694
*Miriam Stansfield
Nov. 27, 1625 -
Jan. 1697

Thomas Draper
Gideon Stansfield
Grace Eastwood

Elizabeth Griggs
- 1761

John Griggs
Jan. 1659 -

John Griggs
Cir. 1622 -
Jan. 23, 1692
Mary Patten
Cir. 1634 -
Jan. 23, 1692

*Thomas Griggs
*Mary Green(tree)
*William Patten
*Mary

Elizabeth Cass
June 4, 1666 -

*John Cass
Cir. 1620 -
April 7, 1675
Martha Philbrick
Aug./Sept., 1631

*Thomas Philbrick
*Elizabeth Knapp

Sarah Fairbanks
Oct. 19, 1724 -

Samuel Fairbanks
Feb. 27, 1693 -

Jonathan Fairbanks
May 1, 1662 -
Dec. 19, 1719

George Fairbanks
—
Jan. 10, 1683
Mary Adams

*Jonathan Fairbanks
Grace Smith

Sarah
- 1713

Susanna Watson

*Matthew Watson

*Mary Orr

* - immigrant

CHAMBERLAIN FAMILY

The most recent research of the Chamberlain family indicates that they are descended from William, Count de Tankerville, of Tankerville Castle in Normandy. The Count came to England with William the Conqueror in 1066. He returned to Normandy, but his descendants lived in England on the land granted to him.

John de Tankerville, son of the former earl, was Lord Chamberlain to King Henry I.

There were five Chamberlains to settle very early in New England. Three, Thomas, William and Edmund, were undoubtably brothers and perhaps the sons of Francis Chamberlain of Virginia who had arrived there in 1621 aboard the *Diligent*. One of the brothers, Edmund, born about 1615, first appears in the records at Roxbury, Massachusetts, where, on January 4, 1647, he was married to Mary Turner, "maide servant", as recorded by Rev. John Eliot, the 'Apostle to the Indians'.

Their first child, Mary, was baptised at Roxbury in April 1648. By February of the next year Edmund Chamberlain, John Parker and William Chamberlain were granted by the Bay town of Woburn "Ten or Twenty acres at that end next Parly (Pearly) Medow Brook, and Adjoining Reding line...". Thomas Chamberlain was already living there.

Woburn was only the first town the brothers farmed in during their search for enough land.

"After a town had been planted and the land taken up, the hardy and adventurous young men who lacked the means to buy land were ready to band themselves with others in like circumstances and resolutely push on and make new homes in the wilderness. The General Court was ready to grant lands for such purposes to men of good character when their numbers promised to be sufficient for mutual protection and for the main tenents of religious worhsip."

A petition by inhabitants of Concord and Woburn was sent to the General Court in May of 1653.

"To the Hon. John Endicot with others of the Hon. Magistrates and deputies at the Hon. Court now at Boston assembled. Humbly Sheweth...that..being encouraged by this court to view the land, that lieth yet undisposed of and unimproved on the other side of Concord river: which we do find a very comfortable place to accommodate a company of God's people upon; that may with God's blessing and assistance live comfortably upon and do good in that place ...and many of your petitioners are destitute of accommodations, some never having had any, and some others very little comedation, for that we cannot subsist, unless we do take some care to look out a way...and now we your humble petitioners do intreat this hon. court to grant us so much land as may be there laid out to the quantity of six miles square of upland and meadow, which parcel of land we do entreate may begin at Merimacke river at a necke of land next to Concord river...intreat...to gratify their humble petitioners with a speedy answer..."

The land requested included the fishing grounds of the Pawtucket Indians where the city of Lowell now stands and where Rev. John Eliot was working to convert the Indians to Christianity. He entered a petition at the same time for a grant to the Indians that they "might not be distrubed in their ancient possessions". The Court granted both petitions.

So it appears that Edmund Chamberlain moved from Woburn across the line to Billerica (Shawshin) where he took a farm next to William's and then moved across the river to Chelmsford after a petition for farms there was approved.

William lived the rest of his life in Billerica. The town's records state, "Rebecca, w. William Sr., Sept, 26, (16)92 died in ye prison at Cambridge". She was one of the unfortunate people accused of witchcraft.

"Chelmsford May: 17: 58 To the honered Coart Assembled at Boston the humble petistion the inhabetants of the towne off Chelmsford Sheweth: that we have as god by his Providenc haveing despoased off us with our famelies into this Remoat Corner of the wilderness...wee have and doe find as the State of things now standeth Much dificalte to : nay imposebile...of procuring such nesesarie suplye...which difecalltie is much increased to uss by beeing prohibeted from tradeing with the indiens which we doe Conseive to bee our Lawfull Liberte: owr humble Requeste tharfore is that yr honers would bee pleased to take this Case into yr Consideration: and grant your petiscioners thare Lawfull Liberte which wee Conceive ought not to bee Menopolised...

James Parker	George byam	Willaim Underwod
William Fletcher	Benjamin buterfild	John Shiple:
Henry Farwell	Daniel Blodget	Richard Hildereth
Tho Chamberlin	John Spalden	John Nutting
Edward Kempe	Roberd Flecher	Abraham Parker
James Blud	Samewill Foster	John Right
Thomas Adams	Joseph Gilson:	Jacob Parker
Edward Spalden	James Hildereth:	Edward Spalden
John Shiple	Josiah Richardson	Roberd Procter
Joseph Parkis	John Riske	Edman Chamberlin
Samewill Kempe	Berabin butterfild	Joseph Parker "

These thirty-three names included nearly all of the adult males living in town. The petition was probably not granted. It would have interfered with a valuable source of income to the colony, "...the Trade of Furrs with the Indians in this Jurisdiction doth properly belong to this commonwealth and not unto particular persons.

150

There in Chelmsford in 1656, the first minister, Rev. John Fiske, recorded that "Mary Chamberlain wife of Edmond Chamberlain, was dismissed to us from the Church of Ooburn (Woburn)". Later that year Mary presented her children to the Chelmsford church "as follows: Mary about 8 y. old, Sarah about 7 y. old, Elisabeth about 5 y. old, John aboute 3 y. old and Edmond about ½ a y. old." (Little Edmond fought in King Philip's War in 1675 and was "slayne in the Swampe Fight".)

Two years after the children were presented to the church, Jacob was born in Chelmsford. Descended from Jacob was Socrates Bacon's mother, Lucy Chamberlain.

"3 May 1665", Edmond was made a freeman. "The several persons underwrit returned by Certificates from the several ministers and selectmen, were by public suffrage of both Magistrates and Deputies admitted to freedom. and took their oaths accordingly.

John Endecott	Eliazer Hauthorne	Joseph Porter
Phillip Cromwell	Deane Winthrop	ffrancis Bacon
Nath. Greene	Edmo. Quinsey	Isak Sternes
Nath. Saltonstal	Edmo. Chamberlaine	Jno. Stevens
Jn. Wright	Stephen Paine	Sam. Ward "

and sixty-two others.

Mary died in 1669 at Samuel Ruggles house in Roxbury and Edmond was married the next year to the widow Hannah Witter Burden (or *Burdett)*, daughter of William and Annis (Churchman)Witter[1], by Rev. Samuel Adams.

Edmond moved next to Malden and then to Roxbury where he rented Griffith Bowen's farm for five years. But Edmond was still looking for something else and with the group of "goers" from Roxbury, he and Hannah moved to New Roxbury (Woodstock) far out on the frontier as early as 1693. With them was their new young family, Susanna and Mary and the son born shortly after Edmond Jr. died in the Great Swampe Fight—a son also named Edmond. Descended from this second Edmond Jr. was Socrates Bacon's father.

Edmond Chamberlain, Sr., at town meeting in Woodstock November 23, 1693, "was allowd a corner of land, about thirty rods, on the north side of Muddy Brook, for fencing". "Granted March 21, 1693/4, 3 acres adjoining the land he purchased of James

[1] William Witter (1584-1659) settled at Lynn in 1629 and later purchased, for two pestle stones from the Indian Sagamore Poquonnum, all the land now occupied by Swampscott, Sagamore Hill and Nahant, Massachusetts. He was a dedicated religious worker.

Frizell of Woodstock." In February, 1696, "the Lot no. 56 of the third range was taken up by Edmond Chamberlain and contained 21 acres."

This year another Indian uprising broke out and the house of John Johnson was invaded in Woodstock and his three children "dashed upon the hearthstone". During these troubled times the growth of the settlement came to a stop.

Son Jacob Chamberlain was awarded 23¼ acres in the third range of lots that year of 1696 but probably he never went to Woodstock, perhaps because of the Indian trouble or because his father died then.

Edmond was deacon of the first church until his death May 8, 1696. His estate was appraised at £77 by Benjamin Sabin, James Corbin and John Johnson. Hannah, as administrator of the estate was aided by Samuel Ruggles, "yeoman" and John Mayon, "Cordwainer both of Roxbury". A grown Edmund, Jr. married Elizabeth Bartholomew November 21, 1699 in Woodstock; daughter of William and Mary (Johnson) Bartholomew. Her parents had been coaxed to Woodstock early by residents who wanted william to build one of his fine grist mills. (See Bartholomew Family on page 131.) Edmund, Jr.'s sister Mary was married the same day.

Edmund, Jr. and Elizabeth had:

Edmund, born 1700; died young.

Demund, 1702, Deacon in the church as was his father and grandfather.
   Twin to:

Elizabeth, married Lieut. Joseph Wright.

William, 1704.

Joseph, 1706.

Samuel, 1708.

Peter, 1709.

JOHN, born May 11, 1712.

Mary, 1714, died 1805. Married William Thompson.

Hannah, 1721.

In 1704, fear of the Indians again gripped the settlers. They were overjoyed when James Corbin's cart, sent to Boston for ammunition, was spied coming close to home. Sixty armed men went out to escort it safely to town.

In 1713, Edmund Chamberlain, Jr. was chosen surveyor to decide boundries of a new land division in south Woodstock. He had a pew in the new meeting house in 1721 and was selectman and sometimes tax assessor. He may have helped divide the remaining territory in 1724; the "Mill Land: Piece in Dry Clay Meadow; Honey Pot Hole; Rocky Hill; Piece northwes and east of piece called Round-About Way; etc. This was divided among al the fifty proprietors of Woodstock. The young Ephraim Bacon had just ar

152
see *Corrections*, page 337

rived the year before with his step-father, Ebenezer Edmonds.

Edmund Chamberlain died January 15, 1751, at 75 years old.

John, Deacon Edmund Jr's, eighth child, was born in Woodstock in 1712 and married, in 1738, Hannah Child, born in Woodstock to Lieut. John and Elizabeth (Wales) Child. Lieut. John was one of that large Child family that first helped to settle Woodstock. One other of the brothers Child married young Ephraim (II) Bacon's sister Elizabeth.

John and Hannah's children were:
Peter, born 1740, married Wealthy Chaffee.
John, born 1742.
HANNAH, born August 9, 1743.
Asa, 1745, married Martha Newton.
Elizabeth, 1747.
Norman, 1752.
Joseph, 1753.

Dauthter Hannah married Ephrain Bacon (III) in 1767 and was the mother of Ephrain, "Jr.", and Rev. Samuel, agents to Africa for the American Colonization Society. She is buried in the little cemetary on Bacon's Lane.

When the first Edmund Chamberlain was living in brand new New England in Chelmsford and was married to Mary Turner, they had a child, Jacob, born in 1658. Jacob took some land in Woodstock when his father did in 1693 but probably never moved there. He had moved to Malden with Edmund in 1670 and both went to Roxbury about 1677 where Jacob, instead of joining the exodus to Woodstock, made his permanent home. He married Mary Childe in 1684, the daughter of Benjamin Child and Mary Bowen, progenitors of the Woodstock-settler Child family. Mary was baptised in 1660 in Roxbury and died there in 1718. Jacob married the widow Sarah Faxon Weld.

Jacon and Mary's four children were:
JACOB, born 1683.
John, 1687, married Hannah Bowen, he was twin to:
Mary, 1687, married Samuel Davis.
Elizabeth, born circa 1690, married Joseph Weld.

In 1713, "Jacob Chamberlain senr. was recieved into full Communion with the Church". He died in 1721 and his gravestone in the Eustis Street Burying Ground, Roxbury, is inscribed "...aged 63 years. He dyd of ye small Pox".

Jacob Jr., born in 1683, married Sarah Payson May 30, 1711, the daughter of Samuel Payson and Mary Phillips.

An accusation of trespass was raised against Jacob in a will:

"I William Heath of Roxbury, ...give unto my son...Marsh in Muddy River...This marsh my Hond. Father Peleg Heath bought of James Morgan, as appears by his Deed...third November 1651, & my Father, Mother, nor I ever sold one foot of it that ever I knew of except one acre my mother sold to Capt. Sem'll Ruggles wch I bot of him again. But Jacob Chamberlain of Roxbury, committed Trespass on the most Northerly Corner of this my Land in the year 1700; I would then have pursued him for his Trespass, but when I came to see for my deed of said land behold it was stole out of my chest, and I saw it not again till about twenty years after & then it was given me by a stranger in the night, as tho' it had been a Letter in the Road, but when I came to light I found not one word in it only this stolen Deed Inclosed & then I was foreclosed in the Law, but Joseph you shall have the Deed of said Land and I hereby desire & Impower you by application to the Honble. General Court to bring Jacob Chamberlin Jr. to Tryal of his Title to my Salt Marsh, you will find the Deed he pretends to hold it by is no older then the false Record I lost so many hundred pounds by & altho' this Record has since been proved false in both superior & inferior Courts & some restitution of my money, yet I have never had any restitution of this my salt marsh to this day."

No record of the trial was discovered.

Jacob and Sarah had these children:

Sarah, born 1712, married Samuel Scott. (It is not certain that she is their child.)

Mary, 1714, married John Trott.

Jacob, 1716, married Phebe Vinton.

SAMUEL, 1718, married Lucy Stevens.

Elizabeth, 1720.

Edward, 1723, married Hannah Edmonds.

Patience, 1727, lived a few days.

John 1729, lived a few days.

Stephen, 1731, lived a few weeks.

There is reason to believe the last three children were by a second wife also named Sarah. Jacob Chamberlain died in Roxbury in 1761.

Samuel, son of Jacob, was born in Roxbury and married, in 1742, Lucy the daughter of Jospeh and Lucy (Ruggles) Stevens. (See the Stevens family on page 173.) Samuel may have fought in the REvolution. He certainly fought in the Louisburg Expedition of 1745 where he was among twenty Roxbury men, one of them Samuel, & impressed to "man the vessels" sent to capture the French bastion on Cape Breton Island in the hostilities between France and England, called King George's War. Samuel probably marched again in 1755 when area men were sent to the front in Col Timothy Ruggles' regiment to fight the encroachment of French into the

154

see *Corrections*, page 337

Ohio Valley.

Samuel Chamberlain died in Dudley, Massachusetts, a town located in the small cluster of new towns near Woodstock. His and Lucy's children were:

Lucy, born in Roxbury in 1744, married Edward Curtis in Dudley. The third Lucy in a line of seven.

Samuel, born 1745.

Samuel, born 1746, married Mary Green.

Sarah, born 1747.

Sarah, born 1748.

Timothy, 1749, married Judith Harding and Mary Coulton.

Mary, 1751.

ELAIKIM, 1753, married Anna Stow.

Joseph, 1755, married Esther Twiss.

Sarah, 1758, married Timothy Sherman. (May be the Sarah recorded above.)

Eliakim Chamberlain was born in Dudley, October 7, 1753. He married Anna Stow, descendant of another Puritan family, in 1780 in Charlton, neighboring town to Dudley. (See the Stow family on page 193.) Elaikim was eighteen years old at the time of the Boston Massacre and a serious Charlton, in common with the rest of the colony, began to prepare for the inevitable struggle.

In England, Massachusetts was declared to be in rebellion. Charlton Minutemen were organized, equipped, and drilled and on the alarm of the 19th, were up in arms and on their way to join the stream of brown clad men from other towns converging on the road to Lexington. Eliakim and his fellow Minutemen followed the British troops to Boston where the colonists held the city captive in a tight ring.

"Our Charlton companies performed good service there and rendered assistance in the erection of the several fortifications on the hills of Cambridge, Dorchester and Charlestown."

Eliakim also marched on the alarm of December 10, 1776, to Providence, Rhode Island, with Captain Abijah Lamb's company, Col. Jonathan Holman's regiment, serving in the same regiment with Ephraim Bacon; their children that would marry not yet born.

In the years after the war boundry disputes between the towns of Sturbridge, Dudley and Charlton erupted. Eliakim lived on one of the disputed lines and had petitioned with others many times for a new town to be formed out of the quarreling three. He would then have been part of the Gore,

see *Corrections*, page 337   155

where the Bacon's lived, and the main body of persons who wished to be in the new town, Southbridge. He even bought a pew in the projected church. But by the time the boundries wre about to be drawn, Eliakim Chamberlain had changed his mind.

So adamant was he that the ensuing difficulties and delays caused a committee to be formed (one whole half of which was Noah Webster). And in the end, the man H. Porter Morse called a real son-of-a-gun, Eliakim, had his way and the final boundry line had to be drawn in a very crooked way around the Chamberlain farm, very reminiscent of Dick Tracy's profile.

Eliakim and Anna had a large family:

LUCY, born May 12, 1782, married EPHRAIM BACON, JR.

Samuel, 1784, married Abigail Tucker.

Nathaniel, 1786, married Patty Streeter.

Charlotte, 1788, married Aaron Tucker.

John, 1790.

Jason, 1792.

Sally, born 1796, died 1800.

Ziph, a son, born 1799, died before 1828.

Benjamin Stow, 1801.

Eliakim, Jr., 1805.

In the early 1800's, Lucy, Samuel, Nathaniel and Charlotte all moved to the wold 7th Range in what is now Maine.

Eliakim died January 5, 1833 at 79 years old.

"...Considering The uncertainty of this mortal life and being of Sound and Perfect mind & Memory Blessed be Almity God for the Same...

1st That all my Just Depts and funeral Charges be paid by my Executor...

2ond I give to my beloved wife Anna Chamberlain one third Part of All my Real Estate...being in the Southwest part of Charlton with one third Part of the Buildings on the Same In Common and undivided with the other Two thirds which I give to Stow Chamberlain & Eliakim Chamberlain as well...Also give to my said wife Anna All my Indore Movables and wearing Apperel & my Chase—Also...to my wife Anna...her right of Dower...'

He stressd that the thirds were never intended to be divided "...for goodness of quallity and quantity". The children in Maine were to receive fifty dollars each, "...for I have given them some things in my lifetime". To John and Jason he gave one dollar, "...why I give them no more now in that I have given them there full Share in my lifetime".

"7th To the Children of my Deceased Dauter Lucy Bacon one Dollar to Each of them Why I give them now know more is that I Advanced to there Mother In my lifetime

see *Corrections*, page 337

what I thought was her full Share.

8th I hereby Apoint my Son Eliakim Chamberlain Sole Executor of this my last will and Testament...this twenty-Sixth Day of may in the year of our Lord one thousand Eight hundred and twentyeight.''

Eliakim's son Benjamin Stow was awarded a guardian, Andrew King, even though Anna was still living. Ephraim and Lucy Bacon's grown daughter, Cendarilla, was living with the Chamberlains, her grandparents, possibly to take care of Anna. After the guardianship was settled, an inventory was arranged:

"Real Estate

The homestead of said decesed situated in Charlton aforesaid Containing by estimation one hundred and thirty acres of land with the buildings there on appraised at- $2850.00

One pew in the baptist meeting house in Southbridge, No. 27- $13.00

Personal Estate

One horse 38.00 One yoak of oxen 68.00 Seven Cows 118.00 One two years old heifer 15.00 one half dito 6.90 ½ of sucking Calf 1.50
One half of six last spring Calves 16.00 One half of four swine 5.00
Hay in the barn 82.00 one winowing mill 2.50 One ox sledge 1.00 One ox cart ladders & hay riging 18.00 One ox waggon & hay rigging 8.00
two plows 6.75 One harrow 4.00 two Iron bars & a half 3.00 Six draft Chains Six ox yoaks & bows 1.00 four staples and rings 1.00 lot of old Iron
One steal trap & hors evener .50 teakle blocks Iron rings & wages .85
One Iron Shovel three dung forks one hoe one grindstone crank and frame 2.92 three hay forks two hay hooks three corn knifes two axes 2 whifletrees[1] .99
One bush cythe & stalf eight old Cythe one Cyder shovel and tub 1.20
One Cutter 14.00 wagon seet one ladder 1.00 One hand cart 3 dragg plant 15.50
One string of bells .10 three plank .25 One half of 29 white pine logs 12.90
172 feet of oak boards 120 feet of 3 by 4 sit work 1.92
One hors wagon and harnes 12.00 one Chais & harnes 52.50
One collar & traices & whifletree chain 1.75 One saddle 2.50 Old saddle saddle bags part of a harness hammers & pincers .61
heards (?) grass Seed one bushel 2.00 One grain riddles[2] .20 One gun and aquipments 2.33 ½ Sheet of Iron .87 Shoe bench & 4 Sickles One white oak log 1.70

Anna Stow Chamberlain died January 16, 1840 at 77 years old and her inventory listed very different kinds of things:

1. Whiffletree, singletree. A horizontal cross bar to which the traces of a harness are attached.
2. Grain riddles, a coarse sieve

1 Chaise and Harness $23.00
1 Clock 3.50 two Mirrors 1.00
1 Bed, bedstead & bedding 19.00
1 Bed, bedstead & bedding 10.50
5 Sheets 7.50 19 Sheets 9.00
13 Sheets 3.00 7 Table covers 3.80
17 pairs of pillow cases 3.75 5 pairs .75
Hearth rugs and Cushions .50
Carpeting 2.60 Underbeds .75
Towels 1.37 Warmingpan 1.50
Earthern ware 4.20 Glassware 3.50
Silver Spoons 4.08 other Spoons .60
Tinware 3.00 pewter ware 2.00
Meal bags & winnowing Sheet .75
Flax hetchel[3] .13 one pr Cards 8 cents
Stone Churn .50 Spinning wheels .20
Loom and apparatus reeds[4] .25
1 pr Steelyards .25 Coffeemill .10
Knives and forks .75 Teapots .75
Five Sets 1.00 Flat Irons .33
Pressing Iron .25 Bellows .17
Old Iron & Crane hooks .60
Iron ware 3.00 Brass kettles 5.00
Brass and Tin dippers .15
Case Drawers 1.25 Chest .50
Meal Chest and Corn .60
1 Set of grain Measures and Sieves .60
Pillow and other feathers .20
Widow Curtins and paper rags .75
Trunks 1.00 Light Stands 1.00
1 Cupboard .50 1 Cupboard .50
Dried Apple .35 Vinegar & Cask .75
Chest .12 Tables 2.00 Chairs 1.50
Whip .25 Close Stool .06
Brushes & Broom .50 Leather .08
Iron Furnace .30 Baskets .33
Wickers and Scissors .10
Old Casks 1.00 Pork, salted 2.00
Potatoes 1.00 Wooden ware .75
Timber logs 2.00 Map & book .10
Worcested .25 flax .25
Woolen Cloth .50
Wearing Apparel 15.63

3. Hetchel (hatchel); An implement for cleaning flax or hemp, consisting of a set of teeth fastened in a board. Also called hackle.
4. Reeds, that part of a loom that drives the filling against the woven fabric; consisting of tw horizontal parallel bars near together.

1 Note Signed April 1st one thousand eight hundred and thirty six, by Benjamin Stow for Twenty seven dollars 11/100: considered doubtful.
1 Note Signed by Edward C. Cleveland, worth $11.06

Anna's bequests, written in 1837, were of a slightly different order, too. She gave to each of her "beloved" children one eighty*part of her estate, including "...heirs of my beloved daughter Lucy Bacon, deceased, (former wife of Ephraim Bacon) one eighth part of my property..." John, the oldest son at home, received one hundred and fifty dollars more. A year after this Anna made a codicil to her will, "...I also hereby give and bequest unto my beloved grand dauther Cinderella Bacon, Fifty dollars" and signed it in a very weak hand.

After Anna's death a month later, Cendarilla traveled to Indiana, married William Armitage and lived on the farm next to her brother, Socrates.

The Chamberlains are burried in the old, silent and secluded Dresser Hill cemetary outside Charlton, surrounded by a stone wall and dark fir trees. To reach it from Sturbridge, take Rt. 20 to Charlton. Turn South at the center of Charlton where Rt. 20 and Main Street intersect. Main street soon takes the name of Dresser Hill Road (Rt. 31). Out in the country the road reaches the Dresser Hill Farm on the left and a small, rough Dairy Bar on the right. Turn there to the right and follow the country road past a fork to the second road on the right, a lettle more than one half mile. Turn right onto this wooded narrow road. Driving slowly, you finally reach an almost upright stone post on the left to mark the entrance to a cart-wide track. A modern house is on the right of the track, set far back. Just a little way down the track an opening appears to a large, ancient, well-kept cemetary.

Some descendants of Edmund Chamberlain: General Joshua L. Chamberlain, chosen by General Grant to give the marching salute for the surrender ceremonies at Appomattox.

Col. Josiah Snelling, hero of the Battle of Tippecanoe. Fort Snelling was named for him.

Levi Chamberlain, missionary to the Hawaiian Islands.

Sources:

Descendants of Edmund Chamberlain by the Chamberlain Association
Glazier, Chamberlain Families of New England and New York
Hazen, H.A., History of Billerica
Billerica Vital Records
Chelmsford Vital Records
Vircus, F.A., Compendium of American Genealogy

see *Corrections,* page 337

New England Historical and Genealogical Register
Linzee, J.W., The Ancestors of Peter Parker and Sarah Ruggles
Bowen, C. Winthrop, Woodstock, An Historicat Sketch, History of Woodstock
Bowen, C. Winthrop, Benealogies of Woodstock Families
Church and Congregation at Chelmsford
Lowell, Mary C., Old Foxcroft
Roxbury Vital Records
Dudley Vital Records
Probate Court Worchester, Mass.
Charlton Vital Records
Massachusetts Soldiers and Sailors
Quinabaug Historical Society Leaflets
Perham, H.S., Papers
Waters, W., History of Chelmsford

BARTHOLOMEW FAMILY

The brothers, John, Robert and Richard Bartholomew were living in Warborough, Oxfordshire, England about 1550 where they, as Gentlemen, held many pieces of land and had the honor to be church wardens. John[1] Bartholomew's son John[2], married Margaret Joyes in 1552 and was made overseer of his uncle Richard's estate by the latter's will. John[2], or his son John[3], is supposed to have been one of the founders of Bartholomew Chapel in Burford, a nearby town.

John[2] and Margaret's fourth son was christened *Will'm Barthlmewe* in Warborough, February, 7, 1567. He married Friswide, daughter of the Mayor of New Woodstock, England, William Metcalfe, and became a dealer in silks and woolens. He was buried in Bartholomew Chapel on May 6, 1635.

William, the son of William and Friswide, was born in 1602 or 3. He was omitted from his father's will, depriving him of his inheritance as second son, because of his religious convictions. In the period before 1630, the slightest opposition to the Church of England met with strong chastisment. It was not uncommon for fathers to disown their sons who opposed the established church as William was doing.

William moved to London and developed a close relationship with Rev. John Lathrop and his congregation which included Mrs. Anne Hutchinson. He was considered a dissenter as was his friend Rev. Lathrop, who had been a clergyman in Kent but renounced his orders and become the pastor of the independent Presbyterian Church in London. Although Lathrop's meetings were held in secret, the congregation was discovered and he and forty-two followers were imprisoned. William may have been one of them.

After four years the Reverend Lathrop was released and sailed for New England with thirty of his congregation. It is certain William Bartholomew was one of that group on the *Griffin* that arrived at Boston September 18, 1634. With him was his wife, Anne Lord, daughter of Sri Robert Lord, and the families of Anne Hutchinson, Rev. Lathrop and Rev. Zachary Symmes.

William was immediately granted several tracts of land at a place just named Ipswich, next to Anne's brother, Robert Lord. He was also granted the privilege to trade with visiting ships. He became a freeman on May 4, 1635, and on May 6, appeared at the General Court at Boston as the chosen representative of the people of Ipswich. The new town had some of the ablest men in the colony, including Thomas Dudley, future Governor of the Bay Colony, and Samuel Appleton. William's prominence in that town was a reflection of his "superior education, family and ability", according to historians.

see *Corrections*, page 337   161

In the next several years, William was re-elected to every session of the General Court, was appointed to "sett out the land at Newbury for keeping sheep that come on Dutch ships", and was feoffee of its public schools, that is, he found and parceled out land for the schools.

On September 19, 1637, William was appointed to a special grand jury in Boston which was to try Mrs. Anne Hutchinson who had adopted theological opinions at odds with the ministers of the colony. She had held meetings in her home where questions of doctrine were raised and discussed and where her "revelations...seduced & led into dangerous errours" many of the people, and caused years of public contention. Leading a person into "dangerous errours" of thought was a serious charge. Perhaps innocent persons would be deprived of their chance to be saved. And then, too, the authority of both the church and the government might be undermined the colonists worried.

William Bartholomew had this to say at Anne Hutchinson's trial,

"I would remember one word to Mrs. Hutchinson among many others. She knowing that I did know her opinions, being she was at my house in London, she was afraid, I concieve, or loth to impart herself unto me. But when she came within sight of Boston and looking upon the meanness of the place I concieve she uttered these words. If she had not a sure word that England should (would) be destroyed her heart would shake. Now it seemed to me at that time very strange that she should say so.

"Mrs. Hutchinson remarked: I do not remember that I looked upon the meanness of the place nor did it discourage me, because I knew the bounds of my habitation were determined...

"Mr. Bartholomew continued: I speak as a member of the court, I fear that her revelations will deceave.

"Governor Sir Henry Vane: Have you heard any of her revelations?

"Mr. Bartholomew: For my own part I am very sorry to see her now here and I have nothing against her but what I said was to discover what manner of spirit Mrs. Hutchinson is of; only as I remember as we were once going through Pauls church yard (in London) she than was very inquisitive after revelations and said that she had never had any great thing done about her but it was revealed to her beforehand.

"Mrs. Hutchinson: I say the same thing again.

"Mr. Bartholomew: And also that she said she was come to New England but for Mr. Cottons sake. As for Mr. Hooker (as I remember) she said she liked not his spirit, only she spake of a sermon of his in the Low Countries where in he said this—it was revealed to me yesterday that England should (would) be destroyed. She took notice of that passage and it was very acceptable with her.

"Mr. Cotton: One thing let me intreat you to remember, Mr. Bartholomew, you never spoke anything to me.

"Mr. Bartholomew: No, sir, I never spake of it to you and therefore I desire to clear Mr. Cotton.

"Governor Vane: There needs no more of that.

"Mr. Bartholomew: Only I remember her eldest daughter said in the ship that she had a revelation that a young man in the ship should (would) be saved, but he must walk in the ways of her mother."

Mrs. Hutchinson was convicted of sedition and banished, "a woman not fit for our society", and the arms of her Ipswich followers put in the care of Mr. Bartholomew. Her banishment was postponed over winter because she was expecting a baby but in the spring she whent to Rhode Island, as had the "Godly and zelous...but very unsettled (in) judgement" Roger Williams, who had left the Bay Colony two years before.

In 1639, William Bartholomew (he pronounced his name *Bartlemy* and wrote it without the second "o") offered to keep the teacher of the Ipswich school at his house for a year without charge "if she have health, but if she prove sick, the charge to be borne by the publicke". That year he was also town clerk, and in 1645 was appointed to a committe to decide the best way of destroying "Ye wolves, wch are such ravenous cruel creatures and daily vexations to all ye inhabitants of ye colony".

William was asked to copy the colony's papers in his clear hand and the "waste book" he copied is the oldest record Ipswich now possesses. He was one of the chosen "seven men", the men who influenced the town most, that included Mr. John Whittingham, Mr. Samuel Applecton, Thomas Emerson, Daniel Foster, Thomas Bishop, and William Adams. He was a deputy. He helped lay out highways. He was one of the largest subscribers for a yearly compensation to Major Daniel Dennison "to encourage him in his military helpfulness", and subscribed towards the purchase of a bell for the town. He and his brother Henry, of Salem, "tendered themselves to supply" money to the colony to continue the Commissioner's Court, an act that proved very important for it was the court basic in the formation of our federated form of government.

In 1651, William bargained for 30,000 hogshead staves, probably for his business as a merchant, and the next year, he was chosen to be on a committee to "establish and regulate a Grammar schoole and schoole master". In 1654, he was chosen treasurer and appointed by the General Court "to divide ye Colonies arms among ye shires". In 1655, he re-conveyed to the town of Ipswich, for a token price, the entire tract granted to him in 1639 for the town's common pasture which has ever since been known as "Bartholomew Hill Pasture", or more correctly, "Bartlemy Hill Pasture". All references to this pasture mention a row of willows running over the crest of the hill.

For the next five years William continued to be mentioned frequently in the records of the business of the town with but one problem. In 1658 he was licensed to sell strong water, (only the best men being allowed to receive such a license) but was fined ten shillings for "selling dear".

William bought a house in Boston from Robert and Sarah Nash and moved there in 1660 where he assisted, as he had always done in Ipswich, in the town's affairs. He was exceedingly busy taking inventories and overseeing estates and persons. He was appointed overseer of William Brown's mill there and it was probably then that William Bartholomew, Jr., learned all he later put to good use building the essential mills in frontier towns. He worked once on a committee to help some Englishmen who had been prisoners of the French when they captured St. Christopher's.

"Mr. William Bartholomew late of Bosteon, now sojourning with Mr. Green in Charlestoune deceased this life 18th day of January 1680/1." He was seventy-eight years old and he and Anne were living with their only daughter. No will was found. He apparently divided his large property among his children before his death. The inventory of his small remaining estate was as follows:

Charlestowne 17. 4. 1681
    An Inventory of an Estate of William Bartholomew Deceased taken and Estimated by us whose names are subscribed

Imprimis To one ffeatherbed & bolsters & 1 pollow two Ruggs & paire of Blankets & old shattred bedsted
Old chaires, joint stooles, Cushions & paire of old bellows
½ doz'n Cushions
brasse: vis't" 2 old Kettles with 2 trivet, other small brasse things, old brasse things
one doz'n Napkins & Tablecloth, 1 paire of old Sheets
2 Cuppboard Cloths, 5 old Table cloths
old sheets 3 paire spaire Course pillow cases 1 course shirt and nine old Course Towells
4 doz'n Childrens stiff Capps
A small Remn't of Cotton Cloth, & of speckled Linnen & of home made cloth and of Kersie[1]
Old Pewter
Books vis't. a bible in q'to: Clarks Martyrologie, etc.
Old blanketts worn out with peices & such like Coverled
old boxes & Chest and Lumber and old Trunk & 3 Chests.
an old fowling piece 1 mach lock mus'yt & sword
two old small Ruggs a blew Rugg
a parcell of Indian Hatchets
1 parcell of hows
2 Iron Potts, Pewter
an old Carpett 8 yd's Canvas 9 yd's narrow Canvas
two old Hammackers[2]
Tin small things
two Earthen Juggs
1 Cutlesse, an old brass Kettle

Estimated by us. Samuel Phipps
Nicholas Meade

[1]Kersie: Kersey, a smooth, light weight, ribbed woolen cloth. From a village in England calle Kersey.
[2]Hammackers, probably "Hammock". Spanish, hamaca.

William Bartholomew's grave in Phipps Street Cemetary, Charlestown, is placed next to that of John Harvard, the benefactor of Harvard College. Anne died in Charlestown two years later. Their children were:

> Mary, married Matthew Whipple and Jacob Greene. In 1667 Mary made her father attorney to settle with John Whipple, her father-in-law, her right to property left to her by her deceased first husband.
> Joseph, born about 1638, returned to England to live.
> WILLIAM, born 1641.

William Bartholomew, Jr., married Mary Johnson in 1663, the daughter of one of the colony's most important military officers, Issac Johnson, who was killed leading the assault against the Narragansett Fort in the war with the Pequots. Her grandfather was John Johnson who held the title of "Surveyor of all ye Kings armies in America". (See Johnson family on page 140.) William himself as a Lieutenant and "was imbued with the spirit and endowed with that capacity for leadership which constituted the statesmanship of the times". He learned the carpenter trade and the mill business. In an address given in 1882, Andrew J. Bartholomew said,

> He became prominent as a pioneer in the settlement of new towns...the early history of Hatfield, Branford, and Woodstock, discloses his varied labors, in erecting the corn and saw mill, the rude church and minister's dwelling, laying out highways, selecting the minister, providing for the school, securing the grant of the privileges of townships, and holding various offices of town government, and in managing its institutions all through his...active life. His qualities for this grand work were so marked and well understood by his compatriots that the settlers of Woodstock commissioned him, with others, to forward new settlements in the wilderness of New Hampshire, Vermont, and New York, and build up new towns from their surplus popluation."

The summer before he married, William was staying near Medfield working as a carpenter or millwright at Robert Heusdale's mill.

> "John Levin aged twenty ffour yeares or thereabout & William Bartholomew aged twenty three...saye that beinge at a ffarme at Mr. Richard Parkers about tenn myles ffrom Medfield about the latter end of June last did see a company of Indians come to ye ffarme afforsaid & did request to have Liquors ffor saving of some wolves but Nathaniell Mott wd not give ym any but tendered ym a pecke of Corn apece to every my ffor their paines in deliveringe the wolves but they refused & were so earnest ffor Liquors that one of the deponents was fforced to thrust them out of doores & told ym yt they would not be orderly he would laye handes ym."

In 1677, William lived at Hatfield and was raising a building when the September 19th raid by the Indians surprised him. They captured his four

see *Corrections*, page 337

165

year old daughter, Abigail.

"Att Eleven of the Clock in ye day time the enemy came upon Hatfield (when ye
greatest part of the men belonging to the Towne were dispersed into ye meadows) and
Shott down 3 men within ye Towne fortification, killed and took women & children &
burnt houses & Barnes..."

The captured were taken "through the forests, over the Lakes" to Canada and
kept eight months until they were ransomed for 200 pounds.

Wars with the Indians (King Phillip's War) made that area uninhabitable
for the next several years so William drew up a contract with the town of
Branford, in Connecticut, to build and maintain mills there.

"The town have agreed to give unto William Bartholomew twenty acres of land as
convenient as any be...provided also he do perfect his agreement...concerning building
a mill in Branford and build and settle in the town."

In January, 1680, they granted William land "below Guilford Road".

"The Towne have given liberty to Wm Bartholomew to set up a saw mill upon the
great river about the foot of the great hill and the town have given him liberty to make
use of what timber he shall sea (cause) for sawing half a mile below said mill and so on
both sides of the river and along his mill as far as he shall see cause."

In April, 1687, young Woodstock, one year after the arrival of the first
settlers from Roxbury, were old aquaintences of William, arrived, passed
this resolution,

"The Company of Planters att a gen'll meeting did then choose Edw'd Morris, John
Chandler, Sen'r., Nat'll Johnson & Joseph White, to treatt and agree with William Bartholomew of Branford for the building of a corn mill on as reasonable terms as they
can...each (town resident) to bere his equal proportion according to his home lott."
"...on condition of his building a corn mill on the falls below Muddy Brook ponds and
finding the Town with grinding good meal clear of gritt as other towns have generally
found..."

Generous offers of land were William's if he would promise to come, bu
his experience at Hatfield with the Indians made him hold back; Woodstoc
was too far out on the frontier. But by the fall, and after an offer of a plac
to "set a mill" and almost 200 acres of upland and meadow, "It was granted att
full meeting of the proprietors: that William Bartholomew should have twenty acres of land.
provided he bring his wife & settle upon it by next June..." Tracts were also grante
each of his sons, Isaac and William, and although nearly fifty years old an

166

already comfortably situated, he accepted their offer.

Soon he was involved in the care of the town. He was commissioned as an ensign upon rumors of Kings James II's loss of his throne and subsequent insurrections in Boston and later, as Lieutenant, placed in command of all subject to military service in Woodstock. He was chosen a selectman "...entrusted with the whole power of the town excepting granting land and admitting inhabitants.", and sent as representative of Woodstock to the Grand General Court at Boston in the town's first election.

In the Spring of 1697 "Mr. Bartholomew died...Two rough unmarked stones at the head of graves probably show his and his son John's last resting places" in Woodstock Hill Cemetery.

William and Mary's children were:

Issaac, born 1664.

William, 1666, left no children.

Mary, 1668, left no children.

Andrew, 1670, married Hannah Frisbie.

Abigail, 1672, married Joseph Frizzel and Samuel Paine.

ELIZABETH, 1676, married EDMUND CHAMBERLAIN, JR.

Benjamin, born circa 1677.

John born circa 1679.

Joseph, born circa 1682.

Sources:

Bartholomew, G.W., The Bartholomew Family
Bartholomew, A.J., Address at First Reunion of Bartholomew
Hammet, Hammet Papers
Ipswich Quarterly Court Records and Files
History of Woodstock

JOHNSON FAMILY

John Johnson was twenty-nine years old when he came with the Winthrop fleet to New England from Lincolnshire, England, in 1630. He settled in Roxbury with his wife and five children. Margery, John's wife, was the daughter of George Humfrey. Their second son was named Humphrey.

John was selected constable of Roxbury that first year and admitted a freeman in 1631. The word's meaning changed just then to indicate, not as it had with the eight original freemen, *stockholder,* but *voter,* or *citizen,* and the number enlarged to more than a hundred men, about half the family heads in the colony. A freeman still must belong to the church and the Puritan church only allowed membership to the "visible saints", those whom God had already chosen for salvation. John was a strong churchman and, in fact, was one of the founders of Rev. John Eliot's church.

John Johnson was a member of the embryo parliment in 1632 and was an elected deputy at the first General Court in 1634. He was elected eighteen times more. It was a post given only to those of "known integrity, mental power, financial ability". Perhaps an example of his good qualities would be the order of the court in 1640, "Samuel Hefford haveing been much misused by his master, Johnathan Wade, hee is freed from the said Mr. Wade, and is put to John Johnson for three yeares, and to have L6 wages per annum."

The Ancient and Honorable Artillery Company, at its first organization in Boston, made him a Captain. He was clerk of the company for three years and, at least once, was sent out to raise "50 more men from each town" for an expedition against the Pequots on the warpath in the Connecticut Valley. After that quieted, the General Court ordered, "the 12th d the 8th mo (October, 1637, on their calendar) to bee kept a day of publike thanksgiveing to God for his great m'cies in subdewing the Pecoits, bringing the soldiers in safety..."

It was that same fall that Anne Hutchinson was taken into custody on the charge of heresy. The General Court ordered "that the arms of her Roxbury adherants bee delivered to goodman Johnson". She stayed in his house from November to the next April and she said, "that except for the fact I must have a companion when I went for a walk, I would have thought my self an honored guest in the house."

John was "appoynted surveyor generall of all ye armyes" and stored the colony's ammunition at his house. Which caused Governor Winthrop to write in his journal,

"1645) 2.6.) The other (fire) was at Roxbury this day. John Johnson the surveyor general of the ammunition, a very industrious and faithful man...having built a fair house in the midst of the town, with divers barns and other out houses, it fell on fire in the day time, (no man knowing by what occasion, and there being in it seventeen barrels of the country's powder and many arms, all was suddenly burnt and blown up, to the value of 4 or 500 pounds, wherein a special providence of God appeared, for he being from home, the people came together to help, and many were in the house, no man thinking of the powder, till one of the company put them in mind of it, whereupon they all withdrew. and soon after the powder took fire, and blew up all about it, and shook the houses in Boston and Cambridge, so as men thought it had been an earthquake, and carried great pieces of timber a great way off and some rags and such light things beyond Boston meeting house. There being then a stiff gale at south, it drove the fire from the other houses in the town. This loss of our powder was the more observable in two respects, 1. because the court had not taken that care they ought to pay for it, having been owing for divers years; 2. in that, at the court before, they had refused to help our countrymen in Virginia, who had written to us for some for their defence against the Indians, and also to help our brethren of Plimouth in their want."

The town records and the school charter were also stored in the house and the loss was an irreparable one. The only thing recovered appears to be the fly-leaf from the original record book, torn and fragmented, but with a list of the earliest inhabitants. One notation has, "John Johnson   6 goats   4 kidds"

"This Court, taking notice of the contynuall paynes & faythfull endevours of Mr. John Johnson in the place of the surveyor generall, lookinge to the country armes & pcureinge many of the country debts, judge it meete he should have due recompence, & doe therefore order, That he shalbe allowed five pounds p annu..."

"Mr. John Johnson, having bin long serviceable in the place of surveyor gen'll, for which he hath never had any satisfaction, which this Court considering of, thinkes meet to graunt him 300 acors in any place where he can find it..."

Many public meetings were held at "Brother Johnson's," a tavern he kept "in Roxbury Street". He was an advocate of the free schools and gave generously to that cause though his family was small for that time, having five children.
   ISAAC, married ELIZABETH PORTER.
   Humphrey, married Ellen Cheney.
   Mary, married Roger Mowry and John Kingsley.
   Elizabeth, married Robert Pepper.
   _____ , a daughter.
John died in 1659 and his wife, Margaret in 1655. John Eliot witnessed his simple will giving Isaac, the eldest "sonne a double portion...according to the word of God". The inventory that was taken listed only these possessions:

2 fether beads 2 bolsters 3 pillows 2 sheets wh 3 blankets and a rugg with curtans and valents with a bed steed
a tabl 6 Joyn stools and a carpet
1 drincking glass i hoar (hour) glass

172

3 hats and wearing apparell with boots stockings bands caps handcherches
2 bibles 1 psalme booke and 8 books more
12 lb yarn 13 scains
1 curtain rod 1 pair of pinser 2 pair sheers
8 silver spoons

In his will he mentioned two grandchildren that lived with him. Probably, the whole family of his son Isaac lived with him and he had moved into one small part of the house, taking meals and the warmth of the fire with the younger Johnsons as was common then. He had his books, his drinking glass, a way to tell time, and a soft feather bed. And honor in his own country.

Captain Isaac Johnson married Elizabeth Porter in January, 1637, when his father's family was well-settled in Roxbury. There is no record of Elizabeth's arrival or any documented link with the one Porter family living in Roxbury.

Isaac was a member of the church his father helped to found and was admitted a freeman in 1635, the same day as William Bartholomew. He became a member of the Ancient and Honorable Artillery Company in 1645, was a lieutenant in 1666 and elected its captain in 1667. He was also Captain of the "Rocksberry" Military Company. He was a Deputy to the General Court. He was also a selectman and appointed in 1652 to stake out highways with that group. Twenty highways were laid out by Edward Denison, Isaac Johnson, Griffith Craft and Peleg Heath. The town then had to set penalties for taking rocks out of the highways and leaving holes in the road. Once Isaac was appointed an arbitrator with Edward Denison in a court case,

"...ordered...whereas no fine can be sufficient for the reparation of a man's name, and considering Job's poverty and necessities, they judge that he should pay the (court) costs,...and for saying that Chandler was a base, lying cheating knave and had gotten his estate by cheating, and had cheated him out of 100 li., he was to make public acknowledgement...Job Tiler should nail up or fasten (it) upon the posts in Andevour and Roxbury meeting houses in a plain legible hand, there to remain fourteen days."

Captain Johnson's name appears often in the histories of the Indian wars and there are several accounts of his bravery. He lead Eliot's band of "praying Indians" and believed these fifty-two men to be "courageous and faithful".

Isaac was in command of the 4th Massachusetts company of seventy-five colonists and the praying Indians on a very cold and stormy December 19, 1675, as they marched to the Narragansett Fort to fight King Philip's warriors. John Bacon was marching to the Great Swamp Fight under Captain

Davenport. During the fight Isaac Johnson started to lead his men over a bridge made of a single felled tree where only one man could walk at a time. "The brave and intrepid Captain Johnson and Captain Davenport were instantly shot down, mortally wounded."

Isaac and Elizabeth's children were all born in Roxbury.

Elizabeth, born 1637, married Lieut Henry Bowen, a member of Isaac's company at Narragansett and later a pioneer to Woodstock.

John, 1645, died at age twenty-two.

MARY, born 1642, married Lieut. WILLIAM BARTHOLOMEW.

Isaac, 1644, married Mary Harris.

Joseph, 1645, died within a few weeks.

Nathaniel, 1647, married Mary Smith.

Elizabeth, widow of Captain Isaac Johnson, died "suddenly" in 1683.

Sources:

Records of the Colony of Massachusetts Bay in New England
Ancestors and Descendants of John Rose Bloom
Porter, J.H., Hannah Johnson and Polly Palmer
Smith, J.J., Certain Early Ancestors
New England Historical and Genealogical Register
Johnson, P.F., The Johnsons of Roxbury, Massachusetts
Ipswich Quarterly Court

CHILD FAMILY

The Child family is represented in England's County Suffolk records as far back as 1327 but the exact ancestry of Benjamin Child is not recorded due, probably, to the secrecy of many of the departures taking place at English docks in 1630. What is certain is that the Ephraim Child that brought his brother William and the ten year old Benjamin, most likely his brother also, was from Bury St. Edmonds. The three accompanied Ephraim's good friend, John Winthrop on the flagship *Arbella*. Ephraim was one of the most affluent of the new settlers and held a leading position in Watertown, where he settled. He was one of the first deacons of the church, one of the original freemen,[1] a deputy to the General Court for twelve years and elected one of the selectmen of the town for fifteen years. He accompanied John Johnson on an assignment to decide the boundries between Newton and Watertown. He had no children and left his large estate to his nephews.

Benjamin, born about 1620 in England, was very active in the affairs of the colony and was said to be "earnest in character...methodical and exact" with a "sterling integrity". He married Mary Bowen, daughter of Griffith Bowen, "late of Wales," and lived near the Great Pond, now called Jamaica Pond, in Roxbury. (The Bowen family is on page 148.)

Benjamin was one of the thirty colonists who gave a part of the £104 needed to build the first church of Roxbury, John Eliot's church. Mary was admitted to this church in 1658.

Benjamin died in 1678. His children and Mary's were:

Ephraim, born about 1654, died September 4, 1675, in the fight at Squakheage against the Indians.

Joshua, born about 1656, married Elizabeth Morris.

Benjamin, born about 1658, married Grace Morris. They were prime planners for the move of the Roxbury people to Woodstock. Seven of his sons moved there and one married the daughter of Ephrim Bacon (I) and Elizabeth Griggs.

MARY, born 1660, married JACOB CHAMBERLAIN, son of Edmund and Mary, and moved to Woodstock.

An infant, died unbaptised. Newborn babies were baptised on the first Sunday after their birth, even in the worst weather, even if their

---

[1]Of the 5 original freemen in N.E., four were Socrates Bacon's ancestors; Mr. George Phillips, John Page, John Johnson, and Ephraim Child.

see *Corrections*, page 337

mother could not attend.

Elizabeth, baptised 1663; unmarried.

Margaret, baptised 1665; unmarried.

John, baptised 1667; died young.

Mehitable, baptised 1669; married Samuel Perrin, moved to Woodstock.

JOHN, baptised 1671, married ELIZABETH WALES, moved to Woodstock.

Joseph, baptised 1673, died within six months.

Benjamin and Mary's first three children were all baptised by John Eliot on February 27, 1658, after their mother was admitted to the church.

John Child married Elizabeth Wales in June 9, 1694, the daughter of Elder Nathaniel and Elizabeth (Billings) Wales of Braintree, and moved to Woodstock. Seven Child brothers, sons of John's brother, Benjamin, Jr., settled in Woodstock very early. A story is told in Woodstock histories about the one cow the brothers owned between them, so scarce were cattle in the new world, each brother kept the cow for only a week at a time. But at Thanksgiving, the eldest brother, Ephraim, kept her a little longer to be able to serve the gathered families a meal of milk-rich hasty pudding.

"On one occasion of the annual gathering of the seven households...the supper was duly prepared, and set forth upon a large "fall-leaf-table", each family provided with their wooden bowls and wooden spoons. According to their custom, all were standing around the frugal supper, while the elder brother...asked the Divine blessing; while thus solemnly engaged, the large watch dog, in passing under the table, moved the leg upholding the leaf, and down went table, milk and pudding. The younger brother...cried out, "Stop, brother! Stop! The pudding is gone, and the milk is gone, and of what use is the blessing now...but let's kill that dog."

The Child brothers operated a saw and grist mill in 1715. William Bartholomew had sold his mill rights to Ebenezer Cass years before and many mills had been built since.

In 1724, the remaining territory in the south half of Woodstock, "some in the tract called Honey Pot Hole were the hearth stones lie...", was divided between thirty-six proprietors, including names familier to us such as Smith Johnson, James Corbin, James Frizzel, Samuel Perrin, Benjamin Griggs Henry Bowen, Edmund Chamberlain, David Holmes, John and Isaac Bartholomew and John Child, mostly of the new generation.

There is recorded only the birth of John and Elizabeth's daughter, Hannah, born in Woodstock in 1709. She married John Chamberlain, son of Edmund Chamberlain, Jr. and Elizabeth Bartholomew.

Sources:

History of Woodstock
Roxbury Vital Records
Child, E., Genealogy of the Child Family
Records of the Colony of Massachusetts Bay in New England
Linzee, The Ancestors of Peter Parker and Sarah Ruggles

BOWEN FAMILY

The following pedigree of Griffith Bowen is deposited in the College of Arms, London.

PEDIGREE OF GRIFFITH BOWEN OF BARRYHEAD IN THE COUNTY OF GLAMORGAN IN THE PRINCIPALITY OF WALES AND KINGDOM OF GREAT BRITAIN

Beli Mawr marr. King of Britain, 55 B.C.; follows the generations of Afflech; Affalach; Owen; Diwc Brichwain; Omwedd; Amwerid; Gorddufu; Dufu; Gwrtholi; Doli; Gwrgain; Cain; Genedawc; Iago; Tegid; Padarn Peifrydd; Edeirn, marr. Gwenllian, daughter of Coel Godebog, King of Britain; Cunedda Vledig; Einion Yeth; Gayer Einion; Llymerini; Cariadoc Vrech fras, who was Earl of Hereford, Lord of Radnor and Lord·of the Dolorous marr. Tegayayr Vron, daughter and heir of King Pelinor; Maynerick (or Maenarch), Lord of Brecknock (Brecon), marr. Ellen (Elinor) dau. of Einon ap Selyff, Lord of Cwmmwd;

(There are some descrepancies in time from the first generation to the following; Blethyn, Lord of Brecknock. The rest is proved correct.)

Blethyn (Bleddyn) Lord of Brecknock (Brecon) marr. Otten (Ellen) dau. of Tudor, King of South Wales;

Gwgan ap Blethyn (Bleddyn), arms: a chevron between three spearheads, marr. Gwenllian, dau. and heir of Philip Gwys;

Cadivor, alias Howel, ap Gwgan of Glyn Tawe marr. Maud, dau. and heir of Llewellyn Vychan ap Llewellyn ap Gwrgan (a great heiress of Gower. Arms argent, a hart lodged proper, hoofed gold, in its mouth a branch vert)ap Iros ap Gwin ap Collwin.

Griffith Gwyr ap Cadivor marr. Catherine, dau. of Sir Elider ap Einion. Arms agent, a chevron between three ravens, sable.

Griffith-Ychan ap Griffith Gwyr marr. Jane, dau. of John Flemming of Mounton (Monkton). Arms : giles, a fret argent, over all a fess azure.

Howell ap Griffith-Ychan marr. Anne, dau. of Gwillm ap Jenkin Grant. Arms: azure, three lion gold a chief argent.

Howell Vaughan (Ychan) marr. Catherine, dau. of Jevan Llwyd of Castel Odyn. Her arms: Gold, a lion rampant.

Gwillim Gam ap Holwell marr. Wenll, dau. of Gwillm ap Savle Jevan Morgan-Yhan Van. Arms: Gules, three chevrons argent.

Howell Melyn of Gwyr marr. Catherine, dau. of Griffith Llewellyn Voythys of Aberglásney in Llangathen. Arms: argent, on a cross sable, five cresents gold; in dexter quarter a deer's head, gules.

Jevan (Evan) Gwyn marr. dau. of Wilcock Cradock.

Jenkyn ap Jevan marr. Joan, dau. of Thomas ap Gwillm Vachan ap Gwillm Phillip ap Elidur.

Owen ap Jenkyn marr. Alice, dau. of Jn. of Swansey, f. Rosser John of Dyffimysk, descendant of Maenarch.

Griffith ap Owen, alis Bowen, of Slade Co. Glamorgan marr. Anne, dau. of Humphry Bury of Burymarbarth in Co. Devon.

Philip Bowen of Slade Co. Glamorgan marr. Elizabeth, dau. of Hopkin John Vaughan.
Francis Bowen marr. Ellen, dau. of Thomas Frankleyn.
Griffith Bowen of Barryhead Co. Glamorgan.

Griffith Bowen was born about 1600. He married Margaret Fleming in Wales, daughter of Henry Fleming of Llanrhidian and Sarah, daughter of Jenkin ap William Dawkins of Gellehir. Ten years later he sold all his lands and brought his wife and most of his children to New England. John Cotton's records of the first church of Boston for the year 1638 state, "Griffyn Bowen & his wife Margarett taken in for members of ye Congregation the 6t of ye 12th month." Other members were Anne Hutchinson and husband "Willyan", Henry Vane, John Winthrop nd family, and some of his servants.

Griffith was made a freeman on May 22, 1639. He was granted land at Muddy River and was chosen to do survey work there, but he lived in a house and garden in Boston. Near his house lot at the corner of what are now Essex and Washington Streets stood the Liberty Tree, said to have been planted by him in 1646 and cut down by the British in 1775.

The large elm became famous at dawn on August 14, 1765, when two effigies were found hanging from it. One was of Andrew Oliver, collector of the stamp tax, and the other, a giant boot with a devil peering out—a pun on the name of Lord Butte, Prime Minister of England. When the figures were discovered it caused such excitement that business in Boston came to a standstill. That evening the effigies were torn down and marched over all the town and finally burned in front of Oliver's house. Later, the Sons of Liberty forced Oliver to resign publicly under the tree in a broad space soon called Liberty Hall

For ten years signs and other figures of those favoring unpopular English regulations appeared on the branches of the tree. A tall pole was placed there which sometimes flew a red flag to call the Sons of Liberty together The British had as much contempt for the tree as they did for the colonists On August, 1775, "armed with axes", wrote the Essex Gazette of 1775, "the made a furious attack upon it. After a long spell of laughing and grinning, sweating, swearing and foaming, with malice diabolical, they cut down the tree because it bore the name of Liberty."

General Lafayette stopped at the place the tree once stood on his visit to America in 1824. A young girl, be-ribboned in red, white and blue, carried silver tray, two goblets and a bottle of old French wine to the General. He toasted the event, "The world should never forget where once stood the Liberty Tree... Now there is a stone replica of only the tree's stump at the spot.

Of course, Griffith Bowen never knew about his tree. He returned to Wales about 1650, after his wife died, and later he moved to London to live

184

see *Corrections*, page 337

the rest of his life. His house in Boston was occupied by John Manard, Benjamin Childe and Joshua Childe, each for a year, and by Edmund Chamberlain for five years.

The children of Griffith and Margaret Bowen were:

Margaret, born 1629 in Wales, married John Weld.

Francis, 1630 in Wales; returned to England and had a quarrel with his father. He probably did not marry as his share of the large estate was assumed by his brother Henry. Francis died in England.

William, 1632 in Wales, married and returned to England after the division of his father's estate. He was a mariner and died about 1687 in Turkish captivity.[1]

Henry, 1634 in Wales, died in Woodstock aged 90. Married Elizabeth Johnson dau. of Capt. Isaac Johnson. Henry was at the Great Swamp Fight.

MARY, born about 1635 in Wales, married BENJAMIN CHILD.

Esther, 1638 in Boston, died 1654, 'Hester Bowen, a young maide.'

Abigail, 1641.

Peniel, 1644, "the sone of Mr. Bowen of Boston Church...he living at a farme neerer to us then to Boston, his wife was delivd. of this child by Gods Mercy without the help of any other woman. God himself helping his pore servants in a straight." Peniel (Penuel) returned to England with his father at age five and died there.

Elizabeth, 1646, married "the Hon'ble Isaac Addington".

Deriah, 1647, returned to England with his father.

Sources:

Bowen, E.A., The Bowens of Woodstock
Linzee, Ancestors of Peter Parker and Sarah Ruggles
Stte Street Trust Company Historical Publications
Virkus, Compendium of American Geealogy

[1]When the Roxbury colonists heard that William was held in a Turkish prison they collected money for his ransom in a box at the church. Learning he had died they decided to use the money for a tomb for the Rev. John Eliot and his wife. The tomb is at the Eustis Street Cemetary in Roxbury.

WALES FAMILY

Nathaniel Wales, 1586-1661, immigrant from England in the *James* to Massachusetts in 1635, was made a freeman in 1637. He was a shipwright and married Susanna Greenaway, daughter of John Greenaway.[1] They were the parents of:

Nathaniel Wales, married Isabel Atherton, daughter of Humphry and Mary (Wales) Atherton. Nathaniel died in 1662 in Boston. He and Isabel were the Parents of:

Nathaniel Wales, born about 1650 in Boston; married in 1675 Elizabeth Billing, daughter of Roger and Hannah Billing of Dorchester. He was an elder in the church and died in Braintree. Their children:

ELIZABETH, married LIEUT. JOHN CHILD; moved to
    Woodstock.

Sarah, married Nathaniel Thayer.

Nathaniel.

---

[1] John Greenaway, immigrant from England, probably in the *Mary and John* in 1629, to Dorchester. He was a millwright, a town officer, and was made a freeman, May 18, 1631.

ATHERTON FAMILY

Humphrey Atherton was born in Winwich Parish, Lancashire, England, in 1609, son of Edmund. He married Mary Wales, daughter of John, and had six children baptised in Winwick before they sailed for Massachusetts Bay on the *James* in 1635 with the Wales family. Five children, Increase, Thankful, Hope, Watching and Patience, were all born in Dorchester, in the new colony.

Humphrey was made a freeman on May 2, 1638, and then a Deputy to the General Court. He was a Speaker of the House and amember of the Council of War for the United Colonies in 1645; Captain of the Dorchester Company, 1646; Captain of the Ancient and Honorable Artillery Company, 1650-1658; Commander of the United Colonies, 1653; Governor's Assistant, 1645-1661; Superintendent of Indian Affairs, 1658 and Major General of the Massachusetts Colony in 1661.

He died of a fall from his horse which stumbled over a cow lying in the road, September 17, 1661, leaving an "extensive" estate.

Humphrey Atherton's daughter, Isabel, married Nathaniel Wales, Jr.

Sources:

Virkus, F.A., Compendium of American Genealogy
Pope, Pioneers of Massachusetts

BILLING FAMILY

The family of Billing lived for several hundred years at their estate, *Billing* in the county of Northampton, England. The name was *de Billing*. The first Billing that can be documented in lineal ascent is John, of Rowell, who had lands in Rushenden and was patron of the church of Colly-Weston. He had two sons, Thomas and John.

Sir Thomas Billing, the eldest son, was called to the bar and was a member of the Inns of Court. He was made Sergeant-at-Law in 1453 and was knighted by Henry VI for taking a prominent part in the Lancastrian side in the War of the Roses. He was council for Henry VI at the bar of the House of Lords when the right to the court was argued. He was later principal law advisor to Edward IV. In 1468 he was Lord Chief Justice of the King's Bench and retained his position in spite of the alternating victories of the White Rose and the Red. He died of apoplexy in 1481 and was buried in Bittlesden Abbey in Oxfordshire where brass figures of he, in his official robes, and his wife are on the large blue marble slab placed over their graves. During Henry VIII's dissolution of the monasteries these were taken to the church of St. Mary's in Wappenham where they still rest. In *Lives of Chief Justices,* Campbell says that "Thomas enjoyed the felicitous fate accorded to very few persons of any distinction in those times—that he never was imprisoned—that he never was in exile—and that he died a natural death."

His first wife, and the mother of his children, was Katherine Geffard, daughter of Roger (Gifford, Giffard), descended from the Scottish royal line beginning with Alpin, who died in 834, and Ecgberht, King of England, 828.

Nicholas Billing, fifth and youngest son of Sir Thomas, lived at Middleton Malzor in Northamptonshire. He died in 1512, leaving money in his will for requiem masses to be performed at Bittlesden Abbey on the anniversaries of his death. He married Agnes, daughter of Stephen Gilbert.

John Billing, died 1526.

William Billing, eldest son of John died at Middleton Malzor in 1557.

Roger Billing, second son of William, inherited Baltonborough, with lands in Somersetshire near Glastonbury with his brother Richard. He died in 1596.

Richard Billing, eldest son of Roger, lived at "Deanes" in Taunton and married Elizabeth, daughter of Ebenezer Strong. In his will he made bequests for the reparation of the Church of Saint James in Taunton, to the poor of that parish, and to his brother Richard, "the younger", to make himself a ring "in remembrance of me".

Roger, second son of Richard, came to Dorchester, New England before 1640. About ten years later, his nephew, William, came to the same town. Roger became a member of the church almost immediately and was admitted a freeman in 1643. He married Hannah and had seven children: Mary, Hannah, Joseph, Ebenezer, Roger, Zipporah and Elizabeth. Elizabeth married Nathaniel Wales in 1675.

Sources:

Billings, F., Genealogy and Descendants of William Billings
Billings, C.H., Ancestors and Descendants of Mine
Virkus, Compendium of American Genealogy

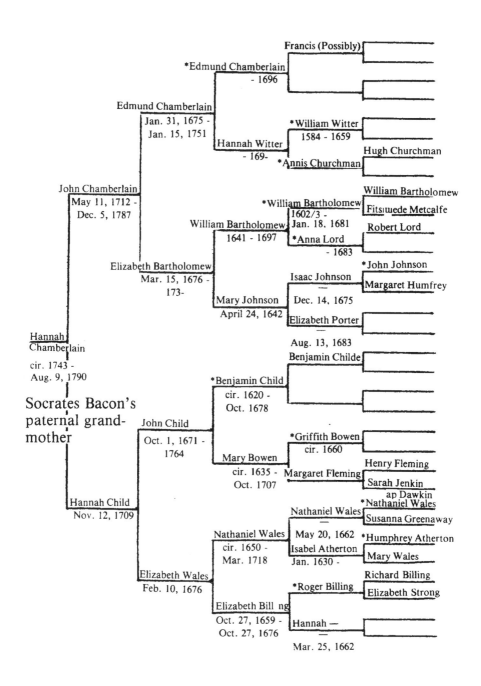

Francis (Possibly)

*Edmund Chamberlain
- 1696

Edmund Chamberlain
Jan. 31, 1675 -
Jan. 15, 1751

*William Witter
1584 - 1659

Hannah Witter
- 169-

Hugh Churchman

*Annis Churchman

John Chamberlain
May 11, 1712 -
Dec. 5, 1787

William Bartholomew

*William Bartholomew
1602/3 -
Jan. 18, 1681

Fitsiuede Metcalfe

William Bartholomew
1641 - 1697

Robert Lord

*Anna Lord
- 1683

Elizabeth Bartholomew
Mar. 15, 1676 -
173-

*John Johnson

Isaac Johnson
—
Dec. 14, 1675

Margaret Humfrey

Mary Johnson
April 24, 1642

Elizabeth Porter
Aug. 13, 1683

Hannah
Chamberlain
cir. 1743 -
Aug. 9, 1790

Benjamin Childe

*Benjamin Child
cir. 1620 -
Oct. 1678

Socrates Bacon's
paternal grand-
mother

John Child
Oct. 1, 1671 -
1764

*Griffith Bowen
cir. 1660

Mary Bowen
cir. 1635 -
Oct. 1707

Henry Fleming

Margaret Fleming

Sarah Jenkin

Hannah Child
Nov. 12, 1709

ap Dawkin
*Nathaniel Wales

Nathaniel Wales
—
May 20, 1662

Susanna Greenaway

Nathaniel Wales
cir. 1650 -
Mar. 1718

*Humphrey Atherton

Isabel Atherton
Jan. 1630 -

Mary Wales

Elizabeth Wales
Feb. 10, 1676

Richard Billing

*Roger Billing

Elizabeth Strong

Elizabeth Bill ng
Oct. 27, 1659 -
Oct. 27, 1676

Hannah —
—
Mar. 25, 1662

GIFFARD LINE

Katherine Giffard, wife of Sir Thomas Billing, was descended from Cerdic, King of the Saxons, 519-534, who was the ancestor of the English royal line; Egbert, born in 775, the first king of all England, whose male line descended to Edward the Confessor, and the female line to the present time; Alfred the Great, 871-901; and several other English Kings, exactly as described in the chapter on Thomas Dudley, page 206.* The lines differ beginning in the 22ond generation from Cerdic. Katherine's line continues:

generation 22. Gospatric I, Earl of Dunbar and Northumberland.
23. Gospatric II, Slain at the battle of the Standard, Aug. 23, 1138, 2ond Earl of Dunbar, Baron of Beanley; marr. Sybil, dau. of Arkil Morel, died 1095.
24. Juliana of Dunbar, marr. Ralph de Merlay, Lord of Morpeth, son of William de Merlay.
25. Roger de Merlay, d. 1188; marr. Alice de Stuteville, dau. of Roger de Stuteville of Burton Agres, d. 1202, Sheriff of Northumberland, 1169-1183.
26. Agnes de Merlay, marr. Richard Gobion, d. Gascony before end of 1230; son of Richard de Gobion and Beatrice de Luielles.
27. Hugh Gobion, d. 1275.
28. Joan Gobion, marr. John de Morteyn, d. 1296, of Tilsworth and Marston, Co. Bedford, son of John de Morteyn, d. ca. 1284, and Constance de Merston.
29. Sir John de Morteyn, d. 1346; marr. Joan de Rothwell dau. Richard de Rothwell.
30. Lucy de Morteyn, living 1361; marr. Sir John Giffard of Twyford, Knight, b. 1307, d. 1369, son of Sir John Giffard de Boef, Knight, and Alexandra de Gardinis.
31. Sir Thomas Giffard, Knight, of Twyford, d. 1394, marr. Elizabeth de Missenden, d. ca. 1367.
32. Roger Giffard of Twyford, Esq. b. circa 1367, d. 1404.
33. Katharine Giffard. Her line now joins the Billing line.

ELIOT FAMILY

PAYSON FAMILY

The large family of Bennett and Lettice Eliot lived in the village of Nazing, County Essex, seventeen miles from London. They were small land owners and had, under pressure from many directions, sent their son John to Jesus College at Cambridge University where he received his degree in 1622. He was hired as a teacher in a school kept by Rev. Thomas Hooker. About eight years after he graduated, not allowed to preach in England because of his non-conformist views, a band of Nazing Puritans asked John Eliot to help them emigrate to New England, "that we might afflict ourselves before God to seek of him a right way for us and for our little ones". And, although they were afraid of the savage beasts and men and the bitter winters in America, but none the less, carrying strong feelings about the English church, several of John's brothers and sisters decided to go with him and the others from home, from Nazing. They did not all leave at once, but "at such time as they could escape, or circumstances would permit".

Two years later, the transplanted Nazing people gathered at a place they named Roxbury and formed their church where John Eliot, now known as the apostle to the Indians, became their teacher. He believed in the words the Indian on the Lady Arbella's embroidered blue banner spoke, "Come over and help us". Wishing to convert the savages, he learned their language to be able to preach to them.

Edward Payson and his wife came with the first Nazing group in 1631 on the ship *Lyon*. He was baptised in England in 1613 and, after his first wife died at the birth of their only child, married John Eliot's sister, Mary. "Edwd Passon" was made a freeman in 1640 in Roxbury where he was a manservant.

Edward and Mary's third son was Edward, Jr., chosen Butler for Harvard by the Overseers in 1675 so he could work while he attended classes. Five years later, he began to preach in the church at Rowley under Rev. Samuel Phillips and married Samuel's daughter, Elizabeth. He stayed there until he died in 1732. He kept records in the church book of his parishioner's births, marriages and deaths and in fine, faint script, noted the death of his daughter, "Sarah, my sweet babe", on March 20, 1702.

Edward and Mary's fifth son was Samuel who married Mary Phillips, another daughter of the Rev. Phillips.

Samuel had twelve children born in Dorchester, Massachusetts:

Mary, born 1689, died 1693.

SARAH, 1690, married JACOB CHAMBERLAIN.
Anne, 1692; died the same year.
Samuel, 1693.
Edward, 1695, married Bethia Wise.
Mary, 1697, married Joseph Snelling.
Dorcas, 1699.
Phillips, 1704.
Elizabeth, 1706, married, probably, Joseph Damon.
Anne, 1708; married, probably, James Jest.
Hannah, 1711.

Sources:

Court Records, Essex Co. Quarterly Court
Blodgett, Early Settlers of Rowley
Thwing, 1st Church of Roxbury, Mass.
Bowen, Genealogy of Woodstock Families
History of Roxbury
Virkus, Compendium of American Genealogy
Sibley, Harvard Graduates

APPLETON FAMILY

The Appleton family is documented as far back as John Apulton, living in 1396 in County Suffolk in England but the family had been living there from the time of the Conqueror. Since their Christian names were Norman, such as William, John, Henry, Edward, it is likely they derived the Saxon place-name *Appleton* from the name of the English lands granted to them. Their arms were *Argent a fess sable* (silver with a black stipe) *between three pomgranets gules* (red apples), *slipped and leav'd vert* (leaves and stalks green). Added later was a crest; an *Olivant's hed coupled sa tusked ear'd or, with a serpent writhed about his noz vert,* an elephant's head with gold tusks and a green snake about his trunk. Their motto was *Difficiles Sed Fructuosae.*

That first documented generation was John Apulton of Walingfield Magna, near Ipswich, Bury St. Edmunds and Sudbury. He lived during the reign of King Richard II and died in 1414.

3. John, of Waldingfield parva, married Margaret, daughter of Robert Willinge. She died in 1468 and John in 1481.

4. John Apulton, Jr. of Waldingfield Magna, married Alice, heiress and daughter of Thomas Malchier.

5. Thomas Apulton married Margaret, only daughter and heiress of Robert Crane of Stoneham parva. Thomas lived until 1507.

6. Robert Apulton, Thomas' oldest son, married Mary Mowntney, a descendant in the sixth generation of Robert Mowntney. The *Appleton Memorial* by Isaac Appleton has a drawing of the brass figure of Mary as it appears on her tomb in the Little Waldingfield Church with her hands in prayer and the clothes she wore etched in detail. The Appleton arms were also placed there in brass and a brass figure of Robert lies on his tomb but is covered by a pew built over it some centuries ago. These 'monumental brasses' were inlaid in stone but in the time of the civil wars when churches were converted into barracks most of the inscriptions were stolen.

"In the yeare 1644 on the 12th of June, there came one Jissope with a commission from the Earle of Manchester, to take away from gravestones all inscriptions on wch hee found 'Orate pro anima'...showing their excessive anti-Roman Catholic zeal which made war upon the words, 'Pray for the Soul'.

In that same church hangs a

"...helmut, part of a leather jerkin or apron, and a sort of coronet which tradition gives our family...these things hang upon an iron peg about twelve feet from the floor, in the chancel. A similar peg is within a few feet of this where the remainder of the armor hung, but it has been stolen or lost, time unknown."

7. William Appleton of Waldingfield parva, son of Robert, married Rose, daughter of Robert Sexton, Gentleman, of Lavenham.

8. Thomas Appleton, Esquire, married Mary, daughter of Edward Isaack of Patricksbourne, Kent.

The Isaack family line is recorded unbroken in County Kent as far back as circa 1450 when James Isaack married Elizabeth, "ye D. & heire (of) Condye vice admirall to Kynge to whom the Kynge gave the manner of Hersinge in Kente after wch he was called Condy of Hersynge". Edward Isaack's mother was Margery Hawte, heiress of a line of five generations of Knights.[1]

Thomas Appleton died in London in 1630. His eldest son was Sir Isaack, Lord of the Manor of Holbrook Hall; Knight.

9. Samuel, fourth son of Thomas, was born in 1586 and married Mary Everard at Little Waldingfield (Waldingfield parva).

The Everard family's earliest record is from the thirteenth century during the reign of Henry III when Ralph Everard, one of the 'landed gentry', lived at Waltham Magna. The *Breviary of Suffolk* in the British Museum states, "This family is very ancient, and had fair possessions in Linstead, Laxfield, Haselton and Dunston".

Samuel and Mary had six children before Mary died and Samuel married again. He and his family and second wife, including a seventh child nearly a year old, sailed for New England in 1635 and settled in Ipswich. He had planned for some time to sail and sent cattle over in 1630 with the first fleet. "There came not on shore one half of them", wrote Winthrop to his son and ordered him to "take no money of Appleton".[1]

Ipswich was a new plantation at a place the Indians had called Agawam. It already had a minister, Rev. Nathaniel Ward, and his assistant, Rev. Thomas Parker. William Bartholomew, Mr. Thomas Dudley, some Emersons, a Philbrick and an Eliot, John Johnson and William Serjeant, and later, the Knowltons, William Buckley, Adams', Averils, Ayres', Bradstreets, Frenchs, Mathias Button, Nathaniel Rogers, Robinsons Henry Archer, E. Chapman, Richard Saltonstall and John Webster, all lived in early Ipswich.

When the Assistants of the Massachusetts Bay Company had met in London in 1629, they decided that every man who transported himself and his

[1] Sir William Hawte, Kt., Sir Nicholas, Sir William, Sir William, Sir Richard Hawte, Kt.

202

family at his own expense to New England would be given at least fifty acres. Later, the freemen parceled out much more land than that and Samuel was given "a farme containing foure hundred and sixty acres more or less medow and upland as it lyeth bounded by the River commonly called the Mile brook..." "All those that have planting ground by the River side beyond Mr. Appleton's are to...lay out a highway as may be most convenient as themselves can best agree..." This is now Waldingfield Road.[2]

In 1637, Samuel Appleton was "assisting in the Ipswich Court, probably as juror or judge". In 1648, he received a grant of "a little p'cell of land lying by the Highway leading to his farm..." as his share of the land granted to men who marched against the Pequods. In 1650, there was granted a "p'cell of ground...beyond the swamp to make his fence straight..." And he acquired Parley's meadow and other land.

"1641, December 3. Mr. Appleton hath promised the Town to have a malt house ready by the first of April next, and to malt such corn as shall be brought to him from the people of this town at such rates as shall be thought equal from time to time. And no man (except for himself) is to have any made elsewhere for the space of five years now ensueing."

Samuel's son was running the malt house by 1665 when, although the law prohibited the cutting of oak or walnut trees, the maltsters were "granted liberty to fell some walnuts for their kilns..." "...being as good Husbands for the Town as they can." It was voted, too, that there should be trees "marked for shade for cattell in all common by wayes..."

Mr. Samuel Appleton was "admitted to the freeman's oath" on May 25, 1636. (Only three others, Robert "Keaine", Henry Flint and Daniel Maude, out of sixty-two persons admitted on that date, were entitled to be called *Mr.*) In 1637, Samuel was Deputy to the General Court and to all the Courts thereafter until he was left out for refusing, along with many of the rest of the Court, to "support the views of the Synod at Newton, which condemned eighty-two errors in religion, as connected with Mrs. Hutchinson and her party". A new Court was chosen which banished Mrs. Hutchinson and several others. (Appleton's) dismission from public life, under these circumstances, is honorable to him."

---

[1] A cow in N.E. was worth L20, at home it cost L5.

[2] A letter received in 1978 from George F. Bradstreet, a structural engineer, said, "The Appleton Farm in Ipswich...remains to this day in the Appleton family. However, the last Mr. Appleton died several years ago and his widow now occupies the farm. They had no children." Mr. Bradstreet, himself, is the eleventh generation to live on the Bradstreet farm settled in 1635.

"...in the first planting of Ipswich, the Tarratines or Easterly Indians had a design to cut them off...when they had but between 20 and 30 men, old and young, belonging to the place (and that instant most of the men had gone into bay about their occasions, not hearing thereof). It was thus one Robin, a friendly Indian, came to this John Perkins, then a young man then living in a little hut upon his father's island...and told him that on such a Thursday morning early, there would come four Indians to draw him to goe down the Hill to the water side, to trick with them, which if he did, he and all neare him would be cut off; for there were 40 burchen canowes, would lie out of sight, in the brow of the Hill, full of Armed Indians for that purpose: of this he forthwith acquaints Mr. John Winthrop, who then lived there, in a house near the water, who advised him if such Indians came, to carry it ruggedly toward them, and when there backs were turned to strike up the drum he had with him beside his two muskets, and then discharge them; that those six or eight young men, who were in the marshes hard by a mowing having their guns each of them ready charged by them, mighttake the Alarme and the Indians would perceive theyr plot was discovered and haste away to sea againe; which was accordintly so acted and tooke like effect; for he told me that presently after he discovered 40 such canowes sheare off from under the Hill and make as fast as they could to sea. And no doubt many godly hearts were lifted up to heaven for deliverance."

From then on, a watch patrolled the town, roads and open places at night and was manned by every adult male over eighteen years old of every family, including "sons, servants and sojourners". A military organization trained every Saturday at first, and later, once a month.

In 1651, Samuel's daughter Sarah married Rev. Samuel Phillips and Samuel lived the rest of his life with them in Rowley where he died in 1670. His children were:

Mary, born 1616.

Judith, 1618, died 1629.

Martha, 1620, married Richard Jacobs, died September, 1659.

John, 1622, Rep. to Gen. Court, Clerk of the Courts, County Treasurer, Capt. of a troop to pursue Indians. For opposing the Provice Treasurer's illegal order to assess taxes here, he was imprisoned, fined and disenfranchised. He left a large estate. Married Priscilla, daughter of Rev. Jose Glover, "at whose charge was established the first printing press in America".

SARAH, born at Reydon, Holland, in 1627, where her family lived for a short time before emigrating to New England. She married Rev. SAMUEL PHILLIPS.

Judith, born Reydon, 1634, married Samuel Rogers, son of Rev. Nathaniel, brother of John Rogers, president of Harvard College.

Samuel, 1625, at Little Waldingfield, as were all but the two above. Married Hannah Paine and Mary Oliver. Commander in Chief of the army defending the towns on the Connecut River, "by whose industry, skill, and courage those towns were preserved ..." and he lead all of the Massachusetts forces at the Great Swamp Fight.

1686 saw a threat different than that presented by Indians. Samuel, Jr., was an Assistant to the Council when Sir Edmund Andros was appointed Governor. A speech made in 1849 explained:

"In that darkest hour of our history; our whole colonial legislature aboloshed; our whole civil power grasped by Sir Edmund Andros; our whole adopted law swept away by a stroke of the pen of the king; the principles of justice silenced; every man's title to his farm requiring to be confirmed by a fine; those little democracies, the town, annihilated by a law forbidding them to meet more than once a year, and that simply for the election of town officers; the gun announcing to Boston that a standing army was quartered there, and over-awing the liberty of the inhabitants; at that moment of peril, Sir Edmund Andros was pleased to lay a tax, and to apportion it upon the town...and a board should be constituted for the assessment of the tax upon themselves.

...On the evening before that day (to choose the board), several inhabitants of Ipswich met...at the house of John Appleton...In that little preparatory caucus...it was ...concluded that it was not the town's duty to consent to that method of raising money. The next day (was) the town meeting...and thereupon it spread upon its records this vote—'That considering that said act, has infringed upon our liberty, as it is of the land, which declares that no taxation shall be laid unless with the consent of the people; they do therefore vote first, that they...decide that the Select men shall not lay such a tax, till it is determined on by the people.' This was circulated in manuscript through the County of Essex, it being illegal to print documents of this kind."

Samuel Appleton denounced Andros' arbitrary assumption of power in a public speech, and three days after the sudden arrest of the selectmen of Ipswich, warrents were issued for the arrest of Dudley Bradstreet of Andover, Samuel Appleton of Ipswich, and Nathaniel Saltonstall of Haverhill, as "persons factiously and seditiously inclined, and disaffected to his Majesty's government". The warrant specified no illegal act.

"...and although Mr. Appleton was convicted of misdemeanor by a jury of Boston, (who, as has well been said by one of the [arrested selectmen], were foreigners), and held confined under bonds, yet this manuscript appreciably kept alive that feeling which...later enforced by the thunder of Faneuil Hall, and by the thunder of Bunker hill ...proclaimed the same principle of English liberty which had long slumbered in the breasts of the people."

Bradstreet and Saltonstall paid their bonds but, even with two warrants out for his arrest, Samuel refused to pay and so hid at, it was said, his son's house in Lynn. He delivered inspired speeches to the townsmen from a high rocky piece of ground still known in Lynn as Appleton's pulpit.

> "...therefore in his Majesties name do charge & Command you, to make dilligent search & enquiry for ye sd Samuel Appleton, in any house or place where you shall be Informed, or Suspect him to be, & to breake open any doore or doores where you shall suspect him to lye hid or be Concealed within yo'r sd County, & him being found, you are to Apprehend, secure and convey to this place to Answer before me in Councill to such matters of High misdemeanor as on his Maj'ties behalfe shall be objected ag't him; Whereof you are not to faile, & for soe doeing this shall bee yo'r Warrt
>
> His Excellency, S'r Edmund Andros, Knight, &c."

When Samuel was apprehended, as apprehended he was bound to be, he was ordered again, to pay his one thousand pound bond to insure his "good behavior untill ye next Superior Court" but still refusing, he was imprisoned in the Boston jail. He lived "in ye Stone Prison" from November until March.

> "No town was probably more glad than Ipswich, that Andros was constrained to relinquish his authority by the threatening attitude of the people in Boston and the vicinity."

Family tradition claims that on the imprisonment of Sir Edmund in 1689, Major Appleton was allowed to hand him into the boat "which conveyed him off".

Descendants of Samuel Appleton include two who made notable marriages: Fanny Elizabeth Appleton who married Henry Wadsworth Longfellow and Jane Means Appleton who married President Franklin Pierce.

An unfortunate trait of the Appleton family, was described by J. B. Felt in his *History of Ipswich:*

> "There are four families in this town called bleeders. Three of them are immediately, and the other mediately, related...They are thus named from an unusual propensity in their arteries and veins to bleed profusely, even from slight wounds...Some of their predecessors have come to their end by wounds, which are not considered by any means dangerous for people in general. This hemorrhage first appeared in the Appleton family, who brought it with them from England."

Sources:

Jewett, I. Appleton, Memorial of Samuel Appleton
Caldwell, A., Ipswich Antiquarian Papers
Everards of Langleys

206

Salem Quarterly Court Records
Hammet, Hammet Papers
Waters, F.P., The Old Bay Road From Saltonstall's Brook
Felt, J.B., History of Ipswich, Essex and Hamilton, Mass.
Heraldric Journal of American Families

PHILLIPS FAMILY

Rev. George Phillips, the first minister of Watertown, Massachusetts, was the son of Christopher Phillips of Raynham, St. Martins, in the district of Gallow, County Norfolk, England. He was born in 1593. Cotton Mather wrote in his *Magnalia Christi Americana* that he was "descended of honest parents, who were encouraged by his great proficiency at the grammar school to send him into the university; where his good invention, strong memory, and solid judgement, with the blessing of God upon all, attained a degree of learning that may be called eminent".

At graduation, he found a place to preach at Boxsted in Suffolk and "found much acceptance with good men; as being a man 'mighty in the Scriptures'." But because of his doubts about church government and his interest in the writings of non-conformists he disturbed some of his congregation who complained to Rev. John Rogers. Mr. Rogers respected George Phillips so highly that he answered he "believed Mr. Phillips would preach nothing without some good evidence for it from the word of God."

Mather wrote,

"When the spirit of persecution did, (with) extremist violence, urge a conformity to ways and parts of divine worships...He, with many more of his neighbours, entertained thought's of transporting themselves and their families into the desarts of America, to prosecute and propagate...the gospel...and being resolved...to accompany the excellent Mr. Winthrop in that undertaking he...embarqued for New England, where they arrived in the year 1630...(on Winthrop's flagship *Arbella* with) the most distinguished company that ever came over."

Governor Winthrop, in a letter to his son written before embarkation, "From aboard the Arbella, riding before Yarmouth...", that they had a day of fasting and Mr. Phillips preached to them the whole day "...so as we have much cause to bless God for him." Mr. Winthrop, in fact, admired him so he had advanced the money "for the transporacon of Mr Phillips & his ffamily...till hee should be chosen to some p'ticular congregacon."

Very soon after they arrived, George's wife, Elizabeth Sargent,[1] died; "the desire of his eyes...(who) had cheerfully left her parents, to serve...in a terrible wilderness."

George Phillips' name appears on the original list of freemen for May 18, 1631, which is the earliest date of any admission, and he was among the group of men led by Sir Richard Saltonstall that chose Watertown in the Charles River for their permanent home. Before they built more than a few houses, they built a church. When it was ready in July, the Watertown colonists set aside a day for fasting and prayer in a proclamation declaring their thanks for God's mercy that allowed them to escape the "pollutions of the world" and to survive the "long and Hazardous voyage from east to west, from Old

England in Europe to New England in America."

Johnson's *Wonder-working Providence,* written in 1646, described the meeting house as "beautifully built". George Phillips took his place as minister and was Watertown's leader for the fourteen years left of his life. He was so sure of the scriptures that,

"...he was able on the sudden to turn unto any text...Indeed, being well-skilled in the original tongues, he could see further into the Scriptures than most other men...Hence also he became an able disputant; and ready upon all occasions to (support) what he delivered from the word of God; for which cause his hearers counted him, 'the irrefragable Doctor'; though he were wo humble and modest, as to be very averse unto disputation, until driven there to by extream necessity."

"He and his people, especially Sir Richard Saltonstall and Mr. Richard Browne, entertained more enlightened views of civil and religious liberty...than then belonged to other planters of Massachusetts Bay...and Mr. Phillips' novel, suspicious and extreme ideas of what should be, and now is, the Congregational Church in New England."

George Phillips and Mr. Browne are entitled to another honor, "much more important than has generally been conceded to them." When the Court passed an order to tax the people of Watertown eight pounds to build a fort at Newtown (Cambridge) without consulting with them Rev. Phillips and Elder Browne "assembled the people, and delivered their opinion that it was not safe to pay monies after that sort, for fear of bringing themselves and posterity into bondage." They were summoned before the Governor and the Court of Assistants and they declared that as English citizens the people of Watertown could not be lawfully taxed without their own consent. Soon after, on May 7, 1632, as a result of the debate Phillips and Browne had sparked, two representatives from every town were ordered sent to the Court to confer on exact ways to run the colony and changes made in its Constitution. They initiated the origin of representative government on this continent, the beginnings of American Constitutional history.

About George Phillips' death, Mather writes,

"He laboured under many bodily infirmities: but was especially liable unto the cholick; the extremity of one fit whereof, was the wind which carried him afore it into the haven of eternal rest, on July 1, in the year 1644, much desired and lamented by his church at Watertown; who testafied their affection to their deceased pastor by a special care to promote and perfect the education of his eldest son, whereof all the country, but especially the town of Rowley, have since reaped the harvest."

Governor Winthrop wrote that he was,

"a Godly man, specially gifted, and very peaceful in his place, much lamented by his

212

people and others...Here lies George Phillips; an incomparable man, had he not been the father of Samual."

George Phillips' children by his first wife, Elizabeth Sargent, were:
SAMUEL, born Boxsted, England, 1625; married SARAH APPLETON. He was minister at Rowley.
Elizabeth, born Boxstead; married Job Bishop, died young and left no children.
and by his second wife:
Zorobable, 1632, married Ann White.
Jonathan, 1633, a magistrate in Watertown.
Theophilus, 1636.
Annabel, 1638, died at four months.
Ephraim, 1641, died 1641.
Obadiah, died young.
Abigail, married James Barnard and left no children.

Samuel Phillips, born to Reverend George Phillips in England in 1625, was educated at Harvard by the church in Watertown because of the members' enormous respect for his father. To be admitted to Harvard, Samuel had to be,

"competent to read Cicero or any other classic author of that kind extemporaneously, and also to speak and write Latin prose and verse with tolerable skill and without assistance and of declining the Greek nouns and verbs...if deficient in any of these qualifications, he cannot under any circumstances be admitted."

Samuel graduated in 1650, and in 1651 was ordained in Rowley to be "colleague pastor" with the Rev. Ezekiel Rogers. That fall he married Sarah Appleton.

"Mr. Phillips was highly esteemed for his piety and talents; which were of no common order, and was eminently useful both at home and abroad. He officiated, repeatedly, at the great public anniversaries, which put in requistion the abilities of the first men in the New England colonies."

It was in 1695 that Samuel and Edward Payson, Jr. were among the seventeen church elders of the Bay Colony who convened at the Salem

---

[1]Elizabeth was the daughter of Richard Sargent and Katherine "Steevenes". Her baptisim was recorded in the Abbey Church, Bath, England, Oct. 28, 1603.

church to urge its members to forgive their pastor for his part in the recent witch hunts.

"Wee judge, That ableit in ye Late and ye Dark Time of ye confusions, wherein Satan had obtained a more than ordinary liberty to be sifting of this Plantation, there were sundry and unwarrentable and uncomfortable steps taken by Mr. Samuel Parris, by ye Good Hand of God brought into a better sense of things...wee now advise them charitably to accept the satisfaction which he hath tendered..."

A statement had been read by Mr. Parris.

"...before the whole Congregation wherein he expressed his regrets for errors of which he may have been guilty—'And by all, I do humbly own this day before the Lord and his people yt God has been rightously spitting in my face'..."

In Rowley in 1681, Rev. Rogers died and left most of his English books and all of his Latin books to Harvard. His copies of the works of St. Thomas Aquinas, he left to Samuel. The same year, Samuel inherited from his step-mother all his father's "Latin, Greek and Hebrew books now in the house."

In 1682, Edward Payson was ordained Teacher at the church and the next year married Samuel's daughter Elizabeth. When Samuel died in 1696, "greatly beloved and lamented", Edward Payson wrote a long, affectionate poem to commemorate his death. Samuel's wife Sarah died at eighty-six in 1714 and her funeral sermon was preached by her grandson, Rev. Samuel Phillips, III. Samuel and Sarah are buried at Rowley under a marble monument placed there by a descendant in 1839.

"In Brechin Hall at Andover, the library of the theological school, in the great halls of the academies at Andover and Exeter, and in memorial Hall at Harvard College, one may see hanging upon the walls portraits of one and another man and woman of this family, which belongs among the untitled nobility of New England, representing the best element of life there—not that which always dwells in the brightest glare of publicity, but that which directs and shapes the current of public opinion."

Samuel and Sarah had eleven children.
Samuel, born 1654, died young.
Sarah, 1656, married Stephan Mighill (Michael?)
Samuel, 1658, a goldsmith in Salem; married Mary Emerson, dau. of Rev. John Emerson. They were parents of Rev. Samuel Phillips of Andover.
George, 1659; died 1662.
Elizabeth, 1661; died 1662.

George, 1664; minister at Brookhaven.

Elizabeth, 1665; married Rev. Edward Payson. They had twenty children. Son Eliot married Mary Todd.

Doras, 1667; died young.

MARY, 1668; married SAMUEL PAYSON, brother of Edward Payson.

John, 1670, died 1670.

Some descendants of Samuel and Sarah are:

Samuel Phillips, founder of Phillips Academy, Andover, Mass.

John Phillips, founder of Phillips Academy, Exeter, N. H.

Samuel Phillips, Lieutenant Governor of Mass.

William Phillips, Lieutenant Governor of Mass.

John Phillips, first Mayor of Boston.

Sources:

Watertown Vital Records
Gage, History of Rowley
Sibley, Biographical Sketches of Graduates of Harvard
Phillips, Genealogy of the Phillips Family
Hoyt, Phillips Genealogy
Blodgette, G.B., Early Settlers of Rowley
Early Sargents of New England
Sargent, E.E., Sargent Record
Bridgeman, Pilgrims of Boston and Their Descendants
Mather, Cotton, Magnalia Christi Americana
Records of the Colony of Massachusetts Bay
The Colonial Society of Massachusetts Collection
Danvers Church Record

STEVENS FAMILY

John Stevens, born in 1605, came "aboard the *Confidence* to New England" from Caversham, Oxfordshire, England, in 1638 with his wife Elizabeth, his mother Alice and twenty-one year old William, probably John's brother. The Stevens family had with them two young servants, John and Grace Lougie.

John and Elizabeth settled at first in Newburyport, but in 1640 moved to Andover, Massachusetts where they were the fifth family to settle. John was made a freeman in 1641 and was a Sergeant in Andover's military force.

The Stevens children were:

Lt. John, born 1639, married Hannah Barnard and Esther Barker. He was killed by Indians in a war "to the east ward" in 1689.

TIMOTHY, 1641, married SARAH DAVIS.

Nathan, born circa 1645, said to be the first white male child born in Andover.

Elizabeth, married Joshua Woodman.

Ephraim, born circa 1649, married Sarah Abbott.

Mary, married John Barker.

Benjamin, born 1657.

John's second son Timothy grew up in Andover and after his marriage to Sarah Davis, daughter of Tobias and Sarah (Morrill) Davis, moved to Roxbury where he was a deacon in John Eliot's church. There it is recorded on "12m 1666 Timothy Stevens solemly owned ye covenant"..."24th 1 mo Sarah Stevens solemley owned ye covenant wife of Timothy."

Deacon now or not, Timothy had played his part in young pranks. In 1661, a court case concerning the many ways John Carr pestered Simon Bradstreet pulled two of Carr's acquaintences onto the record.

"John Bernard, aged about eighteen years, deposed that the night that Mr. Bradstreete's wheels were run into the swamp, he saw three men come by their house at dark, going toward Mr. Bradstreete's whom he thought were Jo. Car, Tymothy Steevens and Steven Osgood, because he had seen them go into Henry Ingalls house a little before night, and they came from that way afterward. Swore 24: 4: 1661...Elizabeth Dane, daughter of Francis Dane, testified that being late in the evening milking, she heard a great rumbling down the hill, which she saw the next morning were the wheels, She heard men come up a little while after from the hedge side, and one said that noghing could be proved, but she did not know who said it, etc. A night or two afterward, she told Steven Osgood that it would be best to put up the wheels again, and he said 'let ym turne ym up that tumbled ym downe'...

Examination and confession of Steven Osgood: That on Wednesday, 5: 4: 1661, about half an hour after daylight, John Carr, Tymothy Stevens and himself were walking in the street by Mr. Bradstreete's house, when said Stevens suggested that they run said Bradstreete's wheels down the hill, and Car bekoned for Osgood to go too. So they ran them down into the swamp, Stevens watching that no one discover them. An hour or two later, Carr and Osgood took another wheel from Mr. Bradstreete's tumbrill, and ran that down, and brought an old wheel from Goodman Bernard's and put it on the said tumbrill, said Stevens not being with them.''

But by 1666, Timothy was married to Sarah and had "solemly owned ye cov nant". By 1684, Eliot's church contained members Timothy, his son Joh and, listed under 'young persons', Sarah Stevens, Abigail Davis, (a cousin and Benjamin Child, son of that Benjamin who was working to start th colony of Woodstock. (The Stevens family seemed immune to Roxbury Woodstock fever.) Timothy's namesake and eldest son, not listed in Eliot church, was studying at Harvard. In 1693, "liberty was given to build pues around the meeting house except where the boys do sit..." Captain Timothy Stevens built h next to the door at the South end.

Ensign Timothy Stevens, in April, 1689, joined with the men of Roxbur under Capt. Samuel Ruggles to help those in Boston overthrow the op pressive royal Governor of Massachusetts, Sir Edmund Andros, by takir part in the capture of Fort Hill.

Sarah died in April, 1695, and Captain Timothy died in 1717 at sixty-s years old. They had ten children.

Timothy, born 1665, first minister of Glastonbury, Connecticutt, ma ried Eunice Chester and Alice Cooke. His son, Joseph, had eleve sons; nine were in active service in the Revolution. One died on th *Jersey,* a prison ship; one was master of a privateer; one a priva on sea and land for seven years; Ashbel, at fourteen years old, wa taken prisoner and never heard of again; Peter was a minute-mar another was a shipbuilder and Daniel, a "wealthy trader, lost tw heavy ships" when the British took Philadelphia.

Sarah, 1668, married Samuel Aspinwall.

John, 1673.

JOSEPH, 1673, twin of John, married, as his second wife, LUC RUGGLES.

Elizabeth, 1675, married Samuel Phipps.

Mary, 1678, married Elijah Harrick, housewright.

Hannah, 1680.

Samuel, 1682, married Dorothy Weld and Mary Calfe. He and Mar had daughter Mary, mother of Dr. Joseph Warren, a leader of th Revolution, best friend of Paul Revere, who died at Bunker Hil sincerely mourned county-wide.

Abigail, 1685.

Nathaniel, 1688, died 1689.

Joseph, Timothy's fourth child, married Joanna Winchester and had six children. When she died in 1715, he married Lucy Ruggles and they had a family of three. (See Ruggles Family on page 182.) Lieutenant Joseph Stevens died in 1756 in his eighty-fourth year. His six children by his first wife were:

    Thomas, born 1699.
    Sarah, 1701.
    Joanna, 1704.
    Mary, 1707.
    Timothy, 1709.
    Abigail, 1712.
Joseph and Lucy's children:
    LUCY, born February 26, 1717, married SAMUEL CHAMBERLAIN. (Her name in the record is written, "mother, Luce.")
    Joseph, 1720. ("mother, Lucia"). Probably the Joseph killed in battle at Lake George, Sept. 1755.
    John, 1723. ("mother, Lucey"). d. 1750.

Sources:

Virkus, Compendium of American Genealogy
Hoyt, Old Families of Salisbury and Amesbury
Records of Massachusetts Bay in New England
Salem Quarterly Court Records
Thornton, Lives of Heath, Bowles, and Eliot
Roxbury Vital Records
Sibley, Biographical Sketches of Graduates of Harvard
Bailey, S. L., Historical Sketches of Andover

MORRILL FAMILY

The *Lyon* sailed from London on June 22, 1632, and arrived at Boston on September 16. "He brought one hundred and twenty-three passengers, whereof fifty children, all in health. They had twelve weeks aboard and eight weeks from Land's End", Winthrop tells us. Perhaps they experienced such good health because the *Lyon's* master was the famous William Peirce who saved the settlement in its first year from the sweep that death, by the almost unknown scurvy, made through the Massachusetts Bay Colony. Peirce made a hurried trip to England and back in midwinter to bring lemons and by spring health was slowly restored to the surviving Puritans.

On the *Lyon* in 1632 were 'Isaac Morrill of Hatfield, Broadoak, Essex', his wife Sarah and two daughters, Sarah and Katherine. Other passengers on board were William Wadsworth, William and John Curtis and Abraham Morrill, Isaac's brother. Abraham was a blacksmith, iron founder and planter, as was Isaac.

Isaac was born in 1588 and, coming to New England, he settled at Roxbury where he was made a freeman in March 1633, before he had been there a year. He was designated to collect the school money and pay the schoolmaster. Isaac joined the Roxbury Artillery Company at its organization and when he died he left hung up in his parlor "a musket, a fowling piece, three swords, a pike, a half-pike, a corselet, and two belts of bandoleers". The guns had matchlocks or firelocks, and to each one there was a pair of bandoleers, or pouches, for powder and bullets, and a stick called a rest for use in taking aim. The pikes were ten feet long and had a spear at the end. Corslets and coats quilted with cotton were worn for defensive armor. Pike men were considered superior to musketeers which out-numbered them two to one in a company.

Isaac's land expanded until by 1652 he had "two houses, two forges, one barne with out housing and two orchyards, and a swamp at the east end of it together with yards belonging to the houses upon the highway west,... to side of the shop of Tobias Davis upon the highway and the orchyard and land of Tobias Davis north." Timothy Stevens, married to Isaac's granddaughter, Sarah Davis, (her father was that Tobias next door to Isaac) later came into possession of much of Isaac's land. Samuel Stevens, Timothy's son, owned the two forges in 1720.

A town job Isaac held was to collect the school money and pay it over to the schoolmaster.

Isaac and Sarah's children were:

SARAH, married TOBIAS DAVIS.

Katherine, married John Smith of Winnisimet.

Isaac, born 1632, died two months old.

Hannah, 1636, married Daniel Bruer, Jr.

Abraham, 1640.

Elizabeth.

Isaac Morril died December 21, 1661, "an aged brother," wrote John Eliot his record book.

"...deposed at a meeting of the magistrates, at Lieu. Turn'rs, 23 Jan. 1661...Wee whose names are under written doe testify that wee heard Isaac Morrell, upon the 19th: 10mo: 1661, declare it to be his will to give unto the Church of Roxbury, L3 for the purchasing of a Convenient Carpet, for the Table of the Meeting house, & a Comely & decent Cushon for the Ministers Deske.

Samuell Danforth, Edw: Denison, John Smith.

Tobias Davis & Sarah Morrell testified that they heard Isaac Morrell upon the 19: 10mo: 1661, declare it to be his mind & will to give unto his Coussine, Isaac Morrell, his Anvile & all his Smiths Tooles & Instrum'ts.

John Smith, Daniell Brewer & Sarah Morrell testified that they heard Isaac Morrell ye day before his death declare it to be his minde & will to dispose of his wearing apparell, as followeth viz't:—His best Cloake unto his Grand Child, Sarah Davis; one of his two best suites to his Brother Abraham Morrell, eith'r his Leath'r or his Cloath Suite. The residue of his Cloathes to be devided betweene his two sonnes."

Inventory of Isaac's estate mentioned his land "at Stony River...a parcell call smal gaines...ground at gravelly point...land upon the great Hill...in the fresh meddow...a in the blacke necke..."

Sources:

Banks, C.E., Planters of the Commonwealth
Historic Homes and Families of Middlesex
Ellis, History of Roxbury Town
Rockwell, S.F., Davis Family of Early Roxbury

DAVIS FAMILY

Tobias Davis was in Roxbury before 1647 but there is no record of when he and his brother Richard and another Davis, William, who is probably a brother, came to New England. Tobias was a blacksmith and may have at first worked for Isaac Morrill. He lived next to Isaac's forge and married Isaac's daughter, Sarah. On February 10th of 1646 or 47 a baby named Sarah was born and a year later Tobias' wife died. The next December Tobias married Bridget Kinsman and they had six children.

The 1652 Roxbury Land Records show that,

"Tobias Dauis bought of John Peiropoynt, a dwelling house and other out housing together with an orchyard and all the fence their unto belonging abutting upon the land of Isaack Morrill west, upon the land of Phillip Tory south, and upon the highway east, And ten acres of land more or lesse, abutting upon the land of Mr. John Eliot North...And a part of the orchyard of his father Isaack Morrills against the sayd Tobis Dauis his shopp and fence, hauing six apple trees upon it, giuen unto him by his sayd father Isaack Morrill..."

Later a grant was made to Tobias of six or seven acres for a corn mill and a fulling mill.

In 1663, the highway committee reported that,

"A Highway from Mr. John Eliots corner and so along to Deacon Parkes and so to Dorchester brooke, where we find between Mr. Eliots and Tobias Davis his shop, is not 4 rods wide and should be rectified."

In 1658, Tobias was chosen constable and the next January one of Roxbury's five selectmen. He was also an Ensign in the Artillery Company.

Toby Davis had four sons but no Davis grandchildren are found in Roxbury. Son John had no sons.recorded; Tobias Jr. died young; Isaac died at twenty-seven and probably did not marry; and Samuel died at eighteen. In his will, Tobias named all grandchildren as Stevenses.

His children:

SARAH, born 1646 or 7 to Sarah Morrill, married TIMOTHY STEVENS in 1664.

John, 1651, blacksmith, ensign, married Mary Torrey.

Tobias, 1653.

Isaac, 1655

Samuel, circa 1658, died 1661.

These four were baptised on June 12, 1659.

Samuel, 1661, "1679 month 2 day 10 Samuel son of Toby Davis dyed of the pox."
Abigail, 1671, married Peter Collamore of Scituate.
Tobias Davis died in 1690.

Sources:

Pope, Pioneer's of Massachusetts
Rockwell, S.F., Davis Family of Early Roxbury

RUGGLES FAMILY

"All the family legends point to the Staffordshire house of Ruggeley, as the source of the Ruggles family of Essex and of Suffolk, ('a very ancient and respectable family'). The first is claimed to trace from William De Ruggele of Stafford, thirteenth century, who having incurred the royal displeasure and suffered banishment from the kingdom...established a new home in Flanders. Although, for service in the Wars, he had subsequently received the pardon of his sovereign, King Edward I, he never returned to England. Three of his sons, however, are said to have crossed the Straits of Dover, and to have settled inthe County of Essex and from them...the early generations in that and the adjoining counties, descended. Children of a fourth son went to Switzerland and the name Ruggle is still perpetuated there."

In the sixteenth century lived Nicholas Ruggeley, Lord of the Manors of Hawkesbeard (now Armitage Park) in Stafford, and Downton-Ruggeley in Warwick. The Ruggeley armorial bearings are described as: *Argent, a chevron between three roses gules.* That translates as silver, (indicating justice, purity and peace), with three roses divided by a chevron. (The red roses indicating boldness.) The crest depicted a flaming tower, pierced with four silver arrows. The motto was *Struggle.* In Christ Church, Philadelphia, is a silver cup of the Communion service, engraved with these Ruggles arms for it was this branch that fostered the later Puritan emigrants to New England.

The first of the authenticated line is Thomas (I) Ruggle, Esquire, of Sudbury, Suffolk, England. His will is dated 1547. His son, Nicholas (II) Ruggle of Sudbury, had Thomas (III) who later moved to Nasing where events were leading towards the emigration of John Eliot's group.

The next Thomas (IV) Ruggles was born in 1584 and was married at Nasing to Mary Curtis, daughter of Thomas Curtis, of an old Nasing family. Her brother William and her uncle John Curtis left for New England as early as 1632. Thomas Ruggles' younger brother John left on the *Hopewell* for New England in 1635 and took Thomas's ten year old son. John Eliot wrote about him later that "He was a lively Christian knowne to many of the Church in Old England where many of the Church injoyed society together." In fact, John looked after the meeting house where Eliot taught in Roxbury.

Two years later, Thomas and his family came to Roxbury to meet waiting friends and family. Eliot wrote of him,

"Eld'r broth'r to John, children of a Godly fath'r he joyned to the Church soone after his coming being as well knowne as his broth'r his first born sone dyed in England his second son John was brought over a servant by Phillip Eliot and Thomas brought two oth'r children with him Sarah & Samuel he had a great sicknesses the year after his coming, but the Lord recovered him in mercy...(Thomas' wife Mary) "joyned to the

231

church wh her husband & approved her self a Godly Christian, by a holy, blamelesse conv'ation being conv'ted, not long before their coming..."

Thomas took the oath of freeman on May 22, 1639. Too soon after, he and another resident of Roxbury, John Graves, died. "Thomas Ruggles a godly broth'r he dyed of a Consumption." "These two", wrote Eliot, "brake the knot first of the Nazing Christians." In his will, Thomas described some of his land:

"...seaven Accres and a halfe for a Lott abutting upon Arthor Gary and one end to Phillip Elliotts railes thether side to the Comon Dedham path going through the same, and Fowr accres and a halfe at Muddy River in two p'ts...and..three accres, less a pole, next to Thomas Grigges land."

Mary died in 1674. "Old Mother Roote who was Tho Ruggles widdow afore. She lived ...till more tedious yn a child. She was in her 89 yeare."

They had these children:

Thomas, Jr. baptised about 1622, died in England.

John, baptised in 1625, married Abigail Craft.

Sarah, baptised 1628, married William Lyon. He married secondly Martha Philbrick Cass, widow of John Cass.

SAMUEL, born 1629, married HANNAH FOWLE and Ann Bright.

Samuel Ruggles was born in Nazing, County Essex, England and came to Roxbury as an eight year old child with his father, mother, and sister Sarah, in 1637. Samuel was for many years a selectman, deputy, representative of the town and was Captain of the Roxbury Military Company after Lieut. Griffin Craft resigned. He was actively engaged in the overthrow of Governor Andros in 1689.

It started as early as 1664. He and other residents of Roxbury, like John Eliot, Joseph Griggs, and Isaac Curtis, afraid of losing the charter for their land in a proposal by the Crown to do away with the colony's self government, petitioned the General Court to stand firm in its resolution "to adher to the Patent and the privileges thereof...to stand fast in our present Libertys...(promising to assist them to stere right in these shaking times." Then, on April 18, 1689, Governor Andros, who had imprisoned Samuel Appleton (see Appleton) and some other members of his council, was seized and jailed with the help of Roxbury men. Roxbury sent Samuel Ruggles and Nathaniel Holmes to meet representatives from the other towns to do "what they can to establish a governmen for the present...". Eventually, the original Governor, deputies and assistan elected in 1686 were reinstated.

Samuel kept the *Flower de Luce* tavern, a favorite meeting place for sett ing town business. Lucy, (or sometimes *Luce* in the erratic spelling of th colonial period,) was a name to be repeated in each generation of the Ruggles family and Bacon family down to the present time.[1]

Samuel married Hannah Fowle, only daughter of George Fowle of Charlestown, in 1655 and they had eight children:

Hannah, born 1656, died young.

Mary, 1657, died young.

SAMUEL, born 1658, married MARTHA WOODBRIDGE.

Joseph, 1660, died young.

Hannah, 1661, died young.

Sarah, 1663, died young.

Mary, 1666, married Ebenezer Pierpont and Isaac Morris.

infant, died young.

Sarah, 1669, died young.

Samuel's wife, Hannah, died in October, 1669, a month before her daughters Hannah and Sarah. The next spring, Samuel married Anna Bright and they had Thomas, who graduated from Harvard in 1690 and became minister of Guildford, Connecticut. Their other children were: Anna, Nathaniel, Elizabeth, Nathaniel again, "Henery" and Hulda, who married Samuel Hill. Almost all lived to maturity.

"Captain Samuel Ruggles died August 15, 1692, age 63 years." He is buried in the Eustis Street Burial Ground.

Samuel, Jr. the third child of Samuel and Hannah, served in Roxbury in the several offices his father had held, including the position of Captain of the Roxbury Company. In 1686, he and seven others purchased a twelve by eight mile tract of land from two Indians, John Nagers and Lawrence Nassawano, where the Massachusetts town of Harwick now stands. The Ruggles family played a large part in the history of Roxbury and for a hundred and fifty years was "rarely without a representtive either in the General Court or on the board of selectmen, holding some position of responsibility or trust either in Church or State."

Samuel, Jr. married Martha Woodbridge, daughter of Reverend John Woodbridge, pastor of Andover, and granddaughter of Governor Thomas Dudley. Their children were:

---

[1] Lucy Ruggles, born to Samuel, Jr. was the first, Lucy Ruggles Stevens,[1] 1682-1750; her daughter, Lucy Stevens Chamberlain,[2] 1717-: her daughter, Lucy Chamberlain;[3] sister of Eliakim; his daughter, Lucy Chamberlain Bacon,[4] 1782-18____; her daughter, Lucy Bacon, 1802-18____,[5] sister of Socrates; his daughter, Lucy Bacon Thompson,[6] Sam's sister; Sam's daughter, Lucy Bacon Kline,[7] 1870-; and finally, Sam's granddaughter, Lucy McCormick[8] Maldeney.

Samuel, born 1681, minister at Hadley, married Elizabeth Whiting and Elizabeth Williams.

LUCY, 1682, married JOSEPH STEVENS.

Timothy, 1685, minister at Rochester, married Mary White. One of their sons was Brigadier General Timothy Ruggles.

Hannah, 1688.

Patience, 1689, married James Robinson.

Martha, 1692.

Sarah, 1694.

Joseph, 1696.

Mary, 1698.

Benjamin, 1700.

Some descendents:

One Samuel Ruggles, and there were many, built Boston's Faneuil Hall and took part in the dedication ceremonies on September 10, 1742.

General Timothy Ruggles was president of the 1765 Stamp Act Congress. he disagreed with the idea of 'disunion' and was censured by the Massachusetts House of Representatives. John Adams, "who claimed relationship with Ruggles and before found nothing in his character but what was noble and grand", praising him to the point of calling him "a man of genius and great resolution" (he was considered one of the best soldiers in the Colonies), *after* the reprimand given Ruggles, discovered "an inflexable oddity about him...his behavior...governed by pretended scruples...held in bitter contempt and derision by the whole continent." Paul Revere made an engraving entitled "A warm Place—Hell" to shame Timothy Ruggles in 1768 when he and seventeen members of the Massachusetts General Court complied with the King's wishes and voted to recind the Townshend Acts. Revere pictured the Devil urging Ruggles at spear point into the flames, the words "Push on Tim", ballooning from Satan's mouth. And there is poor Tim in his tri-cornered hat with one foot in the fire already. Fifty years later, John Adams remembered Timothy Ruggles was "a high-minded man, an exalted soul." Historians agree that he was too severely dealt with. As a military commander he was highly praised—a a lawyer he was an "impressive pleader, in debate able and ingenious...with a brilliant wit and profound judgement", a judgement that mislead him to choose to lead a group of "Loyal Americans" at Bunker Hill, Americans loyal to England. He moved to Nova Scotia during the war and his sons followed.

Benjamin Ruggles, U.S. Senator from Ohio, 1815-1833.

Sources:

Bond, H., Watertown Genealogy
Roxbury Vital Records
Ruggles, H.S., Ruggles Families of England and America
Linzee, History of Peter Parker and Sarah Ruggles
Thornton, Lives of Heath, Bowles, and Eliot
Records of the First Church
Jones, E.A., The Loyalists of Massachusetts
Forbes, E., Paul Revere and the World He Lived In
Colonial Families of the U.S.
Thwing, History of the First Church of Roxbury

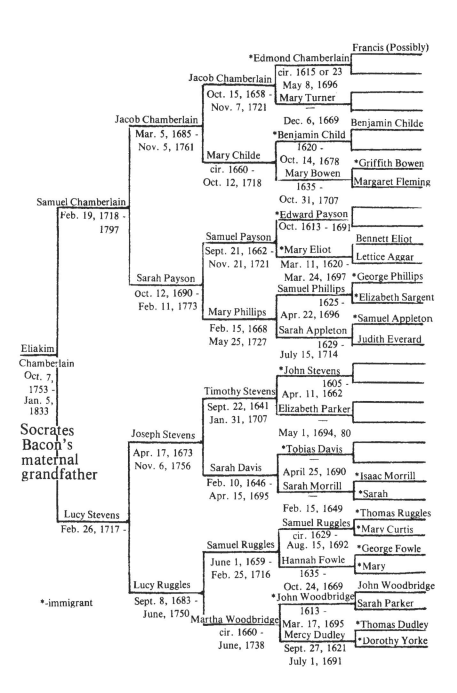

CURTIS FAMILY

The Curtis family is another of the families from the old English village of Nazing and had been there since before 1200.

"...situated only 17 miles from London...one might imagine from the great number of gable-fronted cottages with low thatched roofs that abound...that it had undergone but little change during the past three hundred years. The old parish church is situated on the side of a hill...bounded by the river Lea...We can easily imagine the emigrants worshipping within its old gray walls...The old oak seats which are carved at the ends with a variety of grotesque characters...date back to James I. The parish register...commences in the year 1559.*

And there lies the record of the family of Mary Curtis who married Thomas Ruggles. Mary's grandfather was William Curtis who died in 1582. His will gave "the overplus...equally devyded between Agnes my wife & Thomas Curtis my eldest son excepting...two of my best lambes w'ch I geve to my daughters two children."

Thomas Curtis' baptism is among those recorded, "Thomas Curtis, Aug. 25, 1560", and his marriage, "Thomas Curtis & Mary Camp, Aug. 24, 1585". They had six children. Son William's marriage to John Eliot's sister Sarah in 1618 is recorded, and later, Mary's own marriage, "Thomas Ruggles & Marye Curtis Nov. 1, 1620."

Mary Curtis left with her husband and her children for Roxbury in 1637. William had sailed on the *Lyon* in 1632 and John Curtis, uncle to the two, came after. The Curtis family belonged to John Eliot's church and was considered to be well-educated.

Mrs. P. Curtis of Augusta, Maine, once wrote,

"The first Curtis who came to America brought with him a miniature plow, to be a model from which young Americans might pattern. This passed from generation to generation until it came into the branch of the family at Bowdoinham, Maine, and into the possession of George Henry who had married into the family. He said that he sold it for old silver."

Sources:

Steele, L.E., Ancestry of William Curtis and Allied Families.
Sennett, C.H., The Curtis Genealogy
Hoyt, S.M., English Origins of Curtis Families

FOWLE FAMILY

The first Fowles were settles in Devon County, England, long before t[?] Conquest and,

> "...as you might expect, were the bird hunters. Gamebirds were plentiful, and while they could not be had for the taking, an arrangement could be made with the lord of a manor allowing a certain number to be taken...There are many examples in the old tax records and one is William de Foul in 1271. He and the others are unquestionably at least part-time professional bird hunters. When William the Conqueror had the Domesday Book compiled, written on the margin opposit the Fowle family of Devon was 'An Ancient Saxon Family.' About 1537 the family left Devon and settled at River Hall in Sussex near Battle Abbey."

Their arms are a lion *passant,* with three roses, commemorating t[?] "gallant action of three cadets of the house of Fowle" who saved the life of their ki[?] in a battle during the War of the Roses

George Fowle was born in Wittersham, Kent County, England, where the register of the Church of Wittersham it is recorded, "1610 Jan: George, s[?] of Myles Fowle was baptised." There he married and had two children before [?] emmigrated to Concord, New England. He, and his wife Mary, newbo[?] son John, and daughter "Hanny" arrived about 1637.

"George ffoule" was admitted a freeman of the Colony in March, 1639. C[?] May 22, the proceedings of the General Court show that by their vote [?] that body, "George Foule was allowed & sworne surveyor of the armes for Concord." H[?] duty was to see that the arms were kept in good condition for the time whe[?] they would be needed. Other votes that day chose John Winthrop Govern[?] and Thomas Dudley, Esq., Deputy Governor. Another time, George Fow[?] was appointed for Concord to "have charge of...giving direction...and looking t[?] the order that "every house, or some two or more houses to joyne together for the breedi[?] of salt peeter in some out house used for poultry, or the like" for use in the manufactu[?] of gun powder.

George and Mary lived in Concord until 1648 where four children we[?] born and then moved to Charlestown. George listed his occupation as 'ta[?] ner' and taught two of his sons the trade. They inherited a well-establishe[?] and successful business. When Mary died in 1676 and George in 1682 the[?] were burried in the old Phipps Street Burying Ground, almost in the sha[?] of the Bunker Hill monument with their sons and their son's wives ar[?] children. "Fugit Hora Here Lyes Buried the Bodyes of George and Mary Fowle."

George Fowle left a remarkably detailed will of which only a small part printed here. He "was evidently...a careful, thorough and methodical man..."

"In the nam of god Amen I George ffowle of Charlestowne...being sensibell of the decays of nature growing uppon me yet att present through gods goodnes beinge distinct in my understanding and Memory do declare this my last will and testameant in wrighting the day and year above wreeton...

...I do give to my dear son Jno fowle as an adition to to what I have formerly done for hime my long house at the lower end of my yarde on the south side with the land it stands uppon and the lande lying behind...upon condition yt my son John fowle his heirs exeqotors admenestratrs and asigns do from time to time and att all times & forever make and maintaine a suffishant fence upon ye said line...and forther yt my son John fowle his heirs and asigns forever make and maintaine all the fence att the lower end of my yarde before my hous with two suffishant gats one for carting and another for a foottway as has been formerly and all other fence which he is ingaged by wrighting under his own hand to make and maintaine againste my lande; forther my son John fowle is nott to lay any thing in my yarde so as to hinder the improvement of itt by thos yt shall live in the hous and what dammag is done to gats or fence or houssing threw his means either by carts comming into ye yarde or by leaving open the gats my son John fowle shall make itt good: forther that he shall have no other preveledge in ye yarde only to com to his houssing with barke & other ocations about his work their...to Petter...at all times forever make and maintaine a suffshant board or pale fence between his land & my son Abraham fowls land...I do give to my son Abraham fowle my now dwelling hous with the land itt stands uppon with ye barne and outhoussing to itt...with ye yarde before my hous down to the highwaye leadinge to the penny ferry with the orchard and garden behinde the housse...forther I do give to my son Abraham my hay lote in the lowe Marsh commonly called the dirty Marsh with my lote of upland on the backside of the hill...three cows commons on the stinted comon...Rights...preveleges...all my moveables: except so much as I have disposed of ither by word or wrighting...all my wearing apparell both linning and woolling...I do give to my son Issack fowle tenn acres of my wood lote on Mesteck Side with the lumber and wood and other preveledges aper-taining theirunto and twenty five pounds more...forther it is my will yt my son Abraham shall nott sett lete nor disposs of any parte or parcel of the aforesaid premesis without the consent & aprobation of my exeqoetorr and overseers...forther my will is yt my son Abraham shall not entertain any person or persons into the hous as inmats without the consent and aprobation of my exequotorr & overseers...forther I do hereby declar yt I do...make constitute and apoynte my three loving frinds Samuell Ruggles Senir John Call Senir Thomas White Senir to be my overseers...to se to the true perfor-mans of ye promisis: and forther.I do hereby declar that I do...apoynte my loving son Petter fowle...to give ech of my three frinds beformentioned ech of them a pair of Boots...

George ffowle

The children of George and Mary Fowle were:

HANNAH, born in England, 1635, married SAMUEL RUGGLES.

John, (Captain), tanner, born England 1637, married Anna Carter.
   The arms of the Sussex Fowles are engraved on his tomb.

Mary, born Concord 1640, died young.

Peter, 1641, tanner, married Mary Carter.

James, (Leiut.) 1642, married Abigail Carter. He died of exposure on the Phipps Expedition to Quebec, 1690.

Mary, born 1645.

Abraham, married Hannah Harris.

Zechariah, cordwainer, married Mary Paine. Both died in 1678, the year of the small pox epidemic.

Isaac, 1648, joiner, married Beriah Bright. Their child Abigail married William Smith and had daughter Abigail who married John Adams, future President of the United States. Their son, of course, was John Quincy Adams. It was Abigail Smith Adams who wrote the fine letters to her husband asking him to remind the Continental Congress to 'remember the ladies'.

Jacob.

Elizabeth, born 1656, died young.

Of George Fowle's grandchildren it was written, "None were so fair as the Fowles of Watertown."

Sources:

Forbes, Forbes and Fowle Families
Records of the Colony of Massachusetts Bay
Pierce, Immigrant Ancestors of Fowle
Charlestown Genealogies and Estates
Historical Homes and Families

STOW FAMILY

John Stowe, of Biddenden, Kent County, England is the first positive connection of English Stowes to the John Stow who emigrated to America, although the Stowe name was in England as early as 1200. The first John had three children, the eldest baptised John, January 2, 1540. Young John married Joan Baker and was Parish Clerk in Biddenden. John III was baptised in 1582 and married to Elizabeth Bigge in 1608.

John III and Elizabeth and their six children arrived in New England May 17, 1634, on one of seven ships that landed at Boston that week "with store of passengers and cattle." Wintthrop wrote in his journal that they had enjoyed a short passage.

The next year, Elizabeth's mother, *Mrs.* Rachel Biggs, landed at Boston with another of her daughters, Patience, wife of Hopestill Foster. The Foster and Stowe children received valuable legacies from their uncles, John and Smallhope Bigge of Cranbrook and Maidstone, Kent, England. At Rachel Biggs' death, granddaughter Elizabeth Stowe received a "silver Pott & my Booke of dockter Preston..."

John Stowe was admitted freeman September 3, 1634, at Roxbury where he built his house. He was a Representative to the General Court for two sessions and joined the Ancient and Honorable Artillery Company with his son Thomas. He transcribed the public records for Roxbury and the town repaid him by granting him eighty acres. It may have been there that he kept his twenty goats, almost twice as many as anyone else in town. He paid 'Goodwife Burt for her boy ye full tyme that hee did keepe the goats.'

In the records again, December, 1640, the General Court declared "John Stowe, for selling shot to an Indian, not knowing the law, is respried."

"Father Stowe" as an older John was called, was the first teacher of the Roxbury school and an old school record, dated 1648, allows a sum for his board. Cotton Mather wrote,

"that Roxbury has offored more scholars, first for the college, and then for the public, that any other town of its bigness, or, if I mistake not, of twice its bigness in New England."

John's wife Elizabeth had died only a few years after their arrival and John Eliot wrote about this member of his church:

"She was a very godly matron, a blessing not only to her family but to all the Church and when she had led a Christian conversation a few years among us she died and left a good savor behind her."

Their children were:

A daughter, buried unbaptised in 1610.

Elizabeth, baptised Sept. 12, died Sept. 21, 1612.

Elizabeth's twin, buried unbaptised Sept. 10, 1612.

Thomas, born 1615, married Mary Griggs.

Elizabeth, born 1617, married Henry Archer.

John, born 1619.

NATHANIEL, born October 7, 1621, married MARTHA METCALF

Samuel, 1624, married Hope Fletcher. He, the fourteenth graduate of Harvard, assisted his father as teacher of the Roxbury school while preparing for the ministry under Rev. Maverick. One of his descendants was Harriet Beecher who married Prof. Calvin Ellis Stowe, member of another branch of the family.

Thankful, 1629, married John Pierpont. It is from these two that the Pierpont name originates in this country. He inherited 11½ acres from John Stowe. Their granddaughter married Rev. Jonathan Edwards, "the leading intellectual figure in colonial America." Another of Thankful's descendants was Aaron Burr, who while Vice President of the United States, shot Alexander Hamilton in a duel and was once tried for treason.

Nathaniel Stowe, son of John, born in 1621, married Martha, daughter of Michael Metclaf, a "very zealous non-conformist" who left England hurriedly and closely pursued. (see Metcalf Family on page 200.) It was Nathaniel's second marriege and Martha was the widow of Christopher Smith and William Bignell.

They lived for awhile in Ipswich where Nathaniel and his brother Thomas owned six hundred acres of land at Fairhaven Pond near Stow, Massachusetts. One story claims that the town was named by Governor Bradstreet after his close friend John Stow.

Ipswich records say that in 1656 Nathaniel sued Thomas Smith,

"...for injury to his corne by cattle...Henry Kimball deposed that he saw Mr. Smith's steer in Nathaniel Stowse corn and as he went to get him out he leaped over the five-railed fence of Alicksander Knight's. Samewell Younglove witnessed that he helped to bring fifty head of cattle out of Henry Kimball's and Nathaniel Stow's corn, four of Richard Shatswell's, three of old Kimbal's, two of Goodman Marchant's, three of Goodwife Coolis, one steer of Mr. Smith's...William Dello deposed that there were two oxen of Tho. Smith's...found that twenty-five bushels of corn were destroyed..."

Another time there was a dispute about the identity of a hog that Thoma Harris had killed. Nathaniel testified "that some would have him make fals

246

see *Corrections*, page 337

statements regarding Harris having killed the hog, and, refusing, they called him a simple fellow, etc." Robert Roberts testified "about the mark of the hog, saying that they asked Stow if he could not forget the marks."

Nathaniel and his first wife's children, all born at Concord, were John, 1657, Hannah, died as an infant, Thankful, 1659. Nathaniel and Martha's children, also born at Concord, were:

NATHANIEL, born 1663, married RUTH MERRIAM.

Samuel, 1666, died young.

Ebenezer, 1668, married Abigail Parlin.

Martha died in 1717 at ninety years old.

Nathaniel, Jr., married the daughter of Joseph Merriam, a wealthy Kent man, who with others chartered a chip in London, the *Castle,* for their journey to America. (See Merriam Family on page 198.) Nathaniel and Ruth had nine children born in Concord.

Samuel, born 1694.

Nathaniel, 1696, married Lydie Wheeler.

John 1698, married Mary Wesson.

Thomas, 1699, married Anne Wetherby.

BENJAMIN, 1701, married ZEBIAH MOOR(E).

Ruth, 1702, married Bartholomew Jones.

Jonathan, 1705.

Joseph, married Elizabeth Wooley.

Simon, died in 1701, very young.

When Ruth died at age forty-eight, Deacon Nathaniel married twice again, and although he had five more children in his third marriage none of these lived.

His son, Benjamin, married Zebiah Moor in 1728 in Sudbury, Massachusetts, her home and her family's home since 1632. (See Moore Family on page 235.) The first eight of their twelve children are recorded in Sudbury and the others at Southborough, another step out on the frontier.

Twins, Elizabeth and Hepzibah, born 1729. Hepsibah married Timothy Barton.

Josiah, 1731.

Simon, 1732, died in October, 1755, in the French and Indian War.

Timothy, 1735, died in December, 1755, in the French and Indian War.

Twins, Kezia and Rhoda, 1737, Rhoda died at seventeen, Kezia married Henry Balsom.

NATHANIEL, 1739, married SARAH JONES.

Twins, Eunice and Lois, 1742, died at birth.

Persis, 1744, married Jonas Ward. Jonas Ward married, after 1785, the widow of Nathaniel, above.

247

see *Corrections,* page 337

Jonathan, 1746. married Mary Twiss. Elijah Ward and Richard Dresser told Levi Lincoln on oath that they were present Oct. 14, 1776, when Jonathan told his "last will and testament...when he was absent from home in the service."

"Spoken will of Jonathan Stow of Charlton: It is my desire that my lands may be sold and pay all my debts: also it is my desire that my wife should have such household furniture as is necessary for her to keep house and especially the Books."

Sarah Jones lived in Framingham when Nathaniel Stow married her. It was a town that not long before had been on the frontier, one that her parents and grandparents had helped to settle. Nathaniel and Sarah moved further west to Charlton, one of the cluster of towns bordering Woodstock. They had seven children:

ANNA, born 1762, married ELIAKIM CHAMBERLAIN.

Meriam, 1765. Both daughters were born in Southborough before the move to Charlton. Meriam died in Jan. 1768.

Charlotte, 1766, died the same month as Meriam, Jan. 1768.

Submit, 1768, married Amos Merritt.

Louisa, 1770, married Jesse Merritt.

Sarah, 1772.

Benjamin, "son of late Nathaniel and Sarah, April 3, 1774", married Susanna Eddy and Dolly Dresser.

Nathaniel died just days before Benjamin was born. In 1791, when Benjamin was seventeen,

"To the Honorable Joseph Door Esq'r Judge of the Probate for the County of Worchester I hereby Certify that Benjamin Stow Minor...personally Appeared and made choice of Aaron Wheelock his Guardian Before me.

Caleb Ammidown"

Anna, Sarah's oldest daughter, had married Eliakim Chamberlain eleven years before. They were the grandparents with whom Socrates Bacon and his sisters very probably lived during the time their father worked in Africa.

Some descendants of the Stow family were Vice President Levi P. Morton and Captain Stephen Stowe, "The Martyr", nurse to the American Revolutionary prisoners. And, as mentioned above, Aaron Burr, Henry Ward Beecher, (who in his long, distinguished career, took a moment to cause th turbulent formation of the Second Presbyterian Church in Fort Wayn from the membership of the First Presbyterian Church) and Harrie Beecher Stowe.

Sources:

Stowe, Ancestry and Some Descendants of Captain Steven Stowe
Cutter, Historic Homes and Families of Middlesex
Records of Massachusetts Bay in New England
Pope, Pioneers of Mass.
Records and Files of Salem Quarterly Court
Concord Vital Records
Charlton Vital Records
Reading Vital Records
Sudbury Vital Records
Southborough Vital Records

MERRIAM FAMILY

Merriam was originally spelled *Meryham, Merryham* and *Meriham*. Ham meant home or house and the word in its literal sense meant merry house. Merriam is a very old family and documents show Laurence de meryham of Isenhust in Sussex payed his taxes to Edward 1 in 1296.

William Merriam, county Kent, England, was a clothier, one who combined all the facets of cloth-making and then "critized, accepted or rejected, adjusted the prices of the cloth and put it on the market." He owned land at Sevenoaks, Goudhurst, near Tudley where his son Joseph lived.

Joseph was born about 1600 and married Sarah, daughter of John and Frances (Jefferie) Goldstone, a neighboring family. Joseph, too, was a clothier and was easily able to afford to charter a ship, the *Castle* of London, to sail to New England in April, 1638. They arrived in Charlestown in July and Joseph settled in Concord. Two brothers and a cousin, Isaac Doo̅r, followed. He was received into the church and then admitted a freeman March 14, 1639. Joseph lived only until the next January and left a will instructing that his estate not be appraised until his "eldest child shall come to the age of one & twenty yeares" and that his daughters receive their portion at that age or the day of their marriage. His children were:

William, born about 1625.
Sarah, about 1626.
JOSEPH, about 1628.
Thomas.
Elizabeth, married Thomas Henchman (Hinkesman).
Hanna.
John, born 1641, after the death of his father, married Mary Cooper.

Joseph Jr., lived in Cambridge when he reached manhood on a section called "The Farms" which later became the town of Lexington. He was admitted to the church and became a freeman May 22, 1650. His wife was Sarah, the daughter of Deacon Gregory Stone, prominent both in church and state affairs. By the time of Joseph's death at forty-seven, he had accumulated a great deal of property that was not divided until twenty-three years later. The children

"...Do agree that Sarah Miriam the Relict Widow Shall have the free use of the houseing and lands hereafter Expressed,...The new End of the Dwelling house from top to bottom also the lower room of the oldhouse next to ye new aforesaid, and the use of ye halfe of the Cellar the one halfe of the Barn and halfe of the cowyard and free liberty to cutt halfe her fire wood on ye land of her sonn Jno Miriam and the other halfe to gett off from the land of her son Robert Miriam...And further she is to have about an Acre

253

see *Corrections*, page 337

and an halfe of the Land by the Dore..."

She was given plow land, mowing land, and land in the orchard with "wt moveable Estate she hath in her possession, to be at her Disposall."

The children were:

Sarah, born 1654, married Eleazer Ball and Samuel Fletcher.
Lydia, 1656.
Joseph, 1658.
Elizabeth, 1660, married Isaac Wood.
John, 1662.
Mary, 1664.
Robert, 1667.
RUTH, 1670, maried, in 1690, NATHANIEL STOW.
Thomas, 1672.

Several of Nathaniel and Ruth Stow's grandchildren gave their children the first name Merriam.

Sources:

Appleton, W.S., The Merriam Family and Connections
Pope, Merriam Genealogy
Stearns, Genealogy and Family Histories of New Hampshire

METCALF FAMILY

In 1016, Arkelfrith came to England with King Canute as one of his commanders and for his gallant conduct was given an estate in the north-eastern part of Yorkshire. He was created Lord of Dent, Sedbury and Asknigg. His son was Arkyll, Lord of Dent. The Metcalf descent is:

3. Godpatrick Lord of Dent.
4. Dolphin, Lord of Dent.
5. William, Lord of Dent.
6. Richard, Lord of Dent.
7. Adam Metcalfe, Lord of Dent, 1252.
8. Adam de Medecalfe, 1278. Near Dent are three hills now called "Pennegent Hills" but long ago known as "The Three Calves". In 1278, King Edward I recorded that "Adam de Medekalf" (some assume that meant Adam of the Middle Calf), "was killed by one Stegnebrigge in single combat." The arms granted to a later generation do have three calves *passant sable* that may refer to the hills.

9. Adam Metcalfe of Thornton Rust married a daughter of James of Baynbrigge, Steward and Chief Forester of John of Brittany. In 1304, Adam was a chief to the Earl of Richmond.
10. Adam Metcalfe of Thornton Rust.
11. Richard Metcalfe of Baynbrigge.
12. Thomas Metcalfe of Baynbrigge (Baynbridge).
13. John Metcalfe.
14. Captain James Metcalfe, born in 1389, was Captain, under Henry V, of Wenslydale men in the remarkable Battle of Agincourt in 1415. He married the daughter of Gibson of Ireby Hall, was Lord of the Manor of Nappa in 1422, founded and endowed the Chantry of St. Anne at Askrigg requiring daily mass and prayers for the "good of the King, Queen, himself, his sons and for all their souls when from this life they pass away". One of his sons was a member of parliment in 1478, one was Chancelor to Edward IV and Richard III, and a daughter was prioress of Marrich Abbey.
15. Brian Metcalf married Johanna of Boughton and lived at Beare Park.

Several Leonard Metcalfs follow. One generation who lived at Beare Park in 1569 "joined the rising in the North" in the interest of putting Mary, Queen of Scots, on the English throne in the place of Elizabeth I. He was captured and his name placed first on the list of prisoners taken to Durham Castle in January, 1570. Eleven men were indicted for "Conspiracy, Treason and Rebellion" and all were condemned to die. Four were executed at once at

York, but his turn at the scaffold was stayed to wait for the Queen's attention. It was meanwhile represented to Queen Elizabeth

> "...that Leonard Metcalf rose against her because the Earl of Northumberland did, and too, that he had made over his lands to his wife so that by his life, the Queen should have his lands while by his death, his wife should have them; that therefore, the Queen should win by his life and lose by his death; further, that he was a very quiet, honest gentleman and generally lamented."

Still, the Queen "spared three but thought the four—Metcalf, Lambrt, Claxton and Co nyen—should be made an example; but refer the same to your &the commissioners own judgment." The result was that none of them was executed, probably to get their lands, for the Bill of Attainer names "Leonard Metcalf, late of Beare Parke, County York, Esquire."

After he lost his lands, Leonard Metcalf gave up his Catholisim, the faith of the defeated Mary, Queen of Scots, and left Yorkshire to make a home in Norfolk. There his son, Leonard, took holy orders for the Church of England and became Rector of the Parish of Tatterford.

Leonard, Jr., was born in 1541 at Apperside in the vale of Wenslydale in the North Riding of Yorkshire, the Metcalf home for many generations. He was Rector for over forty years and died in 1616.

Michael was the fifth son of Reverend Leonard Metcalf. He was born about 1587 and from 1619 to 1634 was the warden of Saint Benedict's Church. He wrote his Warden's Account Book "in a sure, clear hand writing ending in a graceful flourish—the handwriting of a well-educated man." But his main business was as a Dornix weaver. The Dornix, or Dornic, was a kind of Damask or tapestry used in hangings and heavy curtains. He had a hundred or more men employed in his shop.

Michael married Sarah Elwyn in 1616. She was born at Heigham near Norwich in Norfolk, the daughter of Thomas and Elizabeth (Benslye) Elwin, "a family having a distinguished lineage."

While Michael was a busy manufacturing man, he was also deeply involved in the religious upheaval pervading England. He became an outspoken Puritan which brought him into conflict with his bishop, Matthew Wren who hated him and cited him into the Bishop's Court. Wren presented testimony that Michael and Nicholas Metcalf had,

> "uttered dangerous words against the King which could no longer be endured...the said michael slippit away and went to New England."

After Michael's first attempt to leave from Plymouth, January 13, 1636

258

he called himself an exile from his wife and children "with whom he would gladly have continued if with liberty." Michael wrote,

"To all the true professors of Christ's Gospel within the City of Norwich—I was persecuted in the land of my father's sepulchres, for not bowing at the name of Jesus, and observing other ceremonies in religion, forced upon me, at the instance of Bishop Wren of Norwich and his chancellor Dr. Corbet, whose violent measures troubled me in the Bishop's Court, and returned me into the High Commissioners Court. Suffering many times for the cause of religion, I was forced, for the sake of the liberty of my conscience, to flee from my wife and children, to go into New-England; taking ship for the voyage at London the 17th of Sep't 1636; being by tempests tossed up and down the seas till the Christmas following, them veering about to Plymouth in Old England: in which time I met with many sore afflictions.

Leaving the ship, I went down to Yarmouth...whence I shipped myself and family, to come to New England; sailed 15th April, 1637, and arrived three days before midsummer following, with my wife and nine children, and a servant.*"..."my enemies conspired against me to take away my life, and sometimes, to avoid their hands, my wife did hide me in the roof of the house, covering me over with straw."

Bishop Wren was tried twenty years later by Cromwell's Long Parliament for his persecution of the Puritans. One of the charges brought against him was,

"his cruelty to Metcalf which compelled him to remove to New England to the detriment of Norwich's manufactures...that during the term of 2 years and 4 months, while he held the See of Norwich...3000 of his Majesty's subjects, many of whom used trades, spinning, weaving, knitting, making of cloth, stuff, stockings, and other manufactures of wool; some of them setting a hundred poor people at work...transported themselves into Holland...and other parts, beyond the seas...in consequence of his superstition and tyranny."

Michael and his family arrived either in the *John and Dorothy,* mastered by William Andrew of Ipswich, or the *Rose,* William Andrews, Jr., Master. Both ships docked on June 8 at Boston and the list of names of the two ship's passengers were unfortunately combined by Winthrop in his journal. Almost at once, Michael settled at Dedham near his good friend Jonathan Fairbanks and from there he wrote his several religious 'epistles' to his friends at Norwich. Dedham "felt fortunate to be able to admit to the town several men of superior character and intelligence. Among these were Mr. John Allin, Eleazer Lusher, Micall Metcalf, Anthony Fisher and Jonathan Fairbanks."

Michael joined the church in 1639, was Selectman for Dedham in 1641 and was made a freeman in 1640 or 42. His name stands first on the com-

---

*Thomas Comberbach, aged 16.

mittee chosen to "contrive the fabricke of a meeting house." He was also the teacher in the first free school. A tax was not levied upon the inhabitants of any other town for the support of a free school before this.

"1644 The sd Inhabitants taking into consideration the great necesitie of providing some meanes for the Education of the youth in ye sd Towne did with an unanimous consent declare by voate their willingness to promote that worke, promising to put too their hands, to provide maintenance for a free shcool in our sd Towne."

It was Michael's duty, established by law, "to instruct youth so far as they shall be fitted for the university". Even as early as 1642, the law had required parents to have their children taught to "read and understand the principles of religion and capitall lawes of this country", to write, and to learn a trade.

"1656 Agreed with Michaell Metcalfe for to keep the Schoole for the yeare insuinge the said Michaell doe undertake to teach the childrin that shall be sent to him to read English and to write...In Consideration whearof wee doe ingage he shall receive from the towne the sume of twentie pounds, two third partes in wheat att the price of the towne or Countree Rate...and the schoole to be keept att the schoolehouse exsept the wether bee exstrm to hinder and then he is to atend it at his owne dwelling house: and the towne is to take care to have the harth layd in the school house forth with and to have the windowes made fitt; & wood for the fiare to be layd in att the schoolehouse: we ingage to cale upon the parents of the children that they carefully provid it in due time...and in the heat of the weather if the said Michaell disire to make use of the mettenge house he maye so doe provided the house be left clene..."

A few years later his contract stipulated he teach,

"...such male children as are sent to him to wright & read & The use of retimtick as they are capable and the Latten tonge so far as he can."

Michael's wife, Sarah, died early, in 1644, and he married the next yea widow Mary Pidge of Roxbury. His and Sarah's children, all born in Nor wich, England, were,

Michael, born 1617, died young.

Mary, 1618, married Henry Wilson.

Michael, 1620, married Mary, daughter of Jonathan Fairbanks.

John, 1622, married Mary Chickering.

Sarah, 1624, married Robert Onion.

Elizabeth, 1626, married Thomas Bancroft.

MARTHA, 1628, married William Brignall, Christopher Smith, an
NATHANIAL STOW.

260

Thomas, 1629, married Sarah Paige and Anne Paine.

Ann, 1631, died young.

Jane, 1632, married Phillip Walker.

Rebeka, 1635, married John Mackintosh.

Michael and his second wife had five children:

Michael, 1645, married Elizabeth Kingsbury.

Mary, 1646, married John Ware.

Sarah, 1648, married Robert Ware.

Jonathan, 1650, married Hannah Kenric.

Eleazer, 1653.

Michael Metcalf was seventy-eight when he died in 1664. At the end of his will he parcelled out his books. He gave son Thomas his "first Book of Martyrs, Mr. Perkins ffirst Book and one silver spoon". To "sonne John...my second Book of Martyrs, Mr. Perkins second Book, Luther on the gala (?); one silver spoone". He was very generous to his grandchild, "Michael Metcalfe, the Elder", leaving him, among many valuable things, his "gray Horsman's Coate" and perhaps some good adventure stories to remember him by.

Sources:

New England historical and Genealogical Register

Vircus, F.A., Compendium of American Genealogy

Lainson, Michael Metcalf and Family

Goodwin, Genealogical Notes

Ye Fayerbanke Historical

Moriarty, G.A., The Elwyns of Norfolk

History of Norfolk County, Mass.

Dedham Town Records

DUDLEY FAMILY

The most well-known among Socrates Bacon's forebearers was Thomas Dudley, Governor of Massachusetts Bay Colony and influential in the course the vibrant colony followed. The Dudley family has been traced to Charlemagne, a line published many times. F.L. Weis, a respected genealogist, describes it as follows: *(for generations 9 to 24, including Charlemagne, see the chapter on Beatrix Bacon which shares the same line for that period.)*

Generation 25(A)

Waleran de Beaumont, born 1104, died 1166, Count de Meulan, Earl of Worcester. Married Agnes d'Evreux, daughter of Amuri de Montfort, Count d'Evreux and Agnes, niece of Stephen de Garland.

26(A) Sir Robert de Beaumont, Count de Meulan, died 1210. He and the Earl of Cornwall walked to the Great Hall at Northampton Castle to tell Thomas a'Becket of his sentence. Married Maud, daughter of Reginald Fitz-Roy, Earl of Cornwall, base son of King Henry I of England (son of William the Conqueror), by Beatrix, daughter of William Fitz-Robert and granddaughter of Robert de Mortain, half brother of William the Conqueror and companion at Battle of Hastings, marr. Maude de Montgomery, daughter of Roger, Earl of Shrewsbury.

27(A) Maude (Mable) de Beaumont, living in 1214, married William de Vernon, 1155-1217, fifth Earl of Devon, son of Baldwin de Reviers and Adelise.

28(A) Mary de Vernon, married Sir Robert de Courtenay, died 1242, Baron of Oakhampton, whose line is,

Generation 23(Aa)

Miles de Courtenay, married Ermengard de Nevers, granddaughter of Robert II, King of France.

24(Aa) Renaud (Reginald) de Courtenay of Sutton, Berks, lost his lands in France, married a daughter of Frederick (or Guy) de Donjon.

25(Aa) Reginald de Courtenay, crusader in 1147, married secondly Hawise de Abrincis, daughter of Sir Robert de Abrincis, hereditary Serhiff of Devon, Viscount of Devonshire, Baron of Oakhampton, Governor of the Castle of Exeter.

26(Aa) Sir Robert de Courtenay, married Mary de Vernon, above.

29(A) Sir John de Courtenay, Baron of Oakhampton, died May 3, 1274, married Isable de Vere, daughter of Hugh de Vere and Hawise de Quincy, and the granddaughter of Robert de Vere, 3rd Earl of Oxford, Lord Chamberlain of England, Magna Charta Surety, 1215, and once called the proudest participant in the Magna Charta ceremony.

30(A) Sir Hugh de Courtenay, Baron of Oakhampton, died Feb. 20, 1291, married Eleanor le Despenser, daughter of Hugh le Despenser, a leader of the Mad Parliment of 1258, appointed Justiciar of England when King Henry III was captured and a government set up in only three days by Simon de Montfort, leader of the Barons. Prince Edward, also being held captive, escaped in 1265 and "slew Montfort at Evesham" with an army he'd gathered. "In...the murder of Evensham, for battle it was not", of 160 knights accompanying Simon de Montfort in the field only twelve survived. Hugh Despenser fell by Montfort's side.

31(A) Eleanor de Courtenay married Sir Henry de Grey, Lord Grey of Codnor, county Derby, Greys Thurrocks, Co. Essex, Aylesford and Hoo, Co. Kent. His line includes Sir William de Mohun who came to England with William the Conqueror and receivd 55 manors in Somersettshire, and Sir Hugh's father, Sir John de Grey, died before 1272. Part of the line is:

Generation 24Ab,

Walter de Gaunt, fought against the invasion of David I of Scotland, died in 1139, Earl of Lincoln, commander in the battle of the Standard, married Matilda of Britany, daughter of Stephen I, Count of Brittany.

23(Ab) Gilbert de Gant, Lord of Folkingham, circa 1086, brother of Emma who married Alan de Percy.

22(Ab) Gilbert de Gant (Gaunt of Ghent), Lord of Folkingham and Hunmandby, Co. Lincoln, died circa 1058, married Alice de Montfort, daughter of Count Hugh de Montfort-sur-Risee.

21(Ab) Gisele of Luxembourg, married Rudolph I of Alost in Flanders, (also called Ralph of Ghent), castellan of St. Peter of Ghent 1030-1056.

20(Ab) Frederick I of Luxembourg, born circa 965, died 1019, Count of Salm and Luxembourg, married Ermentrude of Gleiberg, daughter of Count Herbert. She was also of Carolingian descent.

19(Ab) Siegfried, Count of Luxembourg, born circa 922, died 998 married Hedwig who may have been daughter of Count Eberhard, Count in the Nordigau.

18(Ab) Cunigunde, born ca. 890, married secondly Richwin, Count of Verdun, died 923.

17(Ab) Ermentrude of France, born 870.

16(Ab) Louis II, King of France and Emperor, married secondly

Adelaide of Paris, both descendants of Charlemagne.

32(A) Sir Richard de Grey, born 1281, died 1334/5, married Joan Fitz Payn, daughter of Sir Robert, Lord Fitz Payn and Isabella de Clifford.

33(A) Sir John de Grey, Knight, Lord Grey of Codnor, died 1392.

34(A) Jane de Grey, of Codnor, married Sir William de Harcourt, Knight, of Stanton-Harcourt, Co. Oxford, died 1349. His line, by marriage, now a part of this one, is:

Generation 1(Ac),

Cerdic, King of the West Saxons 519-534, was a Saxon earl who founded a settlement on the coast of England in 495 and became the ancestor of the English royal line. "A.D. 495. This year came two leaders into Britain, Cerdic and Cynric, his son, with five ships...519, This year Cerdic and Cynric...fought with the britons at a place called Charford. From that day have reigned the children of the West-Saxon kings*..."

2(Ac) It is possible that Creoda was son of Cerdic, father of Cynric and belongs here.

3(Ac) Cynric, son of Cerdic, King of the West Saxons 534-560. "A.D. 552, This year Cynric fought with the Britons on the spot that is called Sarom, and put them to flight..."

4(Ac) Ceawlin, son of Cynric, reigned "thirty winters...591, This year there was a great slaughter of Britons at Wamborough; Ceawlin was driven from his kingdom"

5(Ac) Cuthwine, son of Ceawlin, did not rule. "A.D. 577, this year Cuthwin and Ceawlin fought the Britons, and slew three kings...and took from them three cities, Gloucester, Cirencester, and Bath."

6(Ac) Cutha, or Cuthulf, did not rule.

7(Ac) Celowald, did not rule. King Cynegils was his brother.

8(Ac) Cenred, son of Ceolwald, father of King Ina and Ingild, did not rule.

9(Ac) Ingild, did not rule, died 718. Brother Ina, King of the Saxons fought at Wanborough, "went to Rome, and there gave up the ghost."

10(Ac) Eoppa, son of Ingild, did not rule.

11(Ac) Eafa, son of Eoppa, did not rule.

12(Ac) Eahlmund, son of Eafa, "A.D. 784,...King in Kent."

13(Ac) Egbert, 775, grew up in the Frankish Court of Charles the Great, driven there by Offa, saw Teutonic monarchy at its best. He was, through conquest, the first king of all England. The male line of kings descend from him to Edward the Confessor, and the female line to the present time.

Line (A)—Thorne, (Ab)—de Gaunt, (Ac)—Saxon
*From The Anglo Saxon Chronicle

14(Ac) Ethelwulf (Aethelwulf) King of England 839-858, lead "the great slaughter of the invading heathen."

15(Ac) Alfred the Great, King of England 871-901, one of history's greatest men. He was crowned at Winchester, 871, founded the British Navy, organized the militia, compiled a code of laws, built schools and monasteries and invited scholars to live at his court, collected the ancient epic songs of the English, (one was Beowulf,) started the Anglo Saxon Chronicle.

16(Ac) Edward, the Elder, King of England 901-924. Married Eadgifu (Edgiva), a power through two more generations of kings. Edward was the greatest military leader of the Old English period, continued his father's work, gave his sister Ethelfleda a great part of Britain to rule, convinced she was as skilled in all facets of defence, conquest, etc. as the rest of the family. She had a brilliant reign. "These children are in themselves the best testimonies of the greatness and goodness of Alfred."

17(Ac) Edmund I, the Magnificent, King of England, 940-946, married St. Alfgifu (Elgiva). He had to "take to the field" at eighteen to take his crown after his brother, the brilliant Athelstan, died. Edmund died while,

"Keeping the feast of St. Augustine at Puckelchurch when a notorious freebooter, Leofa, who had been recently banished by the king's order, entered the hall and insisted upon taking his seat at the king's board. The king, indignant at the insult, ordered his steward to expel the man. The ruffian resisted, and the king himself joined in the struggle. A knife flashed, and Edmund sank to the floor. The thanes dispatched the outlaw; but the king was dead."

18(Ac) Edgar, the peaceful, King of England 959-975, showed strength and wisdom in a long era of peace and prosperity. He patroled the coasts each year. An elaborate review took place at Chester in 973 in which he was "borne along in a barge rowed by six vassel kings." Twice every year he rode through every shire checking on the authorities and dispensing justice. H married Elfrida (Ealfthryth), an ambitious and unscrupulous woman whose servant stabbed her young stepson king in the back while she gave him a drink as he paused at her castle during a hunt. Her own son by Edga bacame king at eleven or so.

19(Ac) Ethelred II, the Unready, King of England 979-1016, died after fleeing to Normandy to escape the avenging Danes. The death of his son Edmund Ironside left the Danish King Canute ruler of England. After Canute died, another son of Ethelred, Edward the Confessor, ruled badl

Line (A)—Thorne, (Ac)—Saxon

for twenty-four years.

20(Ac) Elgive (Alfgifu) daughter of Ethelred, married Uchtred, Earl of Northumberland, murdered 1016, probably by Canute who was eliminating possible plotters.

21. Edith (Ealdgyth) married Maldred, slain in battle, 1045, Lord of Carlisle and Allerdale and half-brother of Duncan, King of Scots.

22(Ac) Gospatric I, Earl of Northumberland 1067-1072, first Earl of Dunbar, Lord of Carlisle and Alerdale. "The brave Gospatric" who rose with those in the north in another attempt to fend off William the Conqueror.

23(Ac) Waltheof, Lord of Allerdale, living in 1126, he may have been the Waltheof who led the Danes in the north against William the Conqueror. William ravaged the Vale of York in 1069 in revenge.

24(Ac) Gunnild of Dunbar, married Uchred, son of Fergus, Lord of Glloway.

25(Ac) Roland, Lord of Galloway, Constable of Scotland, 1189-1200. Married Elena de Morville, daughter of Richard de Morville, Constable of Scotland.

26(Ac) Alan, Lord of Galloway, Crusader, Constable of Scotland, named in the Magna Charta. Married Margaret, in line for the disputed Scotish throne as great granddaughter of David I, King of Scotland, who invated England in a clash called the Battle of the Standard, 1138. David I's ancestors were nine Kings of Scotland:

1. Alpin, died ca. 837. Son of Eochaid IV, The Venomous, and the heiress of the Picts.
2. Kenneth, killed 860.
3. Constantine I, killed 877 in battle.
4. Donald II, killed 900 in battle.
5. Malcolm I, killed 954 in battle.
6. Kenneth II, murdered in 995.
7. Malcolm II, died 1034.
8. Bethoc, Abbot of Dunkeld, killed in battle.
9. Duncan I, killed 1040.
10. Malcolm III, killed 1093.
11. David I

27(Ac) Helen of Galloway, married Roger de Quincy, d. 1264, Earl of Winchester, a Crusader and Constable of Scotland.

28(Ac) Elena de Quincy, married Sir Alan la Zouche, Baron of Ashby la Zouche, Co. Leichester, Constable of the Tower of London,

Line (A)—Thorne, (Ac)—Saxon

descended from the Counts of Porhoet in Brittany.

29(Ac) Eudo la Zouche, of Haryngworth, died 1295, married Milicent de Cantelow, daughter of William de Cantelow, Baron Abergavenny, and Eva de Braiose, daughter of William, 6th Baron de Braiose, and a descendant of Griffith, King of Wales, assassinated 1020. Her line goes back as:

Generation 27(Ac-1)

Isabel de Clare, married 1189 Sir William Marshall, buried in the Temple Church, London, 3rd Earl of Pembroke, Marshall of England, protector, Regent of the Kingdom 1216-1219. At Stamford, before Runneymede, William Marshall and Steven Langton met the barons on the 10th of April 1215, as envoy from the king and asked to hear the barons demands. Although his sympathies were with the barons, he preferred to bring pressure upon King John within the lines of the constitution. After John's death, and the crowning of young Prince Henry, he was made governor of the "king and kingdom." "The gentle earl" "restored the kingdom to order and put into practice the principal" of the Magna Charta. He had, they said, "a great soul."

26(Ac-1) Richard de Clare, "Strongbow", circa 1130-1176, A Welsch noble, Earl of Striguls, 2nd Earl of Pembroke, Justiciar of Ireland, invaded Ireland and took possession of Leinster in 1166. Married Eva, daughter of Dermot MacMurrough, King of Leinster, granddaughter of Enna (Enda), King of Leinster, 1119-1126. Eva died at Wexford. The King's line goes back as follows:

5. Donnchadh (Donoch), King of Dublin and Leinster, slain at Dublin, 1115.

4. Murchadh (Morrough), King of Leinster, slain at Dublin, Dec 8, 1090.

3. Darbforgaill (Dervorgilla), married Dermod (Eiarmait Mac Mael na mBo), King of Leinster, defeated the Danes, 1052, slain at Odhba, 1071/2. A reputed descendant of Enna Cainnselack, King of Ireland in the 4th century.

1. Brian Boru, King of Munster, renowned King of Ireland, born 941, died Clontarf, 1014. Son of Cenneidig (Kennedy), Prince of the Dalcassians, son of Lorcan.

Continuing Richard de Clare, "Strongbow's", line:

25(Ac-2) Isabel (or Elizabeth) de Beaumont, married first, Gilbert de Clare, Earl of Pembroke, 1138, son of Gilbert Fitz Richard, 2nd Earl of Clare (and Adeliza de Clermont,) grandson of Rohese Giffard and Richar

Line (A)—Thorne, (Ac-1)—de Claire

270

see *Corrections*, page 337

Fitz Gilbert de Claire, great grandson of Walter Giffard, Lord of Longueville. See Giffard Line, page 156.)

24(Ac-2) Isabel de Vermandois, married first, Sir Robert de Beaumont, Earl of Leicester. The rest of this line is on the page with Childebert, King of Cologne, as generation 1.

Concluding the line of Euod la Zouche, page 211, interrupted to describe his wife's family:

30(Ac) Ellen la Zouche, married Sir John De Harcourt, Knight.

31(Ac) Sir William de Harcourt, Knight, of Stanton-Harcourt, died 1349. He married Jane de Grey, generation 34A in the Dudley line, which we broke off previously to follow her husband's line "Ac", the line that brings the Saxon King line to join the Charlemagne-Dudley line. To continue, Sir William and Jane's son was:

35(A) Sir Thomas de Harcourt, Knight, of Stanton-Harcourt, co. Oxford, Market Bosworth, co. Leicester, and Ellenhall, co. Stafford, Member of Parliment, 1376, married Maud de Grey, daughter of John de Grey of Rotherfield, a different branch of the de Grey family that brings in another line of the Saxon King line (Ac). The line corresponds exactly until generation 21, where Jane de Grey's family descends from Ethelred, the Unready's granddaughter, Edith, and Maud de Grey's family descends from his grandson, Edward Atheling, heir to the throne.

21(Ad) Edward the Atheling, 1016-1057, married Agatha of Hungary, a kinswoman of Henry II of Germany. Edward was the son of Edmund Ironside and grew up in exile in Hungary. He suddenly died when he arrived in England to assume the crown.

22(Ad) margaret (St. Margaret of Scotland), 1045-1093, married Dunfermline, Malcolm III Canmore, King of Scots, who planned an unsuccessful invasion with the English nobles of the north against the Conqueror in 1068.

23(Ad) Matilda of Scotland, 1079-1118, married Henry I, Beauclerc, King of England, son of William the Conqueror. The English were happy with this match for Matilda reprsented the Saxon blood line of King Alfred the Great and Edmond Ironside. They had two children, Matilda and William, who was last in the male line of the Conqueror. Henry I was one of England's great kings. His antededants were:

Generation 24 (Ad-1). William I, the Conqueror, Duke of Norman-

Line (A)—Thorne, (Ac)—Saxon, (Ac-2)—de Claire, (Ad)—Edward the Atheling.

271

see *Corrections*, page 337

dy, King of England, natural son of Robert I, 6th Duke of Normandy, by Arlette, daughter of Fulbert of Falaise, a tanner. The sight of "her fair feet had captured the impetuous Robert's heart as she stood in the brook which ran under her father's tannery and washed the family linen." William was born there in 1027. His father died on a "fantastical" pilgrimage to the Holy Land when William was ten. He was protected and hidden for the next ten years. He married Matilda, daughter of Count Baldwin V, of Flanders, a descendant of Charlemagne and Alfred the Great. The Count's wife Adela de France was a sister of Henry I and daughter of Robert II, King of France.

23(Ad-1). Robert, Duke of Normandy, died 1035. Father of William the Conqueror.

22(Ad-1). Judith of Brittany, 982-1017, Married Richard II, the Good, (but sometimes called "the Devil" for his mischiveous ways.) Duke of Normandy. His father was Richard the Fearless, his grandfather was William Longsword, his great-grandfather Rolf the Walker, all Dukes of Normandy.

21(Ad-1) Ermengarde of Anjou, married Conan I, Duke of Brittany. He died 922.

20(Ad-1) Adelaide de Vermandois, married Geoffrey I Grisgonelle, Count of Anjou, son of Fulk II, the good.

To return to Matilda of Scotland, generation 23(Ad), who married Henry I of England:

24(Ad) Matilda, daughter of Henry I, married 1127, Geoffrey Plantagenet, Count of Anjou, Duke of Normandy by conquest, son of Fulce (Fulk) V, Count of Anjou, King of Jerusalem. He was "bright and handsome" Matilda tried to secure the English succession for herself but she was called "Ethelred the Unready in petticoats".

25(Ad) Henry II, King of England and Lord of all Western France called Curt Mantel, 1132-1189. Red-haired Henry married Eleanor of Aquitaine, proud and treacherous, the divorced wife of Louis VII King of France. (She descended from Robert II, King of France, and Constance of Toulouse, the Dukes of Burgandy, the half brother of William the Conqueror, Aimery IV, Vicount de Thouars, the Chastelleraults and Rochefoucaulds.) Henry made Thomas a'Becket chancellor. He died broken-hearted when he saw that a list of those who wished to shift their alliegence from him was headed by his favorite son John. "I have nothing left to care for—let all things go their way." His son Richard took the throne.

26(Ad) William Longespee (Longsword), natural son of Henry II 1176-1225, Earl of Salisbury, married Ela, Countess of Salisbury, descended from Robert II, King of France, and Constance. Longsword was sent in 1213 by his half brother, King John, to assist the Flemings in a war again

272

Phillip II of France. the Germans, Flemings and English met Phillip on the "fatal field of Bouvines." Longsword was taken prisoner. He was named in the Magna Charta.

27(Ad) Ida De Longespee married first Sir Walter Fitz Robert, (whose father was leader of Magna Charta Barons,) descended from the first French Kings, Waltheof II, (beheaded at Winchester, May 31, 1076,) and crusader Ranulph the Rich.

28(Ad) Ela Fitz Walter, married William de Odyngsells, co. Warwick.

29(Ad) Margaret de Odyngsells, married Sir John de Grey of Rotherfield, died 1311.

30(Ad) Sir John de Grey, Knight of the Garter, first Baron Grey of Rotherfield, married Avice Marmion. He died 1359.

The line of Maude de Grey ends, absorbed into the Dudley line, generation 35(A). The Dudley line continues:

Generation 36(A). Sir Thomas de Harcourt, Knight, of Stantonharcourt, son of Sir Thomas and Maud de Grey. Married Jane Franceys, daughter of Sir Robert Franceys of Formark, co. Derby.

37(A) Sir Richard Harcourt, knight, of Wytham. Berkshire, married first, Edith Seint Clere, daughter of Thomas of co. Suffolk.

38(A) Alice Harcourt, married William Bessiles, Berkshire.

39(A) Elizabeth Bessiles, married Richard Fettiplace, Berkshire.

40(A) Anne Fettiplace, 1496-1567, married Edward Purefoy, Buckingham.

41(A) Mary Purefoy, of Yardley-Hastings, Northampton, married Thomas Thorne, gentleman, of Yardley-Hastings.

42(A) Susanna Thorne, married Captain Roger Dudley of Carmons Abby, Northampton, son of John Dudley. They were parents of Puritan Emmigrant Governor Thomas Dudley. Roger Dudley's line goes back as follows:

Generation 9 (B). John Dudley, married Elizabeth Clerke, daughter of John and Alice Clerke. His will was dated 1545.

8(B) Thomas Sutton, grandson of Lord Dudley, married Grace Trekeld, daughter of Lancelot Trekeld. At this time the family started to use the Dudley name instead of the longer *de Sutton de Dudley* as they had done.

Line (A)—Thorne

Line (Ad)—Edward of Atheling, (Ad-1)—Dukes of Normandy

7(B) Sir Edmond Sutton, Knight, present at the coronation of Richard III, married Matilda (Maud) de Clifford. Her line of Plantagenet kings immediately follows this Dudley line.

6(B) John Sutton, 6th Lord Dudley, was prominent in the reigns of Henry VI and Edward IV and involved in the War of the Roses, "serving both sides as circumstances demanded." He was once taken prisoner with the King and put in the Tower.

5(B) John de Sutton, 5th Lord of Dudley, married Constance, daughter of Sir William Blout of Barton.

4(B) John de Sutton de Dudley.

3(B) John de Sutton de Dudley.

2(B) John de Sutton, Member of Parliment, married Isabella, daughter of John de Charlton.

1(B) The first John de Sutton was living in 1325 in Dudley Castle, inherited from his wife's father, when he was accused by Hugh le Despenser, the younger, of aiding the Earl of Lancaster in his rebellion. John de Sutton bought his way out of prison and possible death by giving le Despenser all his rights to Dudley Castle. His son, John, 2(B) above, married the daughter of the subsequent owner of the Castle, and it returned to the family.

The line of Matilda de Clifford, who brought her family of Plantagenet descendants into the Dudley line when she married Sir Edmond Sutton, 7(B) above, follows:

6(Ba) Thomas de Clifford, Matilda's father, was killed at Saint Albans, 1455, in the first battle of the War of the Roses where the knights were at this period, so heavily armored that they could not sit their horses but must stand and wait for the battle to reach them and, unable to move must fight or die. He was 8th Lord Clifford, Sheriff of Westmoreland Member of Parliment, married to Joan Dacre, daughter of Thomas, Lord Dacre of Gillisland, and his wife, Phillippa, daughter of Ralph de Neville Earl of Westmoreland, and Margaret Stafford. de Neville controlled one third of the peerages in England in the 15th century and was possibly the de Neville ancestor of Edward IV and Richard III.

5(Ba) Elizabeth Percey, married John de Clifford, Member of Parliment, 7th Lord Clifford, Sheriff of Westmoreland, died 1421.

4(Ba) Elizabeth Mortimer, married Sir Henry Percy, Knight of the Garter, called "Harry Hotspur," "impetuous and valiant son of old Earl Percy." The Percys had helped Henry IV to the throne by betraying King Richard, but

Line (B)—Dudley, Line (Ba)—Plantagenet

later Henry refused to let them ransom Elizabeth's brother, Edmund Mortimer, the Earl of March, true heir to the throne, and captured in Wales while fighting for King Henry in 1402. The Percy's conspired. One day the king drew a dagger and called Hotspur a traitor. Hotspur left, saying, "Not here but in the field!". They quickly assembled an army but the King caught them at Shrewsbury before their help had arrived. About to fight, Hotspur realized that he had left his favorite sword behind in Berwick, the village where they had slept. Legend tells us he turned pale. Meanwhile, King Henry had dressed thirteen knights near his own size in armor bearing his crest and Hotspur forced to use his second best sword, cut down nearly all of them in an effort to reach the real king when an arrow "Pierced his brain." Without him the battle was lost.

3(Ba) Phillippa Plantagenet, only daughter of Lionel of Antwerp ,and next in line of succession after young King Richard. She married Edmond Mortimer, Sr., an outspoken hater of Duke John of Gaunt, her uncle, who tried to get a measure passed to bar women from ruling. The Duke had control of young Richard, his nephew. Edmund Mortimer, Earl of March, was a member of the council to act during the minority of Richard II. He was the great-grandson of Roger Mortimer,"the dark Lord of Wigmore", captured at night by Edward III and hanged for the misdeeds he and Edward II's wife Isabella executed while they controlled the kingdom in the name of Isabella's step-son Edward III.

2(Ba) Lionel of Antwerp, second son of King Edward III, Earl of Ulster, Duke of Clarence, an "amiable giant". He married Elizabeth de Burgh, daughter of William de Burgh, Lord of Connaught, Earl of Ulster, and his wife Maud de Lancaster, daughter of Henry, Earl of Lancaster, granddaughter of Edmund Plantagenet, "Crouchback", great granddaughter of Henry III. The de Burgh family was considered first among the Anglo-Norman lords of Ireland.

1(Ba) King Edward III, the Black Prince, "a handsome person, pleasant and affable, a fluent tongue and a great energy," married Philippa of Hainault.

Edward's father, King Edward II, did not take the crown seriously. He was murdered in Berkeley Castle in 1327 after Roger Mortimer and Queen Isabella landed in England to lead a revolt.

Edward's grandfather was King Edward I, ruled 1272-1307, married Eleanor of Castile. These Edwards were preceded by Henry III (1216-1272), King John 1199-1216), Henry II and Eleanor of Aquitaine, Matilda and Geoffrey V Plantagenet, Henry I, (1100-1135), and William the Conqueror, the thrid time this line connects to the Dudley line.

To return to 42(A): Susanna Thorne and Roger Dudley were parents of Thomas Dudley, later the Governor of Massachusetts Bay Colony, baptised

1559, married Dorothy Yorke, daughter of Edmund Yorke of Cotton, England. The Yorke line is:

10(C) Gilbert Yorke of Harrington, married Amye Bond.

9(C) Edmund Yorke of Buybrooke, married Grace.

8(C) Richard Yorke of Yorkshire, married Joan Darcy.

7(C) Sir William Darcy, 8th Baron Darcy, married Eupheme Langton in 1460.

6(C) Richard Darcy married Eleanor Scrope. Her ancestors include William le Scrope, Governor of the Ilse of Man in 1393, and the Earl of Willshire who lost his head in the battle to keep Richard II on the throne.

5(C) John, 7th Baron Darcy, married Joan Greystock.

4(C) John De Greystock, Baron Greystock, 1389-1436, married Elizabeth De Ferrers.

3(C) Sir Robert De Ferrers of Willingsham, married Joan Beaufort in 1390.

2(C) John of Gaunt, Duke of Lancaster, married, third, the beautiful Catherine Swynford, sister-in-law of Chaucer, who had already borne Duke John several children, the Beauforts, politically involved for the next cen tury. The "great Lancaster" was intensly ambitious and easily the richest man in England, owning both Kenilworth, the most famous castle in England and the Savoy Palace in London. The Savory was sacked and burned by Kentish men lead by Wat Tyler and John Ball in the Peasant's Revolt of 1351. It was "packed with untold treasures from the cellars to the top of the crenelate walls." John of Gaunt is mentioned on page with generation 3 (Ba), the uncl of Phillippa Plantagenet.

1(C) Edward II, King of England. The generations leading back t William the Conqueror are repeated.

Fourteen of the twenty-five Barons of England "who secured the articles of th Magna Charta in 1215" from King John at Runnymede meadow are in th Dudley, Yorke, and Thorne lines.

Barons in the Dudley line:

William d'Albini, Lord of Belvoir Castle; Gilbert de Clare, Earl of Hertford; John de Lacy, Lord of Pontefract Castle; Richard de Clare, Ea of Hertford; Robert de Ros, Lord of Helmsley Castle; Saire de Quincy, Ea of Winchester

Barons in the Yorke line:

Hugh Bigod, Earl of Norfolk and Suffolk; Henry de Bohun, EArl of Hereford; Roger Bigod, Earl of Norfolk and Suffolk; John Fitz Robert,

Line (A)—Thorne, (Ba)—Plantagenet, (C)—Yorke

276

see *Corrections*, page 337

Warkworth; William de Mowbray, Baron of Axholme
Barons in the Thorne line:
Robert de Vere, Earl of Oxford; William Malet, Sheriff of Somerset
and Devon; Robert Fitz Walter, Leader of the Barons

DUDLEY LINE

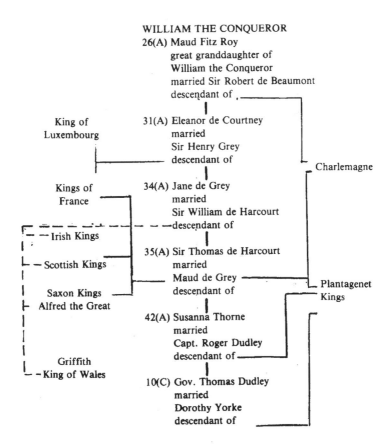

So, as described previously, the Dudleys received their titles and estates from the time of the first John de Sutton of Dudley Castle, descending to Captain Roger Dudley of Cannons Abby, Northampton. Roger Dudley was a cousin of Robert Dudley, Earl of Leicester, the favorite of Queen Elizabeth, and cousin of Edward de Sutton de Dudley, favorite of Queen Mary, Elizabeth's predecessor, and also cousin of Guilford Dudley, unfortunate husband to the unfortunate Lady Jane Grey, Queen of England for nine days.

Captain Roger Dudley married Susannah Thorne and in 1586 was "slain in ye warres", probably in a battle fought during the armed expedition sent to the Netherlands by Queen Elizabeth and led by Robert Dudley. Roger left a son, Thomas, born in Northampton in 1576 and educated in the family of the Earl of Northumberland where he acted as a page.

When Thomas was older he studied law in the office of a relative of his mother, a Judge Nichols, and started practice near the same time he received a Captain's commission from Queen Elizabeth, raised a volunteer company of young Northumberland men and left for the Netherlands to train. "In 1597, he was at the siege of Amiens, but the treaty being concluded before he had any fighting, he returned home." He married Dorothy Yorke "of family and fortune" and settled in Northampton.

Thomas was asked to act as Steward for the young Earl of Lincoln who had inherited his family's large estates and helpless under heavy debt which had accumulated for two generations. By Dudley's "energy and activity, labor prudence and judgement" the whole estate was made solid again and Thomas Dudley, who had become a nonconformist in his religious outlook, left to settle in the English town of Boston to be a part of the congregation of Reverend John Cotton. He returned later to the Earl of Lincoln who "would do nothing without him."

It was at the powerful Earl's manor that the small group of Puritan adventurers held some of their first meetings to form the Massachusetts Bay Company. Thomas Dudley was linked to this venture through the Earl of Lincoln and also by his connections to Reverend Cotton's congregation some of whom were pledging money toward the "Great Migration". By the time he was aboard the flagship *Arbella,* named after the Earl's daughter, he had been chosen Deputy Governor and John Winthrop, Governor Thomas was fifty-six years old and from then on, almost until his death always held a high office in the government of the colony.

On board the flagship with him were his wife, his two sons, several daughters and Simon Bradstreet, son of a nonconforming minister, whom Thomas had raised since Simon was fourteen. Now he was married to Thomas's daughter Anne. As they waited, John Cotton came down to

278

Southampton to preach and to pray for the safety of the hopeful English people loading their goods and families in the eleven ships.

When the ships arrived twelve weeks later on the foreign shore the passengers were sick and dying. The Lady Arbella died, and her husband and the wives of the Reverend George Phillips and Mr. William Pynchon. So did John Winthrop's physician. Thomas Dudley wrote a letter to the Countess of Lincoln,

"...I thought it fit to commit to memory our present condition and what hath befallen us since our arrival here...and must do rudely, having yet no table, nor other room to write in than by the fireside, upon my knee, in this sharp winter, to which my family must have leave to resort though they break good manners, and make me many times forget what I would say, and say what I would not...many of our people brought with us being sick of fevers and the scurvy, and we thereby unable to carry up our ordnance and baggage so far, we were forced to change counsel, and for our present shelter to plant dispersedly; some at Charlestown, some at Boston, some of us upon Mistick, which we named Meadford, some of us westward on Charles River, four miles from Charlestown, which place we named Watertown; others of us two miles from Boston, in a place we named Rocksbury;...

"This dispersion troubled some of us, but help it we could not, wanting ability to remove to any place fit to build a town upon, and the time too short to deliberate any longer lest the winter should surprise us before we had builded our houses. The best counsel we could find out was, to build a fort to retire to in some convenient place, if any enemy pressed us thereunto, after we should have fortified ourselves against the injuries of wet and cold. So ceasing to consult further at that time, they who had health to labor fell to building, wherein many were interrupted with sickness, and many died weekly, yea, almost daily, among whom were Mrs. Pynchon, Mrs. Coddington, Mrs. Phillips, and Mrs. Alcock, a sister of Mr. (Rev. Thomas) Hooker's. Insomuch that the ships being now upon their return, there was, as I take it, not much less than one hundred which returned back again, and glad were we so to be rid of them. The ships being gone, victuals wasting, and mortality increasing, we held divers fasts in our several congregations. And of the people who came over with us from the time of their setting sail from England in April, 1630, until December following, there died two hundred at the least, so low hath the Lord brought us.

"Well, yet they who survived were not discouraged, but bearing God's corrections with humility, and trusting in his mercies, and considering how after a lower ebb he had raised up our neighbors at Plymouth, we began again in December to consult about a fit place to build a town upon, leaving all thoughts of a fort because upon any invasion we were necessarily to lose our houses when we should retire thereinto...

"Half of our cows, and almost all our mares and goats, died at sea in their passage hither, which, together with the loss of our six months building, occasioned by our intended removal to a town to be fortified, weakened our estates...

"If any come hither to plant for worldly ends that can live well at home, he commits an error of which he will soon repent him; but if for spiritual, and no particular obstacle hinder his removal, he may find here what may well content him, viz., materials to build, fewel to burn, ground to plant, seas and rivers to fish in, a pure air to breathe in, good water to drink till wine or beer can be made...If there be any endued with grace and furnished with means to feed themselves and theirs for eighteen months, and to build and plant, let them come into our Macedonia and help us.

"Upon the 25th of this March, one of Watertown having lost a calf, and about ten of the clock at night hearing the howling of some wolves not far off, raised many of his neighbors out of their beds, that by discharging their muskets near about the place where he heard the wolves, he might so put them to flight and save his calf. The wind carrying the report of the muskets to Rocksbury, three miles off, at such a time, the inhabitants there took an alarm, beat up their drum, armed themselves, and sent in post to us at Boston to raise us also. So in the morning, the calf being found safe, the wolves afrighted, and our danger past, we went merrily to breakfast..."

This house in which Thomas Dudley wrote his letter in, "having yet no table, nor other room to write in," seemed such a plain little house to bring down the wrath of Governor Winthrop who wrote to Thomas that he "...did not well to bestow such cost about wainscotting and adorning his house in the beginning of a plantation both in regard to the expense and the example." But, said Mr. Dudley, "It was for the warmth of the house and the charge was but little, being but clapboards nailed to the wall in the form of a wainscot."

New England prospered after the first frightening winter. Thomas Dudley moved to Ipswich for a short while with his children and their husbands and then to Roxbury where he built one of the finest homes in a town with many new, large, and comfortable homes, two stories high, with mammoth center chimneys and "roofs and walls clapboarded on the out syde..." His land was bounded by Smelt Brook and sat across from the Apostle Eliot's house. At one hundred and fifty years old, the house, having always been lived in by a Dudley, was torn to the ground just a few days after the battle of Bunker Hill and its brick basement walls used for the angle of the breastworks thrown up by the Americans. It had been a house with more books than most people had, "mostly religious treatises and law books and some history books." (His daughter Anne called him a "magazine of history.") "Some Latin books...some that indicate a taste for literature", and the poem, "ye Vision of Pier. Plowman."

Thomas Dudley was chosen Governor in 1634 and again in 1640, 1645 and 1650. He was Deputy Governor thirteen times. He was one of the commission to frame the laws for the colony. In 1643, he was appointed commissioner to frame articles of confederation between the colonies. The next year, he was chosen Sergent Major General of all the military forces, "the highest military office in the colonies." He was one of the founders of Harvard deep in plans "for a colledge at Newetowne" (later called Cambridge), "...and was directing mind in its affairs."

Thomas Dudley and John Winthrop were at odds throughout all the years of their alternating governorships, Thomas, stern and harsh, contrasted with Winthrop's tolerant attitude. And in spite of the few high

280

tempered and bitter exchanges in the minutes of the court and in their own letters, they often seemed like friends. Once they walked from New Towne inland to Concord to set off the boundries of grants they had each been given on the East bank of the Concord River. From Winthrop's journal,

"The Governor and deputy went to Concord to view some land for farms, and, going down the river about four miles, they made choice of a place for one thousand acres for each of them. They offered each other the first choice, but because the deputy's was first granted, and himself had store of land already, the governor yielded him the first choice. So at the place where the deputy's land was to begin were two great stones which they called the Two Brothers in remembrance that they were brothers by their children's marriage[1] and did so brotherly agree, and for that a little creek near those stones was to part their lands."[2]

But Thomas Dudley, "Bold-spoken and irascible in manner", so intelligent and with such force of character, "coming to find an asylum for his opinions, hating heresy and intolerance, he was himself most intolerant." He took a large part in the banishment of Roger Williams, Anne Hutchinson and others. "Whatever cause he did espouse, had his whole heart. Whatever he was against, found him a good hater." He became one of the largest land owners in the colonies but was accused of a "too great eagerness for pecuniary gain", but it was well known that though he "drove a good bargain, he was a man of exact justice" and that he gave of his goods and money liberally. His door was open to all, to Indians, to the poor, to strangers. "His knowledge of the law was good and served him and the new colony well...Perhaps it is not too much to say that the State is a monument to his knowledge, his judgement..." And he was a poet. When he died, these lines were found in his pocket:

Dimme eyes, deafe eares, cold stomach shew
My dissolution is in view.
Eleven times seven years lived have I,
And now God calls, I willing dye.
My shuttle's shut, my race is run,
My sun is set; my deed is done;
My span is measured; my tale is told;
My flower's faded and grown old;
My life is vanished; shadows fled;

[1] Rev. Samuel Dudley, oldest son of Thomas, married John Winthrop's daughter, Mary.
[2] "The two Brother's Rocks served as a landmark for early exploration teams traveling along the Concord River...Access to the rocks is in the National Wildlife Refuge...reached from the Dudley Road in Bedford, Mass." according to *The Bedford Sampler*. That Refuge was once known as Bacon's Woods.

My soul's with god; my body dead.
Fare well, dear wife, children and friends,
Hate Heresy. Make blessed ends,
Bear Poverty. Live with good men.
So shall we meet with joy agen
Let men of God in courts and churches watch
O'er such as do a toleration hatch,
Least ye ill egg bring forth a cockatrice,[1]
To pay you all with heresy and vice,
If men be left and otherwise combine
Mine epitaph's I died *no libertine.*"

During his funeral in 1653, the fire arms of the colony were set off from all the forts. He was profoundly missed as a symbol of that first number who guided the daring venture.

Thomas Dudley and his wife, Dorothy Yorke, had these children:

Thomas, (no proof) born circa 1606, graduated Emmanuel College, Cambridge in 1630.

Samuel, 1608, a minister at Exeter, N.H., graduated Emmanuel, married Mary Winthrop.

Anne, circa 1612, married Simon Bradstreet who was elected Governor in 1679. She was America's first poet and was called "the Tenth Muse"[2] when her collection of verse was published in London.

— , a daughter who married a man named Page.

— , a daughter who married Major Keayne.

MERCY, 1621, married Rev. JOHN WOODBRIDGE.

Hugh, settled on Chickopee Plain in 1654.

Patience, married Daniel Denison, Deputy to General Court, Justice, Commander-In-Chief of the Colony's troops.

Dorothy.

Deborah, 1645. May have been one of the daughters whose name is lost above.

Joseph, 1647, Governor of the Massachusetts Colony, 1686.

Sources:

Weiland, Dudley and Allied Families
Mather, Cotton, Magnalia Christi Americana

[1]Cockatrice, a fabulous serpent, said to be hatched from a cock's egg, deadly to those who its breath or met its glance.

[2]In Greek mythology any of the nine goddesses presiding over poetry, the arts, sciences,

Dudley, C.W., The Dudley Family
Thwing, History of Roxbury
Weis, F.L., Ancestral Roots of 60 Colonists
Ancestry of the Jones Family
Roxbury Colonists
Developments of Our Town Government, Ipswich Historical Society Pub.
Records of the Colony of Massachusetts Bay in New England

WOODBRIDGE FAMILY

Thomas Dudley's daughter, Mercy, married the Reverend John Woodbridge, sixth John Woodbridge in a line of English ministers. The first was a follower of John Wycliffe, an early critic of the Church of England, and the fifth John Woodbridge was the respected pastor of a Puritan church in Stanton, Wiltshire, "so able and faithful", said Cotton Mather. This Woodbridge married Sarah, daughter of Reverend Robert Parker whom Mather called "one of the greatest scholars in the English Nation, and in some sort the father of all Non-Conformists of our day", lavishly honored in Queen Elizabeth's reign but eventually driven out of England to Holland. Mather said of Sarah Parker that she was one "who did so virtuously, that her own personal character would have made her highly esteemed if a relation to such a father had not farther added unto (her) luster ..."

John and Sarah's son John, born in 1613, was sent to Oxford to study but was forced to leave when he refused to take the oath of conformity, "neither his father, nor his conscience approving." He studied with private tutors until 1634 when he had the opportunity to go to New England on the *Mary and John* with his cousin, Reverend James Noyes, and uncle, Reverend Thomas Parker, who had also been driven from Oxford to Holland at the same time his father was for his resistance. On the voyage over Thomas Parker "led the music at the devotional services..." Thomas loved music and "had a very sweet voice, and was a remarkably good singer..." In fact, "it was the sweetest music that mine ears ever heard."

The *Mary and John* was one of a group of nine shops "lying in the river Thames, bound for New England", when the crown's authorities ordered the ship detained while they checked for proof that every passenger "hath taken both the Oathes of Alleigeance and Supremacy." The ships masters had to furnish one hundred pound bonds as assurance that all passengers were approved passengers.

John Woodbridge settled at Newbury and found occupation as town clerk and Surveyor of Armor, studying all the while, until in 1638 his father's death caused him to return to England to settle the estate. When he returned to America he brought his brothers with him, Benjamin, who became the first graduate of Harvard, and another who died on the passage.

In 1641, he married Mercy Dudley and began to teach school at Boston. Only a few years later he was ordained, the second minister to be ordained in New England, and was retained as pastor of the church at the new town of Andover which he had helped to settle, even leading the delegation to buy the land, Cochichewick, from the Sagamore of Massachusetts for six pounds and a coat. He treated for the Indians to retain the right to fish for alewives inthe Cochichewick River "for their owne eating" and receiving their promise to take care to not spoil any corn or fruit.

Discontented, John and his family and Benjamin sailed back home to England where he was a pastor, started a school, and was Chaplin to the Parlimentary Commissioners who were dealing with the King on the Ilse of Wight. But sixteen years later, Charles II was restored to the throne and John and his brother and many other Puritan ministers were expelled from the country again for their unsettling non-conformity. He brought Mercy and his eleven children back to the refuge of America where "one fact stands out above all others, the intellectual leadership of the clergy, and that...among a laity neither ignorant nor weak."

John settled again in Newbury to become an assistant to his uncle, Reverend Parker, now "a blind and aged bachelor", but there were differences between John and his congregation concerning church discipline. He was seen as too broad and liberal. He decided to resign his ministry. As he was "remarkably blest in his private estate", he didn't mind the loss of his salary and, after all, "he had little tendency to preach." But because of the value the country's citizens put upon him, he was appointed one of the associate magistrates for Essex County. He was an Assistant to the General Court in 1683 and 1684 and Justice of the Peace until his death.

John and Mercy had been married fifty years when she died in 1691. He was overwhelmed by the death of his "most religious, prudent, and faithful consort" and felt "torn away from the desire of mine eyes." From that time, he seemed to lose interest in his world for she was "the best part of it."

He had been all his life "wonderfully compsed, patient, and pleasant" and "had a great command" of his temper. He was forgiving to the extreme and would not allow disappointment to bother him. Once he was told of a "sore disaster" to his cattle and would only say, "What a mercy it is, that this is the first time that ever met with such a disaster!" He was a great reader and a great scholar.

"The strangury arrested him" at the age of eighty-two in 1695. He had suffered for some time and near the end, refusing a glass of wine, said, "I am going where I shall have beter."

His and Mercy's children:

Sarah, born 1640, married in England and did not return to New England with her family.

Lucy, 1642, married her cousin, Rev. Simon Bradstreet of New London, Conn., and Capt. Daniel Epps. (Rev. Bradstreet was once introduced with, "Here is a man who can whistle Greek.")

John, 1644, minister in Conn., married Abigail, daughter of Conn. Governor William Leete.

Benjamin, 1645, minister at Conn., R.I., Maine and Mass. Marrie

288

Mary Ward and Deborah Cushing.

Thomas, 1648, Captain, married Mary Jones. Judge Sewell wrote in his diary, "Thos. Woodbridge is so burnt in his own fire that he Dyeth..."

Dorothy, 1650, married Nathaniel Fryer, mariner, Representative and Member of Council, N.H.

Anne, 1653.

Timothy, 1656, minister in Hartford, Conn. Helped found Yale, member of Saybrook Convention. Married Mehitable Wyllys, a Mrs. Howell and Abigail Warren.

Joseph, 1657, inherited the homestead because he "always continued with (his father) and ,hath bin servicable to our Affaires." Married Martha Rogers.

MARTHA, circa 1660, married Capt. SAMUEL RUGGLES. Three of their sons trained at Harvard for the ministry.

Mary, 1662, married Samuel Appleton of Ipswich.

John and Mercy Woodbridge were the antecedents of sixteen colonial clergymen by the name of Woodbridge and of many more bearing other names. A few other of their descendants were: Anson Greene Phelps, founder of Phelps, Dodge & Co., Oliver Wendall Holmes, Richard H. Dana, author of *Two Years Before the Mast,* William Ellery Channing, a founder of the Unitarian Church, and William Woodbridge, Governor of Michigan and a U.S. Senator.

Sources:

Jones, E.F., Ancestry of the Jones Family
Vircus, Compendium of American Genealogy
Currier, J.J., History of Newbury
History of Andover
Mather, C., Magnalia Christi Americana
Mitchell, L., The Woodbridge Record
N.E. Historical and Genalogical Register

STONE FAMILY

The exact date has never been found nor the name of the ship Gregory Stone sailed on with his wife, Lydia, their six children and Lydia's two grown children, but it was about 1635 that he settled in Watertown very near his brother Simon. The two brothers were from Great Bromley in Tendring Hundred, county Essex, near the town of Colchester. Their Anglo-Saxon ancestors had lived there for over three centuries.

The first Stone on record was Philip atte Stone, "late servant of Robert de Vere, Earl of Oxford", who with several others, was called to an inquisition before the sheriff of Essex in 1302 for "forcibly enter(ing) the park of the said earl of Great Bentleye and hunter therein against his will." Living in Little Bentley was Walter atte Stone, a Yeoman, descendant of a family that was probably of the *villein* class. Records show Walter atte Stone taxed by Edward II in 1320 and by Edward II in 1327.

Great grandson, Walter atte Stone, born in 1390, at the Court of the Manor of Bovills: "To this court came Walter atte Stone, and made fealty to the lord for a tenement and garden adjacent, held by copy of court roll, which late was of William atte Stone, his father."

John Stone, born about 1420 in Ardleigh, Stone home for two generations, occupied a small estate called for centuries *Barons,* but more recently *Old Shields.* It was during John's lifetime the prefix "atte" as part of the family name went out of general use.

His eldest son, Walter, inherited *Barons* in 1487 and Simon, his second son, received an estate in Ardleigh, *Walles,* and the one he lived in called *Godewyns* in Great Bromley. These years were peaceful as the Wars of the Roses wound down. They had taken a terrible toll of the old feudal families but not much harm was done to the yeoman.

Simon died before 1511, a "prosperous...yeoman...buried inside the church...significant of his superior local position..."

Then "Davye Stonne' inherited *Godewyns.* Although his records are some of those destroyed by Henry VIII when he appropriated the monestaries, it is sure he had sons John and Simon and probably Thomas and Matthew.

Second son, Simon, lived at *Hunts,* an estate gived him by his uncle, Walter. he and his cousin Robert Stone were church wardens in Great Bromley, a mark of local distinction.

Simon's son Davy, born about 1540, lived during Queen Mary's short reign when twenty Protestants from surrounding parishes were burned at the stake in a field near Colchester. A family of three named Munte who died may have been related to the Stones.

Davy Stone had eleven children, the youngest four by his second wife,

see *Corrections,* page 337

Ursula. Her first child was Simon, the fourth, Gregory. Both emigrated to New England in 1635.

Gregory Stone received an education of some sort for he could read and write, rather a rarity among the yeomen. He was married in 1617 at Nayland, near Bromley and the home of John Winthrop, an area from which nearly two-thirds of the colonists to New England emigrated. The Diocesan Registry still has the record of the visit of the Archdeaconry of western Suffolk for 1629 and there is Gregory Stone's name, one of the parishioners presented for refusing to kneel to receive communion. All but one of those were in New England a few years later.

Settled in Watertown at first, Gregory moved everything a little over the line to Cambridge. By 1642, by grant and purchase, he owned more than four hundred acres, some of it bordering his brother Simon's land on the Watertown line. His house and seven acres on Garden Street sat just across from Linnaean Street on what is now Harvard's observatory grounds. His orchards were famous in the colony and grew on the site of the present Botanic Gardens of Harvard College.

Gregory Stone was admitted a freeman on May 25, 1636 with Simon. He joined the Cambridge church. In 1643, "Gregory Stone, Deacon of this Ch: & Lydia his wife in f. C. (full communion) whose children, John Daniel, David, Elizabeth, Samuel Sarah, Also John Cooper, Son of the forsaid Lydia and Lydia Fiske her daughter (also come..." Gregory was deacon for thirty-four years. He was a deputy to the General Court and continuously served on committees to manage town affairs. In 1671 he was assigned "for the Cattichising of the youth at the farmes", a settlement out on the fringes of the town grant.

He and his wife exhibited a solid common sense when they signed a certificate on behalf of Winifred Holman, accused of witchcraft, stating that they "never knew anything in her life concerning witchery."

"But the most noteworthy committee on which Dea. Gregory Stone served was in 1664 when he and three other men presented to the General Court a petition signed by a hundred and forty other residents...protesting against the...proposed government of New England by a Royal Commission...in which they were not represented, and contrary to the intent of the original patent of the Colony.

"19 Oct. The Court being mett together & informed that several persons, inhabitants of Cambridge, were at the doore, & desiring liberty to make knowne theire errand, were called in, & Mr. Edward Jackson, Mr. Richard Jackson, Mr. Edw: Oakes, & Deacon Stone, coming before the Court, presented a peticon from the inhabitants of Cambridge...

"To the honoured Generall Court of Massachusetts Colonie...we whole names are under written, the inhabitants and housholders of the towne...doe hereby testify our unanimous satisfaction in and adhearing to the present government so long and orderly established, and our earnest desire of...all the liberties and privileges pertaining

see *Corrections*, page 337

theirunto which are contained in the charter granted by King James and King Charles the First of famous memory, under the encouredgment...of which...we or our fathers ventured over the ocean into this wildernesse through great hazards...and difficulties; and we humbly desire our honoured General Court would address themselves...to his Maiesty in that we may not be subjected to the arbitrary power of any who are not chosen by this people..."

"Deacon Gregory Stone was thus prominent among the first to protest in Massachusetts against government without representation by the governed..."

He has been described as "a man of vigorous physique and vitality; of uncompromising convictions and strict integrity..." He served on committees to his eightieth year and died in 1672. In his will he wrote,

"To my grandchild Jno. Stone sonne of David Stone, I do give my little cow called mode, & my little young colt, or five pounds, provided he live with my wife one year after my decease, & do her faithful service according to his best ability, during which time my wife, shall find him his meat, drink, and cloathing, & at the end of the year deliver him the above named cow & colt..."

Gregory Stone's estate inventory included a long list of farm impelements, livestock and household goods and "A winescot Cubard" now owned by the Concord Antiquarian Society. Its photograph shows a leggy cabinet, large, square, and ornate in the Jacobean style. All of his wearing apparel amounted to:

"...shirts bands and hancherifs and Caps, A grey sute a payer of Red drawers, A murry Coate,[1] A tany Coate, A blacke Coate, A serge[2] Cloake, A grey lined Jackit, A grey Jackit, A black serge Jackit, An olde Cloth Jackit, a blue payer of brechis and drawers, A Red wastcoate, A grey wastcoate, A mans hoode, A new payer of gloves, A payer of old gloves, A payer of mittins, A payer of moose leather gloves, two payer of stockins, A blacke hat and band, two old hats, three payer of shooes, A payer of bootes."

He had seven children, the last three by his wife, Lydia Cooper:
John, baptised 1618, built Framingham's first mill, married Anne How.
Daniel, 1620, called *Doctor*.
David, 1622.
Elizabeth, 1624-1626.
Elizabeth, 1629, married Anthony Potter of Ipswich. He was taken to

[1]Murrey, of a purplish-red or mulberry color.
[2]serge, a strong twilled fabric made of wool, with a diagonal rib on both sides.

court for allowing his wife to wear a silk hood but was discharged on proving he was worth L200.

Samuel, 1631, married Sarah Sterns.

SARAH, 1633, married JOSEPH MERRIAM of Cambridge "farmes".

Sources:

Bartlett, J., Gregory Stone Genealogy
Stone, W.R., English Ancestry of Simon and Gregory Stone
Historical Homes and Families
Vircus, F.A., Compendium of American Genealogy
New England Historical and Genealogical Register

MOORE FAMILY

An historian of Puritan families wrote that "Moores were as numerous in the New England woods as mosquitoes." and there were several John Moores settled here at the beginning. The John Moore that the Bacons descended from was born in England about 1610 and arrived in Massachusettes perhaps as early as 1637 with Elizabeth and John, his two children by his first wife, and with his second wife, Elizabeth Whale, and her parents. They settled in Sudbury with several other families belonging to the Bacon history and bought a houselot and twenty-two acres from Edmund Rice. Later, he bought more land and a house from Gregory Stone's son, John, the deed giving him "all the boord and shelves" about the house, "fast or loose" in that part of Sudbury now Wayland.

John Moore and his father-in-law, Philemon Whale[1] were among the non-freemen who took the oath of alegiance to the town July 6, 1645. John was several times a selectman, fence viewer, and surveyor of roads, and once a constable and "invoice taker", unusual responsibility for a man who refused, or was not allowed, to become a freeman.

He died in 1674, "a prosperous planter", and willed his lands, bordered by Edmund Rice, Peter King, John Maynard, John "How" and Edmond Browne, to his sons. He also included a paragraph that was unusually worded for this period:

"I doe hereby nominate authorize & Constitute & appoint Elizabeth my loveing & tender wife to bee the Lawful true & only Executrix of this my last will & Testament...who I know will bee carefull & tend'r of my children, & so I comitt her & them to ye Lord, who hath promised to bee a ffather to the ffatherlesse, & the widows husband, requireing & chargeing all my children to (know fear) love and serve the Lord: to honor obey & cherish theire mother to live in love & unity among themselves, & in peace with all men according to the word of God to bee faithfull & dilligent in theire gen'll & particular callings; & this with the blessing of the Lord I heartily pray might bee their portion & the portion of theire children & posterity to the worlds end..."

"I doe hereby desire Authorize & appoint my Reverend Pastor M'r Edmond Browne & my worthy loveing ffriends Leiften'nt: Edmond Goodenow & M'r Thomas Steevens all of this Towne of Sudbury, to bee the overseeres of this my will, my last will..."

John Moore's last seven children were born to his second wife Elizabeth

[1]A Philemon Whale, weaver, lived in Berkhampstead, England, near friends Thomas Axtell and Edmond Rice. Now in Sudbury he lived not far from the mill pond near the present Concord Road, first laid out in 1639. Philemon's wife died soon after they settled here and he married Sarah Cakebread, daughter of the miller.

Whale after arriving in America.

Elizabeth, born about 1628, married Henry Rice.

JOHN, 1630, married ANN SMITH.

William, 1640.

Mary, 1642, married Richard Ward and Daniel Stone.

Lydia, 1643, married Samuel Wright and James Cutler.

Jacob, 1645, married Elizabeth Loker.

JOSEPH, 1647, married LYDIA AXTELL. (raised *Maynard)*

Elizabeth, 1649, died young.

Benjamin (Sgt.), 1651, married Dorothy Wright.

Eldest son, John, born in England before his father sailed for America and Sudbury, married Ann, John Smith's[1] daughter, and that year, 1654, became a Lancaster landowner. Lancaster was a new grant out on the edge of civilization and was on the site of Nashua, the home of Sholan, the sachem, who invited the Englishmen to his valley. And it was peaceful for twenty-one years.

The Indians started harassing Lancaster in September, 1676, and, by the spring that also saw Sudbury brutally attacked, had planned a final blow for the little settlement:

"About the 10th of February, after some hundreds of the Indians, whether Nipnets or Nashaway men is uncertain, belonging to him they call Sagamore Sam, fell upon Lancaster, a small village, of about fifty or sixty families, and did much mischief, burning most of the houses that were not garrisoned. And which is most sad and awful to consider, the house of Mr. Rowlandson, minister...which was garrisoned with a competent number of the inhabitants: yet the fortifications of the house being on the back side closed up with fire wood, the Indians got so near as to fire a leanter, which burning the hous immediately to the ground, all the persons therein were put to the hard choice, either to perish by the flames, with the house, or to yield themselves into the hands of those cruel savages, which last (considering that a living dog is better than a dead lion) they chose, and so were forty-two persons surprised by the Indians, above twenty of the women and children they carried away captive, a rueful spectacle to behold; the rest being men, they killed in the place, or reserved for further misery: And many that were not slain in fighting, were killed in attempting to escape."

Two who died were a Fairbanks father and his son. Captain Gookin wrote about the rescue attempt:

"Upon the report of this disaster, Capt. Wadsworth, then at Marlborough, with about forty resolute men, adventuring the rescuing of the town that was remaining: And having recovered a bridge, they got over safe, though the planks were pulled off by the

[1] John Smith was also a first proprietor of Lancaster. A wealthy man, he died in 1669.

300

enemy, and being led up in a way not discovered by them, they forced the Indians for the present to quit the place, after they had burnt and destroyed the better half of it."

The remaining garrisons were crowded with families. Thomas Sawyer's house had almost as many people as Rowlandson's, including "widows & many ffatherlesse children", and Laurence Waters' sheltered John Moore's family and others.

"Lancast'r March 11th 1675/76
Our state is very deplorable in our incapacity to subsist; as to remove away we cannot, the enemy has so encompassed us; otherwise for want of help and cattle, being most of them carried away by the barbarous heathen; and to stay disenabled for want of food...many of us heare in this prison, have not bread to last us on mongth & our other provision spent & gon, for genraliyty our Town is drawn into tow Garisons wherein are by the Good favours of yo'r Hon'rs eighteen soulders, which we gladly mayntayn soe long as any thing lasts, & if yo'r Honors should call them of, we are seartaynly a bayt for the enemy if God do not wonderfully provent...We are sorowful to Leave the place, but hoplesse to keep it...it troubles our sperits to give any Incurigm't to the enemy, or leave any thing for them to promot their wicked designe, yet better save our Lives than lose Life & Estat both, we are in danger emenent, the enemy leying Above us, nay on both sids of us, as dus playingly Apeare, our womens cris dus dayly Increase beand espresion which dus not only fill our ears but our hearts full of Greefe, which makes us humbly Request yo'r Hon'rs to send a Gard of men & that if you please so comand we may have Carts About fourteen will Remove the whool (of us)...

Jacob Ffarrar	Job Whittcomb
John Houghton Sen'r	Jonathon Whittcomb
John Moore	John Houghton Jrn'r
John Whittcomb	Cyprian Steevens"

Troops were sent with the carts and the garrisoned people were scattered to former home towns.

"Then the Indians, who seemed to have been lurking around, came out of their lairs, and set fire to the buildings still standing; and...there was nothing left but smoking and blackened ruins in this lovely valley."

John Moore took his family to Sudbury to live again but not many years passed before he and the old residents went back to Lancaster to rebuild. During 1689 Indian frays again alarmed them.

"Whereas we ye Inhabitants of sd Lancaster being under som fears of being surprissed by the Indians we being by foremer experience sencsible of their mallice and crueltie...doe mutually Nominate Mr. Thomas Wilder for a Leauten't and sergeant John Moore to be ensigne..."

John Moore was Selectman with his son John, a deputy, and sometimes delegate, to the General Court. He once wrote of "My new dwelling house Wataquadock", where his sons John and Jonathan lived until they were ol Some say it was a garrison house. Ann Smith Moore died in 1671 at th birth of their daughter, Maria. "Ensigne John Moore, late of Lancaster...yeoman died in 1702. His estate was divided into six equal parts, the eldest son John, to have a double share.

Mary, born 1655, married MATTHEW GIBBS.

ELIZABETH, 1657, married MATTHEW GIBBS.

Lydia, 1660, married — Witherby

John, 1662, married Mary Whitcomb and Hasadiah Fairbank. One c
    his sons was named Fairbank Moore.

Joseph, 1664.

Ann, married — Hildrick

Jonathan, 1669.

Maria, 1671.

The first John Moore and his wife Elizabeth Whale had a fourth son Joseph, who like his brother John, was also an ancestor of Socrates Bacon. I stead of moving to Lancaster like brother John Jr., he lived all his life i Sudbury. It was during the most dreadful time in its history. King Philip War was especially destructive to that settlement. Joseph's home was th "dwelling house...with all the pasture lands aboutt it" inherited from his father. H married Lydia Axtell, called Maynard in all the records. her father, Thoma Axtell, died when she and her twin were very young. Her mother, Mary Ric Axtell, then married a close neighbor, John Maynard. Other clos neighbors were Mary's father, Edmond Rice, and the Moores.

Joseph and Lydia's children were:

Benoni, born 1669.

JOSEPH, 1670.

Hannah, 1673, married Joseph Gleason.

Thomas, 1676.

Mary, 1681.

John, 1683.

Elizabeth, 1685, married Henry Rice.

Lydia, 1687.

Obadiah.

Their son Joseph, Jr., married and had four children:

Sapphira, 1710, married John Woodward.

ZEBIAH, 1704, married BENJAMIN STOW.

Eliab, married Susann Thompson, and/or Keziah Stone, fifth genera

302

tion from Deacon Gregory Stone.
Mary.

Brigham Young's mother was a descendant of John Moore and Elizabeth Whale, his father descended from Thomas Axtell, and his wife from our Gibbs family.

Sources:

Holman, Ancestry of Col. John H. Stevens
Seaver, Moore Family History
Hudson, A.S., History of Sudbury
Cutter, Historical Homes and Families of Middlesex Co. Mass.
Powell, S.C., A Puritan Village
Virkus, F.A., Compendium of Amer. Genealogy
Kathan, History of Capt. John Kathan
Annals of Lancaster
Barry, W., History of Framingham
Hudson, A.S., Annals of Sudbury
Marvin, History of Lancaster
Lancaster Vital Records.
New England Historical and Genealogical Register
Vital Records of Sudbury

AXTELL FAMILY

In the records of St. Peter's Church, Berkhamstead, Hertfordshire, England, are written the important dates in the life of William Axtell, his wife Tomasine, his sons John, Thomas, William, Daniel and Samuel, and his daughter Sarah. There were other children mentioned in the will of one of them, Nathaniel, written as he waited to sail for New England.

Daniel, William's fourth son, was born in 1622 and enlisted in the army of Parliament. Col. Daniel Axtell was in command of the guard under Oliver Cormwell sent to preserve order and "repress violence" during the trial that resulted in the beheading of King Charles I. Four years later Col. Axtell was arrested as the troop of horse he'd joined to oppose the re-establishment of the monarchy disolved due to lack of support from the people. He was put on trial for treason.

One charge against him was his supposed "wanton and barbarous cruelties upon the Irish people" when he was sent to Ireland to subdue the rebels, even though he was one of the officers who resigned in protest against the parlimentary governor's harsh treatment of those islanders.

> "he defended himself with great skill and persistence, quoting from the statutes...The Chief Justice complimented him on his manifest diligence in the study of law, but...overruled his plea..."

Col. David, Lord Axtell, was executed at Tyburn, in 1660. He prayed, at the request of Francis Hacker who was to be executed with him, for both of them:

> "One portion of the prayer...filled with earnest pleadings for the people standing near, to the City of London, for the magistrates and hangman and for the Chief Magistrate...offered while he stood in the handman's cart with a rope around his neck...After...no one was found to put forward the horse, the cartman saying, 'I would lose both the cart and the horse before I would have a hand in hanging such a man.' "

But it was his brother who emmigrated to New England, Thomas, who married Mary Rice in 1638, the year before her father, Edmund Rice, and others from the village left for New England. When Thomas and Mary sailed five years later, they had two children. They bought land from Edmund Rice next to the Rice house and lived there almost three years before Thomas died. Edmund bought back the land. Mary wed neighbor John Maynard.

Thomas Axtell and Mary Rice had:

305

see *Corrections,* page 337

Mary, baptised 1639, died young.

Henry, 1641, married Hannah Merriam and lived in Marlboro, killed in the 1676 Indian up-rising. He was likely named for his grandfather's brother who died shortly before his birth.

LYDIA, 1644, married JOSEPH MOORE, her next door neighbor. His father bought the Rice house in 1655.

Mary, Lydia's twin, married John Goodnow, had eleven children.

Mary Rice Axtell and John Maynard had:

Zachary, 1647

Elizabeth.

Hannah, 1648.

Mary, married Daniel Hudson.

Sources:

Axtell, Axtell Genealogy

Hudson, A.S., History of Sudbury

Pope, Pioneers

Virkus, F.A., Compendium of American Genealogy

Vital Records of Sudbury

N.E. Historical and Genealogical Register

Holman, Ancestry of Col. John H. Stevens

Mass. Bay Court Records, petitions of Oct. 5, 1669

RICE FAMILY

Edmund Rice was one of the group who came to Sudbury early in 1639 from Barkhamstead,* Hertfortshire, England. Several genealogists present the following as the Rice family line.

Coel Codevog, King of the Britons. His daughter Helena was the mother of Constantine the Great, 272-337.

Fifth in descent from Coel Codevog is Uryan Reged, Prince of North Briton in the sixth century, expelled by the Saxons and fled to Wales where he was Prince of Reged, Lord of Kidwelly, Carunllou and Iskennen. He married Margaret La Faye, daughter of Gerolus (Gorlois), Duke of Cornwall.

The next nine generations were each Lord of Kidwelly: Pasgen, Morr, Llarch, Rhyne, Cecilt (Cecil), Gurwared, Kynbathwye, Lloarch, Eynion and Gronwey. The decent continues:

Rice, Lord of Iskennen, married Margaret, daughter of Griffith of Kiddz, Lord of Gwynvay (Cwynav).

Elider ap Rice of Iskennen, married Gladis, daughter of Phillip, son of Bah, son of Gwath Voed, Lord of Efginwriath.

Sir Elider Ddy (Dhu), Knight of the Sepulchre, married Cicely, daughter of Siscilte ap Hyn, son of Morithigne, Lord of Cantresclife.

Phillip ap Elider Fitz Uryan, married Gladis, daughter of David Uras.

Nicholas ap Phillip Fitz Uryan, married Joan, daughter of Griffith ap Llewellin Voythes.

Griffith ap Nicholas Fitz Uryan, married first, Mabel, daughter of Meredith ap Henry Dune of Kidwelly, Wales. Griffith was a Yorkist slain at Wakefield.

Thomas ap Griffith Fitz Uryan, married first, Elizabeth, daughter of Sir John Griffith, of Abermarlais, North Wales, a descendant of Howell ap Griffith, Lord of Kansadorne, a great great grandson of Yerworth, Lord of Krickheath.

Sir Rice (Rhys) ap Thomas Fitz Uryan of Elmalin, Carmarthenshire, Wales. Married first, Eva, daughter of Henry ap Gwilliam. Sir Rice went with a considerable number of choice soldiers to King Henry VII (the Earl of Richmond) on his landing at Milford Haven with a small force in 1485. They marched to the battle of Bosworth Field. He was make a Knight of the Garter and was Captain of the Light Horse at the battle of Therouenne and the siege of Tournay. "...never more than a knight, yet little less than a Prince in his native country."[1]

Sir Griffith Rice, married Katherine, daughter of Sir John St. John. Sir

see *Corrections*, page 337

309

Griffith was made a knight of the Bath at the wedding of Arthur, Prince of Wales, in 1501.

Sir Rice Griffith (Fitz Uryan), born circa 1500, married Lady Katherine Howard. He was beheaded in public ceremony on Tower Hill Jan. 4, 1531/2 during the reign of Henry VIII for a political offense. Lady Katherine's line is the same described on page 209 from Egbert through Alfred the Great to generation 19, Ethelred, the Unready. It then follows his son Edmund Ironside who married Algitha, daughter of Segefrith the Dane, through their son Edward the Atheling, generation 21(Ad), to Henry II of England, generation 25 (Ad) and includes William the Conqueror. It continues from Henry II to his son:

John, King of England, born December 24, 1167, married secondly, Isabel, daughter of Aymer de Taillifer, Count d'Angouleme, and Lady Alice de Courteney, great great granddaughter of Henry I, King of France, and Anne, of Russia.

Henry III, King of England, born October 1, 1207, married Eleanor daughter of Raymond Berenger IV, Count of Provence (descendant of Sancho III, the Great, King of Castile, Bavarre and Aragon), and Beatrix daughter of Thomas, Count of Savoy, great grandson of Humbert II Count of Maurienne.

Edward I, King of England, born 1239, married secondly, Margaret daughter of Philip III (Philip the Hardy), King of France, (descendant of Robert the Strong of France) and Mary, daughter of Henry III, Duke of Brabant, descendant of Emperor Charlemagne.

[1] Fuller, *Worthies*

Thomas Plantagenet, Earl of Norfolk, Earl Marshal of England, married first, Alice, daughter of Sir Roger de Hales, coroner of Norfolk.

Margaret Plantagenet, Duches of Norfolk, born circa 1320, maried first John, third Lord Segrave.

Elizabeth de Segrave, married John de Mowbray, crusader, killed fighting the Turks in Thrace, 1368. His mother was Joan, daughter of Henry Plantagenet, third Earl of Lancaster, grandson of Henry III of England. Lord Mowbray's father was son of the Sheriff of Yorkshire and Governor of the city of York and was hanged there after the battle of Boroughbridge in 1321.

Thomas de Mowbray, Duke of Norfolk, Earl of Nottingham, Earl Marshal of England, married secondly, Elizabeth, daughter of Richard Fitz Alan, tenth Earl of Arundel (descendant of Henry I of France and Anne of

Russia), and first wife, Elizabeth, daughter of William de Bohun, Earl of Northampton, (descendant of Henry I of France and Anne of Russia), and Elizabeth, daughter of Edward I, King of England, and Princess Eleanor of Castile. Thomas Mowbray died of plague in Venice, 1399, after Richard II banished him "for a hundred wynter."

Margaret Mowbray married Sir Robert Howard of Stoke Neyland, Suffolk, son of Sir John Howard and second wife, Alice, daughter of Sir William Tendring of Tendring, Norfolk.

Sir John Howard, Duke of Norfolk, Earl Marshal of England, married first, Catherine, daughter of Sir William de Moleyns. Howard was an eminent Yorkist, held several offices of trust under Edward IV and Richard III, was killed support Richard at the battle of Bosworth Field, 1485.

Thomas Howard, second Duke of Norfolk, Earl Marshal of England, Earl of Surrey, married secondly, Agnes, daughter of Hugh Tilney of Skirbeck and Boston, Lincolnshire. Howard was taken prisoner at the battle of Bosworth and imprisoned three years in the Tower. He was the victor at Flodden Field in 1514.

Lady Katharine Howard, who married the soon-to-be beheaded Sir Rice ap Griffith (Fitz Uryan), as mentioned on page 244. Their two lines come together here in their son:

William Rice, of Boemar, Buckinghamshire, England, born 1522. Granted armes in 1555 by Queen Mary.

Thomas Rice, born about 1555.

Edmund Rice, born in Buckinghamshire, England, about 1594, was twin to Robert who came to New England in 1631.

Edmund married Thomasine Frost in 1618, the daughter of Edward Frost, clothier, of Stanstead, Co. Suffolk, and nine children were born to them before they sailed for Sudbury in 1638. The eldest, Mary, sailed later as the wife of Thomas Axtell. In New England, "with Rice and Maynard to lead the way, they shouldered their packs and followed the Indian trail to a spot on the river that runs to Concorde." and "found homes for the group who surreptitiously embarked...from England."

When the Sudbury meadows were divided, Edmund's land was on the east side of the Sudbury River. Today that is Old North Street in what is called Wayland. Next to his lot was his son Henry's and next to that John Maynard built a house. Edmund bought land from Henry Dunster, the first president of Harvard (and once a companion of John Milton. in England), nd land near Lake Cochituate and land from Philemon Whale next to the place his daughter used to live with Thomas Axtell. There he started to build while he collected more land "for his sons."

311

The Rice homestead stood for a very long time and a picture of it shows an Elizabethan frame house one and a half stories high. It likely was the end result of years of adding on to the small house Philemon Whale built there first.

Edmund then had a house built on the property he'd bought from Dunster. It was to be,

> "...thirty foote long, ten foote high stud, one foote sill from the ground, sixteen foote wide, all the doores well-hanged, and staires, with convinient fastenings of lock or bolts, windows, glases, and well planked under foote, and boarded sufficiently to lay corne in, in the story above head...the barne...fifty foote long, eleven foote high in the stud, one foote above ground, the sill twenty foote, of no leantes or eighteen foote with leantes on the one side, and a convenient threshing floare between the doares."

Edmund took the freeman's oath in 1640, was appointed magistrate to hear small cases and peform marriages (which was a civil ceremony), "lay out" the town's lands, and was many years a Selectman. 1648 saw him become a Deacon of the church, a position to which only men of "unimpeachable character" were appointed. He was a Deputy to the General Court five times. In 1661, "he was appointed to meet with some of the Nipmuc Indians to negotiage the payment of a debt owed by one *Netus*. The son of Netus, who was a Praying Indian, had attended a school kept in Cambridge...Being unable to pay the bill of seve pounds ten shillings for tuition, the tribe agreed to let Netus make a payment in land." H and John Maynard, now his daughter Mary's husband, were fence viewers "chosen to judge the sufficiency of the fences about men's particular properties in case of damage and difference..."

Edmund Rice and John Maynard were two of the thirteen petitioners who asked the General Court for a new plantation in 1656.

> "Whereas your petitioners have lived divers years in Sudbury, and God hath been pleased to increase our children, which are now, divers of them, grown to man's estate, and wee, many of us grown into years, so as that wee should bee glad to see them settled before the Lord take us away from hence; as also God having given us some considerable quantity of cattle, so that wee are so straightened, that wee cannot so comfortably subsist as could be desired; and some of us having taken some pains to view the country, wee have found a place, which lieth Westward about eight miles from Sudbury, which wee conceive might bee comfortable..."

Edmund moved to the new plantation they called Marlborough Tomasine died two years earlier and so it was his second wife, mercy, widow of Thomas Brigham, that helped him raise the rest of his family. He lived i Marlborough until his death in 1663.

Edmund and Tomasine's children:

MARY, baptised 1619, married THOMAS AXTELL and John
Maynard.
Henry, 1621, married Elizabeth Moore, John Moore's daughter. He
was killed in King Philip's raid in 1676.
Edward, 1622, married Agnes Bent and Anna —.
Thomas, 1626, married Mary King.
Lydia, 1628, married Martha Lamson.
Daniel, 1632, died within a few days.
Samuel, 1634, married Elizabeth King.
Joseph, 1638, born on the voyage to America, married Mercy King.
Benjamin, 1640, married Mary Brown and Mary Chamberlain. Daniel
Pond once told that in 1675, "Benjamin Rice came to my house with his
feet frozen...Dr. Avery's son cut off one foot at the lowest joint, and staunched the
blood with a musquash skin."
Edmund, 1653, married Joyce Russell, may have died in Philip's raid.
Edmund Sr., and Mercy's children:
Ruth, 1659, married Samuel Wells.
Ann, 1661, married Nathaniel Gary (Gerry).
Edmund's granddaughter, Abigail Rice Smith, was great grandmother
(paternally) of Abigail Smith, the wife of John Adams and mother of John
Quincy Adams, sixth generation from Deacon Edmund Rice. The descent
of the Fowle family to Abigail Smith is through her mother.

Sources:

The American Genealogist Vol. 9-10, 15-16
Rathbone, William Rice and Wealthy Cottrell
Smith, E.H., More About Those Rices
Smith, E.H., Edmund Rice and His Family
Ward, Rice Family
Cutter, Historical Homes and Families of Middlesex
Rice, C.S., We Sought the Wilderness
Rice, C.E., By The Name of Rice

see Corrections, page 337

GIBBS FAMILY

Long before the conquest of England, the Gibbs family lived across the channel in Normandy. They probably came to England in the Norman Conqueror's time.

The first Gibbs to emigrate to New England was Matthew. He lived in Charlestown by 1650 but moved to Sudbury out on the frontier, joining the Moores, Rices, and Axtells, who settled it early, about 1637. "...it was proposed that a company proceed westerly, and settle at what is now Sudbury..." The land was tempting because a large stream ran through it "with abundance of fresh water marsh...also it hath a store of plow-land." The territory was divided, to the amazement of many men who had never had so much, and common fields were designated where men who worked together were safer. Then they built small, plain houses, for material was extremely difficult to carry over the Indian's Old Bay Path meandering this way. It is doubtful that anyone had a cart, but highways were laid out to Thomas Reed's saw mill and Thomas Cakebread's corn mill where, on the mill pond, Philemon Whale built this house. By spring, 1639,

"Ordered by the commissioners of the town, that every inhabitant shall come forth to the mending of the highway or forfeit 5 shillings...The poorest man shall work one day. For every 6 acres of meadow land a man hath he shall work one day."

Matthew was newly married to Mary, daughter of Robert and Mary Bradish of Cambridge whose house lot in that town had just been purchased by Harvard College.[1] Young Mary joined the Charlestown church before the couple moved.

Gradually, Matthew became a large land owner, buying Sudbury land from Thomas Reed and Rev. Edmund Brown, (Thomas Reed and*Mary Reed Bacon's uncle). He served on town committees and was one of the residents who arranged to receive "the public stock of ammunition into their hands", stores put to desparate use in King Philip's raids on Sudbury in 1675 and 76.

Sudbury had been left alone by the Indians until then. Matthew Gibbs, Jr., was among nine men impressed to defend towns closer to the Bay but Sudbury asked to have them released "considering our condition as a frontier town and several of our men already being in the service...and very much scattered." Rev. Edmund Browne wrote,

[1] Item in the Harvard inventory of 1654, "A small piece of land lying before the Colledge & formerly the houselott of Rob't Bradish .

315

see *Corrections*, page 337

"It is reported that our woods are pestered with Indians. One Adams within our bounds was shot at by a lurking Indian or more. He was shot through the coat and shirt near to the arm-pit...One Smith walking the woods was assailed by 3 or 4 Indians, whom he discovered swooping down a hill toward him, but Smith saved himself by his legs...One Joseph Curtis...rode for it..."

When the attack came it was from "mostly invaders—not parties who had ever had claim to the soil...as a general thing the whites and Indians lived on friendly terms." "Mischief was done and several lives cut off by the Indians" on that day, March 10, 1676. On the 27th, a band of three hundred, led by Netus, the Nipmuck captain, again advanced on the town, taking people and goods that were found outside the block-houses but they were suddenly surprised by armed townspeople and forced to retreat. Netus was killed. They waited another month until King Philip arrived to lead them into Sudbury. The great Captain Daniel Gookin stated,

"...upon the 21st of April about mid-day tidings came by many messengers that a great body of the enemy not less as was judged than fifteen hundred, for the enemy to make their force seem very large there were many women among them whom they had fitted with pieces of wood cut in the forms of guns, which these carried, and were placed in the centre..."

"The strength of Our towne upon ye Enemey's approaching it consisted of Eighty fighting men."

Help was sent from Concord, Watertown and Boston. From Chelmsford, Corporal Phipps' troop and Captain Hunting's company of forty Indians were on their way. All the twelve Concord men were killed in a meadow before they reached the garrisoned Sudbury people. The other troops joined the fight but twenty-nine of the fifty Watertown men eventually lost their lives, some in a forest fire Philip set to drive out Captain Wadsworth's well-placed English forces, some as they raced from the fire to Hop Brook Mill a half mile away. It was running a gantlet and turned into a slaughter. The few men who reached the mill were safe but the several who were captured were "cruelly tortured" that night.

Richard Jacobs wrote the next day,

"This morning, about sun two hours high, ye enemy alarmed us by firing and shouting toward ye government garrison house...they came in great numbers on Indian Hill, and, as their accustomed manner is after a fight, began to signify to us how many were slain; they whooped seventy-four times, which we hope was only to affright us, seeing we have had no intelligence of any such thing, yet we have reason to fear the worst...After burying the bodies of the Concord men at the bridge's foot, we joined

316

ourselves to Capt. Hunting (with his Christian Indians who had arrived during the night) and as many others as we could procure, and went over the river to look for Capt. Wadsworth and Capt. Brooklebank, and we gathered them up and burried them.''

Earlier that morning these Christian Indians,

"having stripped themselves and painted their faces...went to make discovery of the enemy...and if they had met with them to beat up their quarters...But God had so ordered that the enemy were all withdrawn...''

The men of Sudbury, "Mathew Gibs, Joseph Moore", and others, wrote,

"Many Observables worthy of Record hapened in this assault, vizt: that noe man or woman seemed to be possessed with feare; Our Garisonmen kept not within their Garrisons, but issued forth to fight ye Enemy in their skulking approaches:...The Enemy was by (a) few beaten out of houses which they had entered & were plundering, And by a few hands were forced to a running fight which way they could...was there with us any towne so beset since ye warr began...''

It wasn't over. Matthew was impressed for Captain Davenport's company, the same company John Bacon belonged to, to fight the freezing, bloody Swamp Fight the next winter. A decade later, the French and Indian War involved the Sudbury men again, in "dreadful service".

Matthew and Mary's children were,

MATTHEW, married in 1678 Mary Moore, who died the next year, and ELIZABETH MOORE, both daughters of John Moore.

Mary, 1652, married John Goodrich and Thomas Frost, Jr.

Hannah, 1654, married Samuel Winch.

Thomas, 1656, died young.

Elizabeth, 1658, married John Russell.

Thomas, 1660.

John, married Anna Gleason and Sarah Cutler.

Matthew, Jr., and his wife, Elizabeth Moore, lived in Framingham before 1719. They may not have moved from Sudbury. Framingham territory was taken from Sudbury's land and Matthew owned "Rattlesnake Meadow" which he described as between Sudbury and Framingham. So only the boundry lines may have changed.

Their children were,

MATTHEW, 1680, married SARAH PAGE in Framingham.

John, 1682, moved to the "Island of Bermudas".

Samuel, 1685.

Joseph, 1687.

Jonathan.

Josiah.

The third Matthew Gibbs married Sarah Page, the sister, probably, of the town physician, John Page, and descended, (again, probably) from John Page who came to New England on the *Jewel* in that first fleet of 1630. "A company of about 100 persons, of whom John Page was a member, purchased the entire peninsula...now occupied by the city of Boston...for a sum equalling about $150. They became the first real settlers..." He was born at Middle Temple in London and died at about ninety years old. John Page's wife, Phoebe Paine, lived to eighty-seven.

Matthew and Sarah had these children,

Sarah, born 1708, died young.

Sarah, 1710, married JOHN JONES, JR. She died young.

ELIZABETH, 1717, married JOHN JONES, JR.

Phinehas, died unmarried.

Hezekiah, 1715, married Elizabeth Pratt.

Matthew, 1720, died unmarried.

Jonathan, Capt., 1723, married Mary Winchester.

Micah, 1727, married Elizabeth Hobbs.

Sources:

Gibbs, G., Gibbs Family of Rhode Island

Temple, J.H., History of Framingham

Burr, History of Framingham

Jones, M.E. and N.D., Jones Ancestry

Hudson, A.S., History of Sudbury

Wyman, T.B., Genealogies of Charlestown

Sudbury Vital Records

Abstracts of Early Wills, 1855

Colonial Society of Massachusetts Collections

Boston Transcripts

Hudson, A.S., Annals of Sudbury

Soldiers in King Philip's War

Powell, S.C., Puritan Village

Peirson, C.L., Page Descent

JONES FAMILY

The Jones name is Welsh but Hugh Jones, born about 1635, came to New England from Wincanton, a small parish in Somersetshire, England. He was fifteen years old when he sailed "on Mr Strattons ship" as an apprentice to Robert Gutch. They settled in Salem where by law he was taught to read along with the master's children, and instructed in other matters. "Young Persons wont much...regard good laws made by Civil Authority is they are not well counsel'd and govern'd at home."

Hugh received a homestead grant from Salem of three acres "near the brook running down to the mill" at about the same time he married Hannah Tompkins in 1661. She was granddaughter to Ralph Tompkins who arrived in New England on the *Truelove* in 1635. "Hugh Jones, planter" later sold this firs property and purchased five acres in the North Neck from a former master Thomas Gardner.

"Mar. 1671 Serg't Nathaniel ffelton & Hugh Jones are Appointed Survey'rs of the ffences belonging to the Northfeild and of all the ffences from strong Watter brooke to Sam'll Ebbornes Sen'r..."

"Mar. 1678— imprimis, that ye generall fences belonging to ea. proprietor shal be suficiently made upp by ye 30th day of this instant month upon ye penaltie of 12s p diem...Hugh Johnes is hereby appinted & Impowered to aske, demand, sue for Levy & recover all ye fines & penalties.'"

He took the oath of allegiance in Salem October 2, 1678. The General Court ordered this measure be taken by "every male inhabitant 16 years of age and upward" because of the political conditions prevalent in England. This same year, a disturbing note appeared in the record:

"Nov 1678: The complaint of John Roudin, Mary Rowdin and Danell Rolle: that Hue Joanes came to his house one Sabbeth day morning last Indian harvest and demanded a pair of fetters. He told him that it was not a day to come for fetters. Then Jones called deponent and his wife vile names. Isack Read and Joane Read testified that Rowden strick Joans..."

And, most interestingly, the following was recorded during the Salem witch trials in 1692 after Hugh Jones' death four years before (which must have been a mysterious one). Elizabeth Booth testified in front of Judges Danforth, Sewell, Addington, Hawthorne, Corwin and Samuel Appleton that on the eighth of June,

> "...the uneasy ghosts of four murdered persons appeared to her and the spectre of Hugh Jones assured her that Mrs. Elizabeth Proctor killed him because he had a poght of syder of her which he had not paid her for."

Elizabeth Proctor said to her accuser, "There is another judgement, my child and was sentenced to hang along with her husband even though half t town signed a petition declaring, "as to what we have ever seen or heard of them, up our conscience we judge them innocent of the crime objected." Goodwife Proctor w not hung with the others condemed, she was expecting a child and was lat reprieved. Salem was not alone in its hysteria, *witch crazes* were occuring various parts of Europe.

Hugh's wife, Hannah, died in 1672 after the birth of their eighth chil Hugh married Mary Foster, Hannah's cousin, and seven more childr were born. After Hugh's death, Mary moved most of the family to Wobu where two sons-in-law gave bond ensuring against any expense to the tov for the Jones family. No doubt Mary and the children were staying with t married daughters and were well provided for, but every town took simul precautions against the possibility of any new resident becoming a burde

Hugh and Hannah's children were:

Hannah, born 1661, died Oct. 1, 1662.
Sarah, Born 1662, died Oct. 12, 1662.
Sarah, 1663, died soon.
Elizabeth, 1664.
Mary, 1666, married John Pudney of Salem.
JOHN, 1667, married MARY KNOWLTON.
Deborah, 1670.
Samuel, 1672.

Children born to Mary:

Rebecca, 1673, married William Butters of Woburn.
Abigail, 1675, married Samuel Snow of Woburn.
Hannah, 1677.
Rachel, 1679, married Daniel Snow of Woburn.
Sarah, 1681, married Abraham Jaquith of Woburn.
Hugh, 1683.
Lydia, 1685.

Rachel, Sarah and Hugh were all baptised June 8, 1689, in the fir church of Salem with several young Tompkins cousins.

A nineteenth century historian wrote of Hugh Jones,

> "It is evident that he had a hard struggle in life rearing his large family, but he left a race of hardy descendants who have been noted as farmers and blacksmiths, con-

322

spicuous for their vigor and long lives.''

Son John grew up in Salem, served in Sir William Phipps' unsuccessful expedition against Quebec in 1690 and in 1696 married Mary Knowlton of Reading, Massachusetts. Very little is known about Mary Knowlton. There is no record of who her father was although there were seven Knowlton cousins raising young families at the time Mary would have been a child. She was living in REading in 1689 when a baby, called Benony, was born to her. The town records name no father and there are no other Knowltons in Reading. Likely, she was working for a family there, no one person ever lived alone in the Massachusetts Bay Colony. It was seven years later that she and John Jones married.

They had a baby boy, John, who died soon. Then when John Jones was thirty-five years old, they moved to Framingham, another new plantation out on the frontier, and bought forty acres just east of the Hemenway place. A second son named John was born and Mary joined the Framingham church.

John Jones, Jr. born in 1709, inherited his father's farm and lived there until he died in 1778. He and Samuel Fairbanks were members of Col. Joseph Buckminster's company of Framingham militia in the spring of 1757 when New England regiments were called to duty following news of the seige of Fort William Henry on Lake George.

Long before that, John had married Sarah Gibbs whose family was part of Framingham. Sarah died very soon and John married her sister Elizabeth (See Gibbs Family, page 249.) His children were all by his second wife:

SARAH, born 1739, died at ninety-two, married NATHANIEL STOW. '

Elizabeth, born 1741, died at ninety-two, married Silas Winch.

Mary, 1744, married Isaiah Fairbanks.

Samuel, 1746, married Mary Gates.

John, 1751, Minute Man, fought at Bunker Hill under Captain Jesse Eames. Married Mary Belknap and Margaret Trowbridge.

Daniel, 1755, inherited the homestead, Minute Man in Jesse Eames company, married Lucy Eames and Mary Drum.

Sources:

Temple, J.H., History of Framingham
Stearns, E.S., Genealogical and Family History of N.H.
Bartlett, J.G., Hugh Jones of Salem, Mass.

see *Corrections*, page 337

Perley, S., History of Salem.
Clark, M.B., Jones Genealogy
Tuttle, Hugh Jones of Salem, Mass. and His Descendants
Morgan, E.S., The Puritan Family
Salem Vital Records
New England Historical and Genealogical Register
Salem Records and Files of the Quarterly Court
Reading Vital Records

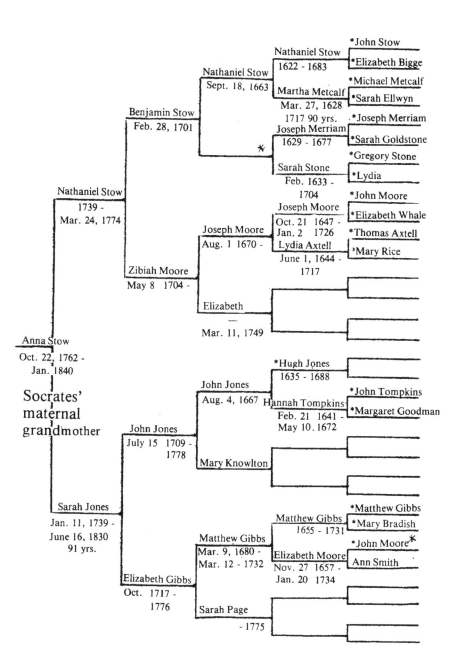

Anna Stow
Oct. 22, 1762 -
Jan. 1840

Socrates'
maternal
grandmother

Nathaniel Stow
1739 -
Mar. 24, 1774

Benjamin Stow
Feb. 28, 1701

Nathaniel Stow
Sept. 18, 1663

Nathaniel Stow
1622 - 1683

*John Stow

*Elizabeth Bigge

Martha Metcalf
Mar. 27, 1628
1717 90 yrs.

*Michael Metcalf

*Sarah Ellwyn

✱

Joseph Merriam
1629 - 1677

. *Joseph Merriam

*Sarah Goldstone

Sarah Stone
Feb. 1633 -
1704

*Gregory Stone

*Lydia

Zibiah Moore
May 8   1704 -

Joseph Moore
Aug. 1 1670 -

Joseph Moore
Oct. 21 1647 -
Jan. 2   1726

*John Moore

*Elizabeth Whale

Lydia Axtell
June 1, 1644 -
1717

*Thomas Axtell

'Mary Rice

Elizabeth
—
Mar. 11, 1749

Sarah Jones
Jan. 11, 1739 -
June 16, 1830
91 yrs.

John Jones
July 15 1709 -
1778

John Jones
Aug. 4, 1667

*Hugh Jones
1635 - 1688

Hannah Tompkins
Feb. 21 1641 -
May 10. 1672

*John Tompkins

*Margaret Goodman

Mary Knowlton

Elizabeth Gibbs
Oct. 1717 -
1776

Matthew Gibbs
Mar. 9, 1680 -
Mar. 12 - 1732

Matthew Gibbs
1655 - 1731

*Matthew Gibbs

*Mary Bradish

Elizabeth Moore
Nov. 27 1657 -
Jan. 20 1734

*John Moore ✱

Ann Smith

Sarah Page
- 1775

see *Corrections*, page 337

KNOWLTON FAMILY

"Knowlton Parish and Knowlton Hall still designate a Manor and Baronial Residence in Kent County..In the fifteenth year of the Conqueror, the estate...passed by Knight's service to Perot...In the thirty-third year of Edward I, Perot assumed the title of Lord Knollton...He left the estate to his daughter who married William de Langley, High Sheriff under Edward III (1327-1377). Their son was William Knollton, Esq. His son, John, came into possession in 1505 and married Dorothy, daughter of Sir John Tyndal, Governor of the Tower of London...Their grandson and heir was Thomas...To 1728, the Knowltons...appeared only in Kent County and somewhat in Middlesex."

Richard Knowlton of Kent, born in 1553, married Elizabeth Cantize and was the father of four sons. The eldest, George, was a contributor in 1624 to a fund for repairing the parish church at Chiswick, which Cromwell's troops had desecrated, converting it into a barrack and stable for his men and their horses during Henry VIII's destruction of monasteries, shrines and churches. The youngest, William, emigrated to Massachusetts as captain of his own ship in 1632.

With Captain William Knowlton was his wife, Ann Smith, and his four young sons. Tragically, he died off the coast of Nova Scotia and his body was buried ashore. His widow sold the ship and friends arranged passage to Hingham in the Bay Colony. Ann and her son Samuel, a mariner, decided to make their home in Hingham but when they were grown the others moved to Ipswich where John became a shoemaker, William a bricklayer, and Deacon Thomas a coordwainer.[1] When William died, Deacon Thomas raised his seven children, "ye youngest about 1 yr & ½ old...till shee Maried". He also raised one of John's sons. He had no children of his own. Many of this next generation seemed from the many court records, a quarrelsome, mischievous, gossipy and rather Devil-may-care lot. Not necessarily Mary, who married John Jones, granddaughter of either William or John, who doesn't seem to have ever gone to court.

Sources:

Hammet Papers, Early Inhabitants, Ipswich, Mass.
Woodward, Genealogy of the Knowlton Family
Stocking, History and Genealogy of the Knowltons of England and
Caldwell, Ipswich Antiquarian Papers
New England Genealogical and Historical Register

327

TOMPKINS FAMILY

Ralph Tompkins, from a musical family (two Tompkins were organists at Kings College, Cambridge), was fifty years old when he "imbarqued in the *Truelove*, Jo: Gibbs, Mr (Master) 19 Sept. 1635" from London for "New ingLand". With him was Katherine, his wife, and three of their children, Elizabeth, Martha and Samuel. Their home had been Buckinghamshire where son John hesitated before he sailed for a new home in Salem. His family joined him there after first living in Dorchester for nine or ten years. His father had become a freeman in Dorchester in 1638. Now in Salem, Ralph Tompkins was granted a "small piece of meadow lying in a corner by a small brook and a great swamp."

When Katherine (Aborne) Foster Tompkins died (she had been a widow when she married Ralph Tompkins) her husband married again, another Aborne. Samuel, brother of Tompkins' deceased second wife, testified,

"...that at her burial as soon as the company had departed, he went in to said Ralph, who was weak and not likely long to survive...to put him in mind of making his will...did heare him sevreall times say that itt was his will yt Mary ffoster should have his Kow and all his household goods...in regard whe Had ben such a good nurs unto him, for said Hee, she has don more for mee and my poore wife than anybody else would have don."

Mary was the child of Ralph Tompkin's daughter Martha and became Hugh Jones' second wife. Ralph and Katherine's children were:

JOHN, born about 1610, married MARGARET GOODMAN and Mary Reed.

Samuel, circa 1613, married Lettice Handford Foster. In her first marriage she had been married by Captain Miles Standish in Plymouth.

Elizabeth, 1617.

Martha, 1621, married John Foster. (The *Truelove's* passenger list incorrectly calls her Mary.)

John Tompkins, "yeoman," married in Edlesborough, Buckinghamshire in 1632, before he left England. When he arrived in Salem he was granted five cares of land at a town meeting in July, 1637. His holdings steadily increased. He was notified in 1661 of one grant of twenty acres and was promised he could "have it layd out if he can tell where to find it."

John was admitted a freeman in May, 1642, with his son, John, Jr., served on juries and committees and was one of the "Survei'rs for fences Northfield", petitioned for a new meeting house and, in 1679, refused to take the oath as tythingman with John Rogers and other neighbors of his. They were fined ten shillings. At about the same time, he and John, Jr. and the Fosters resisted taking the oath of allegiance "to his Majesty". John died in 1681, leaving:

Nathaneil.

HANNAH, baptised 1641, married HUGH JONES.

Sarah, 1643, married John Waters.

John, 1645, "yeoman", married Rebecca Knights and secondly, Mary Reed.

Elizabeth, 1646.

Mary, 1649, married John Felton.

Deborah, 1651, married Nathaniel Silsby.

Priscilla, married Samuel Marsh.

The Taft genealogy claims that President William Howard Taft was descended from John Tompkins.

Sources:

Salem Quarterly Court Records
Town Records of Salem
Salem Vital Records
Ipswich Quarterly Court Records
Records of the First Church in Salem
Plymouth Colony Marriages to 1650
Tompkins, R.A., Tomkin, Tompkins Genealogy
Banks, C.E., Planters of the Commonwealth
Morris, Ancestry of Lydia Foster
Perley, History of Salem

BEATRIX BACON

This line was made a part of the Bacon line several times. First by marriage to Margery Thorpe, page 4, and then through the Dudley family and the Rice family.

This line is recognized by *Colonial Order of the Crown.**

Generation 1.

Childebert, King of Cologne, living in 450, son of Clovis the Riparian, Frankish King of Cologne.

2. Siegbert the Lame, King of Cologne, murdered 509 by own son at the instigation of Clovis I, a kinsman, King of the Salic Franks.

3. Cloderic the Parricide, King of Cologne, murdered 509 by agents of Clovis I. He married a kinswoman of St. Clothide. (These first three generations must be accepted tentatively.)

4. Blithilde, marr. Ansbertus, the Gallo-Roman Senator. His chart reads, gen. 1a Afranius Syagrius, Gallo-Roman Consul, 381.

2a A daughter of Syagrius, marr. Ferreolus.

3a Tonantius Ferreolus, Consul at Rome, 469-475, friend and relative of Sidonois Apollinaris.

4a Tonantius, brother of Ruicius, Bishop of Uzes.

5a Ansbertus, above, marr. Blithilde.

5. Erchenaud, brother of Modericus, Bishop of Arisleum, 578.

6. Leuthanus, marr. Gerberga, daughter of Duke Ricomer.

7. A daughter, marr. Ansoud.

8. Sigrada, mother of Didon, Bishop of Poitiers, 656-670.

9. Count Warinus, died 677, brother of St. Leger, Bishop of Autun, marr. Kunza, sister of Bazin, Bishop of Treves.

10. Leutwinus, St. Lievin, Bishop of Treves, 685-704.

11. Rotrou, marr. Charles Martel, the Hammer, rankish ruler, Mayor of the Palace in Austrasia, victor over the Saracens at Tours, 732 descended from Cloderick, the Parricide, above, through Colderick's son Munderick.

gen. 5. Munderick, of Vitry-en-Perhois, marr. Arthemia, sister of Sacerdos, the Gallo-Roman Archbishop of Lyons. Munderick was killed by Thierry I.

6. Bodegisel, brother of St. Gondulfus, Bishop of Tongres in 599. Marr. Palatina, dau. of Gallus Magnus, Bishop of Troyes, ca. 562.

7. Bodegisel II, marr. Oda, a Suevian. He may have been Governor of

*From *Ancestral Roots of Sixty N. E. Colonists* by Frederick L. Weis.

see *Corrections*, page 337

331

Aquitaine, murdered at Carthage returning to Constantinople, 588.

8. Saint Arnulf, Mayor of the Palace and tutor of Dagobert, Bishop of Metz, 612, marr. Dode (Clothilde) who became a nun at Treves, were parents of St. Clodulf, Bishop of Metz, ca. 650.

9. Duke Ansgise, Mayor of the Palace to Siegbert, marr. St. Begga, dau. of Pepin of Landen, Mayor of the Palace in Austrasia, d. 694, and Itta, dau. of Arnoldus, Bishop of Metz, and niece of St. Modoald, Bishop of Treves, sons, it was said, of Ansbertus.

10. Pepin of Heristal, Mayor of the Palace in Austrasia, d. 714, father of Charles Martel by his concubine, Aupais. Martel marr. Rotrou.

12. Pepin the Short, child of Martel and Rotrou, Mayor of the Palace, first king of the Franks 751-768, marr. Bertha, dau. of Count Canbert of Laon, "a great warrior."

13. Charlemagne, King of France, 768-814, crowned Holy Roman Emperor, marr. Hildegarde, dau. of Count Geroud of Swabia, descended from Godefroy, Duke of Allemania. At the height of Charlemagne's power, the French empire covered what we now call France, Germany, Switzerland, Holland, Belgium and a great part of Italy. "A greater leader in history than ever fiction would have it."

14. Pepin, bapt. at Rome by Pope Adrian I, 781, was King of Italy, and consecreated King of Lombardy.

15. Bernard, King of Italy, 813-817, marr. Cunigunde.

16. Pepin, Count of Senlis, Peronne and St. Quentin.

17. Herbert I de Vermandois, murdered ca. 902, Count of Vermandois Seigneur of Senlis, Peronne and St. Quentin, marr. Bertha de Morvois dau. of Guarri, Count of Morvois, and Eva de Rousillion, dau. of Gerard

18. Herbert II, Count of Vermandois and Troyes, marr. Liegarde, dau of Robert I, Duke of France, Marquis of Neustria, King of the Wes Franks, King of Cologne, and his first wife Adele. Robert I was also descended from Childebert, the head of this chart.

19. Albert I, the Pious, Count de Vermandois, marr. Gerberga of Lorrain dau. of Giselbert, Duke of Lorraine and Gerberga dau. of Henry I, th Fowler, of Saxony. Gerberga of Lorraine descended from Charlemagne an his wife Hildegarde. Her chart reads,

gen. 14. Louis I, the Fair, Emporer, 814-840, son of Charlemagne, marr Ermengarde, dau. of Ingerman, Count of Hasbaye.

15. Lothair, I, King of Italy, 817-855, Emperor, 840-855, Marr Ermengarde, dau. of Hugh II, Count of Orleans.

16. Ermengarde of Lorraine, marr. Count Gieselbert.

17. Reginer I, Count of Hainault, marr. Alberade of Mons, d. 916.

18. Giselbert, Duke of Lorraine, marr. Gerberga of Saxony, d. 984. Father of Gerberga of Lorraine, gen. 19, above.

20. Herbert III, son of Albert I, the Pious, and Gerberga of Lorraine, was Count fo Vermandois, marr. Ermengarde, dau. of Reinold, Count of Bar.

21. Otho (Eudes or Otto), Count de Vermandois, marr. Parvie, d. 1045.

22. Herbert IV, Count de Vermandois, marr. Adela de Vexin, dau. of Raoul III the Great, Count of Valois and Vexin.

23. Adelaide de Vermandois, d. ca. 1120, Countess of Vermandois and Valois, marr. Hugh Magnus, Duke of France and Burgundy, Marquis of Orleans, Count of Amiens, Chaumont, Paris, Valois, and Vermandois and leader of the First Crusade. He descends from Childebert, the head of this chart, to gen. 10 where, instead of Leutwinus, his ancestor is the borhter, Lambert:

gen. 10. Lambert.

11. N., brother of Robert, Duke of Hesbaye, 722-742.

12. Robert, marr. Williswinda, dau. of Alleume.

13. N., borther of Thurimbert and Cancor, Count in the Rheingau.

14. Alleaume, brother of Humbert, Count of Worms, 778.

15. N., brother of Guy, Marquis of Brittany, and of Robert, Count of Worms.

16. Witichin, Count of Soissons.

17. Robert the Strong, Count of Paris, Marquis of Neustria, d. 866, marr. secondly, Adelaide of Alsace.

18. Robert I, Duke of France, Marquis of Neustria, King of the West Franks.

19. Hugh Magnus, d. 956, Count of Paris, marr. Hedwig, dau. of Henry I, the Fowler, Emperor of Germany.

20. Hugh Capet, King of France, 887-996, marr. Adelaide of Poitou, a descendant of Charlemagne.

21. Robert II, King of France, 988-1031, marr. second, Constance of Toulouse.

22. Henry I, king of France, 1031-1060, marr. Anne of Russia, dau. of Jaroslas I, Grand Duke of Kiev, and Ingegard, dau. of Olaf III, King of Sweden. Henry I was father of Hugh Magnus of gen. 23, page 263.

24. Isabel de Vermandois, dau. of Adelaide de Vermandois and Hugh Magnus, b. 1131, was Countess of Leicester, marr. first, Sir Robert de Beaumont, Lord of Beaumont, Pont-Audemer and Brionne, Count of Meulan, first Earl of Leicester, companion of William the Conqueror at Hastings.

Beatirce Bacon was descended from Elizabeth, daughter of Isabel de Vermandois and Sir Robert de Beaumont, and from Hugh de Mechines de Kyvellock, 5th Earl of Palatine, a great grandson of Henry I of England, youngest son of William the Conqueror. This line is detailed in the Dudley chapter.

Her father, Sir Roger Bacon, was commander in the wars of Edward II and Edward III of England, he was the Son of Sir Henry Bacon and grandson of Sir Henry Bacon, Sr., a judge itinerant in the time of Henry III. The ascending generations are, next, Sir Thomas Bacon, and his father, Sir Robert Bacon, contemporary of Grimbald and, according to some, a relative.

Grimbald was the man we started with at the beginning of this history, traveling with William the Conqueror, he was the first Bacon in our direct line to come to Britain. He put down English roots that spread for fifteen generations and then reached New England, and florished. And it is the history of each of Socrates Bacon's ancestors that underlines the truth of Sir Walter Scott's belief,

"There is no heroic poem in the world but is at bottom the life of a man."

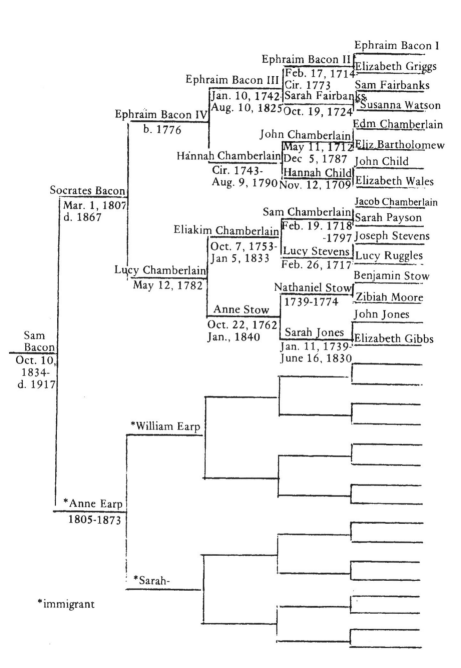

Ephraim Bacon I

Ephraim Bacon II
Feb. 17, 1714-
Cir. 1773

Ephraim Bacon III
Jan. 10, 1742-
Aug. 10, 1825

Ephraim Bacon IV
b. 1776

Socrates Bacon
Mar. 1, 1807
d. 1867

Sam
Bacon
Oct. 10,
1834-
d. 1917

Elizabeth Griggs

Sam Fairbanks

Sarah Fairbanks
Oct. 19, 1724

Susanna Watson

Edm Chamberlain

John Chamberlain
May 11, 1712-
Dec 5, 1787

Hannah Chamberlain
Cir. 1743-
Aug. 9, 1790

Eliz. Bartholomew

John Child

Hannah Child
Nov. 12, 1709

Elizabeth Wales

Jacob Chamberlain

Sam Chamberlain
Feb. 19. 1718
-1797

Eliakim Chamberlain
Oct. 7, 1753-
Jan 5, 1833

Lucy Chamberlain
May 12, 1782

Sarah Payson

Joseph Stevens

Lucy Stevens
Feb. 26, 1717

Lucy Ruggles

Benjamin Stow

Nathaniel Stow
1739-1774

Anne Stow
Oct. 22, 1762
Jan., 1840

Zibiah Moore

John Jones

Sarah Jones
Jan. 11, 1739-
June 16, 1830

Elizabeth Gibbs

*William Earp

*Anne Earp
1805-1873

*Sarah-

*immigrant

CORRECTIONS

Page
1. Green Street
3. Ranulf, first to take name
   'Bacon'
5. change *Norfolk* to *Suffolk*
11 a. Town name is *Dedham.*
   b. All are ancestors of
   Socrates Bacon
13. a.Quote marks after 'later' and
    before 'whereas'
    b. Literary
21. Note belongs on previous pg
25. 'one' cow
44. Fill in '115'
46. Nova Scotia
59. Year should be 1765
66. Kezia marr. Luther Farnum
    Enoch marr. Lydia Dresser and
    Sally Walker
67. Hannah marr. James Fairbands
    and Erastus Higbee
68. add *'apply to Bacon 'exper-
    ience'* to bottom of page.
    as a note
69. Delete *'apply to B. experience'*
76. Enoch *'owed her'*
77. a. change to *'studying'*
    b.Tipton Rock Road. Lane is
    bordered by stone wall built by
    Ephraim III and his sons.
    i n 1978, the very elderly vol-
    untary guide H. Porter Morse
    called it beautiful. It was still
    standing in perfect condition.
83. 124 Summer Street. Torn
    down in late 1980s
94. Bushrod Washington inherited
    Mount Vernon
120. Connection proved. Mary's
     brother next in age to herwas
     gr-grandfather to Pres J.Adams.
136. of
145. correct to pg. 270
152. Name is John Mayo
154. correct to pg.'231'
155. correct to pg. '245'
156. a. chg. 'wold' to *'wild'*

b. A Foxcroft, Maine history says
that "Eliakim Chamberlain was...in
religious belief...a Universalist".
159. read *'eighth*
161. read *'Sir'* R. Lord
165. *'was'* a Lieutenant
177. correct to pg. *'183'*
184. comma should be after *'Co.'*
195. correct to pg. *'255'*
246. correct tio pg. *'257'*
247. a. Moore family, pg. 299 .
     b. Merriam family, pg. 253
     c. Nathaniel marr. Lydia
253. change to *'D o r r'*
270. change 24(AC-2) to (AC-1)
271. change 24(AC-2) to (AC-1)
276. *'Savoy'*
293. *'hunting'*
294. *'whose'*
305. John Moore, *Jr.*
309. Berkhamstead
313. Lydia marr. Hugh Drury
     Next in the list should be
     Martthew. He marr. Martha
     Lamson
315. 'was'
323. Gibbs family, pg. 315
325. Nathaniel Stow's wife is
     Ruth Merriam 1670-1718
331. *'Frankish"*

INDEX

9 i

18 i

23 i

Vachan family (2), 183
Valois, 333
Vane, Henry, 162,184
Vaughn, Elizabeth, 184
  Hopkin John, 184
  Howell, 183
Venice, 33
Verdun, 266
Vere, Hugh de, 265
  Isabel de, 265
  Robert de, 265,277,293
Vermandois, 332-3
Vermandois, Adl. de, 272,333
  Elizabeth de, 333
  Isabel de, 271,333
Vermont, 165
Vernon family (2), 265
Vexin, Adela de, 333
Vinton family (2), 265
Virginia Colony, 68
Vitry-en-Perhois, 331
Vledig, Cunedda, 183
Voed, Gwath, 309
Voythes, L'wil, 183,309
Vrech fras, Cariadoc 183
Vron, Tegayayr, 184
Vychan family (2), 183

Wabash-Erie Canal, 142
Wabbaquasset, 39
Wade, Jonathan, 171
Wadsworth, ___, 300,316
  William, 225
Wakefield, 309
Waldingfield, 201-2
Waldingfield Road, 203
Wales, 184-5,270,309
Wales, Elizabeth, 133,`78,189,
  193
  Isabel, 189-90
  John, 190
  Joseph, 178
  Mary, 189-90
  Nathaniel, 178,189-90,193
  Sarah, 189
  Susanna, 189
Walker family (2), 261
Waltham Magna, 202
Wambourough, Eng., 26
war, 28,41,90,135,154,173
  274,300,302,315

Warbourough, 161
Ward, Elijah, 248
  General, 65
  Jonas, 247
  Mary, 289,300
  Nathaniel, 202
  Parsis, 248
  Richard, 300
  Samuel, 151
  Sarah, 248
Ware family (4), 261
Warkworth, 277
Warley, 116
Warren, Abigail, 289
  Joseph, 132,220
  Mary, 220
  William de, 3
Warwick, 231,273
Washburn, Eliph., 82
Washington, Bushrod, 94
  George, 47,94,66
Washington, D.C., 18,91
Washington Street, 184
Waters, John, 328
  Laurence, 301
  Sarah, 328
Watertown, 10,12,24,116,142
  145,177,211,213,279-80,
  293-4
Watheof, 269,273
Watson family (11), 127
  Susanna, 44,122,127
Webster, Daniel, 93
  John, 202
  Noah, 17,156
Weld, Dorothy, 20
  Elizabeth, 153
  John, 33
  Joseph, 33,153
  Sarah, 153
Wells family (2), 313
Wenham, 16
Wenslydale, 257-8
Wesson, Mary, 248
West Indies, 111
West Riding, 115,131
Westmoreland, 274
Wetherby, Anne, 247
Wexford, 270
Whale; ship, 9
Whale, Elizabeth, 299

27 i

28 i

Made in the USA
Middletown, DE
23 August 2021